I0213028

Call Me Cousin George

A Personal Look
at the Life
of Senator George L. Radcliffe

George M. Radcliffe, Jr.

Copyright © 2021 by George M. Radcliffe, Jr.

All rights reserved.

ISBN 978-1-62806-340-0 (print | hardcover)

Library of Congress Control Number 2022900310

Published by Salt Water Media
29 Broad Street, Suite 104
Berlin, Maryland 21811
www.saltwatermedia.com

Salt Water
M E D I A

Interior photographs courtesy of the author or from sources used with permission including: image of Rev. Lovick Pierce from *Men of Mark in Georgia Vol. 2*. A. B. Caldwell Publisher (Atlanta, Georgia); image of Johns Hopkins University Mile Relay Team from *Hullabaloo '99* yearbook by Williams & Wilkins Company Press (Baltimore, Maryland); image of Sen. George L. Radcliffe and his Christmas books from *The Baltimore Sun*, 22 December 1946; image of George L. Radcliffe with the bronze lion from *The Baltimore Sun*, 7 February 1954; image of shot tower from the Library of Congress; The USS Constellation from the National Archives at College Park; image of Judge Samuel K. Dennis from the Maryland State Archives; image of the 1935 bridge dedication from the Dorchester County Historical Society; image of the *SS Patrick Henry* launching from the National Museum of the U.S. Navy; image of the Truman hunting party from the Harry S. Truman Library & Museum; image of students entering the MHS from the Maryland Center for History and Culture

Call Me Cousin George

Contents

Preface i

The Life of George Lovic Pierce Radcliffe (1877–1974)

The Early Years: 1877-1903 1

His Early Career: 1904-1934 10

The Political Years: 1935-1947 20

The Civic Years: 1947-1974 35

Essays

Early Influences

1. A Confluence of Genes and Environment 43

2. Just a Farm Boy 51

3. The Mysterious Middle Name 62

4. The Runner 72

5. A Teacher at Heart 80

The Historian

6. One Foot in the Past, One in the Future 93

7. "Born a Red-Hot Rebel" 100

8. Wood Fires, Dickens, and Bayberry 110

9. Saving a Lion 122

10. "Fine Old Timbers" 126

Key Individuals

11. The Little Woman 143

12. The Judge 159

13. Chimleys, Zinks, and Bull Turkles 167

14. The Picture on the Dining Room Wall 175

Politics

    15. An Unusual Friendship 187

    16. The Gentleman Politician 198

    17. The Merchant Marine 209

    18. A Friend from Missouri 218

    19. The Contradiction 226

    20. The 1946 Election: His Only Defeat 232

Civic Responsibility

    21. Mr. Chairman 241

    22. His Society 246

    23. The 200-Pound Birthday Cake 257

Family

    24. The Promise 269

    25. The Dreams of a Ten-year-old Child 280

    26. The Power of Concentration 288

    27. Just a Grandfather 293

    28. Cousin George 300

Appendices

    1. George L. Radcliffe's Civic Involvement by Year 311

    2. Christmas Essay: "Heigh Ho" 322

    3. Senate Campaign Brochure (1934) 329

    4. Birthday Ball Address (1949) 334

    5. Radio Address: "The Merchant Marine" (1941) 345

    6. Senate Speech: "Freedom and Liberty" (1942) 351

    7. Senate Speech: "The Equal Rights Amendment" (1945) .. 354

    8. Campaign Speech: "My Message to My People" (1946) .. 369

    9. Sam Hopkins' Memorial to George L. Radcliffe (1974) .. 372

Endnotes 379

Preface

I sat at the dinner table in 1966, stewing about the American history assignment I had been assigned earlier that day. My father, sensing I was somewhat out of sorts, asked me how school had been. After I reeled off the standard high school student answer, "OK", he probed further, hoping to get some family conversation started. The hardest job any parent of teenagers has is getting his children to give more than a one-word answer to a question. After a couple more tries, he finally got me to share what was aggravating me. I explained that we had been assigned a major term paper on an American history topic of our choice, but we had to use mostly primary sources. "Where in the world will I get primary sources?" I interjected. My father had to be dying inside at this point, wondering if there had been a mix-up at the hospital sixteen years earlier when he brought his first child home. Amazingly, he kept his mouth shut and just let me ramble on as I decried the idea that history had to be a part of the curriculum. "Why do we need to learn about dead people; after all, they're—well—dead."

My father had grown up in a house that was a veritable museum of history and antiquity, served in the Pacific during World War II, and grown up as the son of a United States senator, and here was his oldest son ranting about the uselessness of history; clearly the apple had fallen from the tree and had rolled a long way down the hill. But then, at this point he was used to the constant complaining of a teenage son. He was also one of the most patient humans on Earth. However, he finally could stand it no longer and asked me, "Do you know anyone who has played a part in recent history?" hoping this might end his son's tirade. That flew well over my head as I reminded my father that history was about "dead people". That did it. His son was clearly not his offspring. Then, by pure chance, dessert appeared; a sweet potato pie, a staple of our household and a regular item which my grandfather brought us every time he returned from a visit to Cambridge, Maryland, his boyhood birthplace and part-time residence throughout his life. Seizing on this unexpected prompt, my father stated the obvious. "Your grandfather brought this up from Cambridge, didn't he?" Another clue sailed high over my head. Dad continued, "Your grandfather had quite an active life, didn't he?" Finally, something registered, and I piped up, "Grandfather was in the US Senate, wasn't he?" Of course, I knew this fact well, but it was taking a while to jump start my brain. "Hey, he would be a primary source, wouldn't he?" I wasn't looking at my father at this point, but he had to be breathing one massive sigh of relief.

I certainly am not the brightest bulb on the *Homo sapiens* tree, but then one must realize that at this point in my life, George L. Radcliffe was just a lovable, often absent-minded grandfather, one year shy of his ninetieth birthday. I knew well that he had befriended Franklin Roosevelt, had served two terms in the US Senate, and been as civically active as almost anyone in Maryland, but being amazingly modest, he never boasted. The grandfather I knew was all about family, recounting lengthy stories of growing up as a boy on a family farm before cars, electrification, and modern plumbing; literally a human history book, recanting historic speeches and documents verbatim. He could tell you the date of seemingly every battle in history, name and dates of every English king and U.S. president, and recite long poems he had learned in Latin eighty years earlier.

That 1966 history project opened a door for me on the grandfather I had never known, revealing a politician, statesman, and key historical figure. Twelve evenings I trekked the two blocks down to his house to interview him. "Interview" is not the correct term for what happened, as my first question each evening would launch him into a two-hour dissertation on some aspect of his career. He talked casually about individuals he had interacted with, ones that were only entries in a history book for me: Roosevelt, Truman, Marshall, Churchill. I taped those talks, and sadly, they were thrown away several years later as my parents were cleaning out my room. However, the impact of the talks stuck with me and changed me. It was during those talks that I first learned of the immense pride he took in helping build up this country's Merchant Marine before World War II. The details are recorded in many places, but his attitude, core ideas, perspective on past, present, and future were indelibly inscribed in me. He remained my lovable, absent-minded grandfather because that was the role he was proudest to assume, but I knew that he was so much more.

He lived to attend my wedding, speaking so long at the rehearsal dinner that the restaurant had to end his talk so they could close, and he held his first great-grandchild before his death. My parents have passed on, and my three siblings all died young, many years ago. Because my father was an only child and my grandfather's two brothers had no children, I am all that is left of family that remember him. This book is being written out of love—but also of necessity; I knew the person he was. My father, George M. Radcliffe, always wanted to write a biography of his father, but died only having written the table of contents for a book he was going to call "Cousin George". I am using the idea of that title not only to honor my father, but because it fits my grandfather so well. Although he walked on the world stage, he remained the simple country boy and the ultimate champion of family.

My effort is also partly dedicated to my brother, Bill, who tragically died in a car accident many years ago. An award-winning news reporter, Bill would have written this book and done it justice. As the only family member left, the task falls to me, but I only wish my gifted brother could have done this. My work will be a poor second.

Environmental education became my career, but my grandfather's indoctrination made me a historian for life. With apologies to my numerous history teachers who were subjected to a less than motivated student, I present what is more a work of love than a literary accomplishment. George L. Radcliffe was unique. The more I plow into this life of mine, the more I realize that I grew up in the presence of an amazing person. I have never encountered anyone who lived a fuller life than he did. Not only did he live almost ninety-seven years, but he packed more into each year than many do in a lifetime. His passion for history and life experiences gave him an insight into matters that few have. I remember asking him in the peak of the Cold War in the 1960s if there would be a World War III. He thought for a second and then completely surprised me with his answer, "Yes, George, there will be another world war, but it won't be fought with conventional weapons or bombs. It will be an economic war." When I asked him if the Soviet Union would be our main adversary, he said "No, it will be fought with China," explaining then in detail how Chinese history and ingenuity would eventually make them a world economic power. Over fifty years later, I still can't believe that he was able to answer my question that way.

History has largely forgotten him. He left the U.S. Senate seventy-four years ago so few alive today remember him. He was an officer of the Maryland Historical Society (now the Maryland Center for History and Culture) for over sixty years, seeing the group grow from a small organization in one old building to a massive one housed in numerous buildings, yet many of the young employees have never heard of him. He was one of the early leaders in the March of Dimes organization when polio was the most dreaded disease in the news, but thankfully the vaccine has made that aspect of the organization largely a topic of history. There were many more politically impressive U.S. senators, but then George L. Radcliffe was not a politician. He never sought attention, but had a work ethic unequalled by most. He accomplished much in the Senate, but was content to stay mostly behind the scenes, feeling the job was about public service, not making a name for oneself. He was completely nonjudgmental, and no one could ever recall him saying a derogatory word about anyone. He was, however, an unabashed historian and teacher, and his professional life is best viewed through those lenses. He was first and foremost a family man; "Cousin George," as virtually all called him.

However, to those who knew him, his public life was not what was most remarkable. He was a gentleman in a period when being a gentleman was a badge of honor. He claimed on several occasions to have answered every letter he ever received in his two terms in the Senate, and I have no reason to doubt this claim, as the Maryland Center for History and Culture has over 100 boxes loaded with both letters he received and carbon copies of the replies. These were not just simple records of receipt, but often long letters with lengthy answers to questions—tidbits of history, and often, advice. He did keep a simple daily diary which illuminates how busy the man was every day. The sum total of these numerous letters, speeches, and documents paints a picture of his life, dreams, and ideas. As an example of the extreme he would go to in his prolific letter writing, we have a response he wrote to *Who's Who* when the organization wanted to remove him from their latest volume in 1965. Most at age eighty-eight would have just discarded the basically form letter, but not George L. Radcliffe. He penned a two-page single-space letter thanking them for their support of him over the years and agreeing that it was wise of them to give his "space" in the book to others.

> I will, of course, miss some advantages of *Who's Who* because of the withdrawal of my name from your current publication. I realize, however, that you must find curtailment necessary from time to time, and I thank you for what you have done for me in the past. Since the duties of yourself and your associates must be very arduous, you should not have bothered to take the time to explain

to me the reason for your action, and I appreciate your courtesy in doing so.[1]

In this way, this remarkable gentleman from the Eastern Shore of Maryland made his mark in history. He wanted to preserve and teach history, never to be a part of it. He understood better than most that the present is just a steppingstone between the past and the future, and he was more the learned historian than a politician. Listening, for him, was far more important than speaking, and he could wear down an opponent with patience and kindness. This modest gentleman, however, could get things done, and his list of accomplishments in many areas is mind-boggling.

While I had tens of thousands of letters and documents to base the facts on, this is also a personal voyage, a homage to a relative who played a key part in my first twenty-five years of life. The factual basis is there, but I cannot always write about him in the third person. My opinions will surface at times, but I have tried to keep the facts as accurate as possible, as I have almost unlimited access to his own words and ideas. However, I knew the man better than anyone still alive, and his humanity is far more significant than what he accomplished.

His specialties—banking and insurance—are clearly weak areas for me as almost anyone could do a better job of analyzing this aspect of his life, but then this is more an account of the man. He accomplished much with his patient and persistent style, and he left his mark on history. He has much to teach us about what is profoundly important in life. He would be lost in the fast-paced technologically-based world of today; he considered himself too old to learn to drive a car when they became commercially available, and he would frequently call me at night to come down to his house to turn on his television, which he never mechanically mastered. However, what he valued is what we should value today.

The following pages are organized into three parts: a simple chronological biography; a series of essays, organized around several themes; and an addendum of some of his speeches and writings. It is the essays which really define the kind of person that he was—the influence of his parents; his childhood home, Spocott; his passion for history; his lifelong fascination with Christmas; and an amazing wife who helped shaped the person he became. He never knew this, but he became—and still is—a major shaper of the person I am. In many ways I am not fit to walk in his shadow, much less write this book, but "Cousin George" affected many lives in so many ways. He defined the term "gentleman" as well as anyone ever has. He has been gone for forty-seven years at this point, but he still inspires me every day.

<u>Note:</u> There is some minor duplication in the biography and the essays. Each essay was written as a self-contained unit that can be read independent of the biography; thus, minor background information, even if slightly repetitive, was sometimes added to make an essay stand on its own. Because of this, the essays can also be read out of order, even though they are loosely arranged by topic area.

George M. Radcliffe, Jr., 2021

The Life of George Lovic Pierce Radcliffe

(1877-1974)

THE EARLY YEARS: 1877 - 1903

George Lovic Pierce Radcliffe was born into history on August 22, 1877 and remained enshrouded in it for almost a century. He was the last child born to John Anthony LeCompte Radcliffe (1818–1901) and Sophie Delila Travers Robinson Radcliffe (1837–1927). This was the second marriage for both parents; each had lost their first spouse. Born to a sixty-nine-year-old father and a forty-year-old mother, George was child number nineteen of the collective family, but he would go on to become the most prominent member of this large family, staying active throughout those ninety-seven years. He was born just after the invention of the telephone and well before the automobile would enter the world, yet he would live to see a man land on the moon. He would not own a television until the ninetieth year of his life. His life would span more than half of the U.S. presidents to that time, and he would die shortly before the resignation of Richard Nixon. He would get to know three of those presidents well. George would see the Spanish-American War, both World Wars, the Korean War, and the Vietnam War. Deemed too old to fight in either of the World Wars, he would nonetheless play a critical role on the home front of both. Born in the immediate aftermath of the Civil War, his life would span the uncomfortable and turbulent roller coaster improvement of race relations in this country. He was born into a country where a woman's place was in the home and where they could not vote, yet he would see the Equal Rights Amendment passed, introducing himself the amendment's predecessor in 1945. He remained engrossed in history, and became a part of it himself, both in the political realm and through a lifetime of historical preservation. George was born on a farm in an isolated part of the Eastern Shore of Maryland where most transportation was by boat, and would live to see the area well connected to the world by roads, bridges, and rail. His life in many ways parallels the second century of our country. Deemed sickly by his older parents, he would outlive most of his generation and leave a lasting impact on many.

George was born on Spocott Farm, the property settled by his fifth great-grandfather, Stephen Gary, in 1663. His ancestors were some of the earliest settlers to Dorchester County on the Eastern Shore. Both his father and maternal grandfather were prominent shipbuilders and farmers, a logical pairing of careers since Dorchester County was largely isolated from the rest of the state by the Chesapeake Bay and Choptank River, and no location in the county was more than one-quarter mile from water. George was born twelve years after the end of the Civil War, and his family still bore active wounds from the War. Spocott had always been a community inhabited by family, white and Black workers, and at one point, enslaved workers. The family was land-wealthy but cash-poor, but George never went without. He learned the importance of family early on, as he was surrounded by many siblings and children of siblings, but Spocott was a place where family was defined on a larger scale—with all in the Spocott community living, working, and celebrating together.

His father had previously married Rebecca Beckwith (1824–1870), and the two had ten children, but five died tragically within one year of birth. His mother had originally married Andrew Jackson Robinson (1832–1869), and they had six children, four of whom were still alive when George was born. John and Sophie both lost spouses within one year of each other, and with both living in the same area and having young children, it was logical they would end up marrying in 1871, less than a year after the death of John's wife. Both had been hardened by the loss of not only a spouse, but, collectively, seven children, and in the next six years, they would have three more children. Tragedy would continue to hover over the couple as two more of John's children, Nehemiah and Olin, would die in the first two years of George's life. The 1880 census showed John and Sophie living at Spocott with eight children, ages two to thirty-four, including George and his two brothers, Tom and Sewell, and five children from the parents' first marriages. The large family became huge when one included all George's aunts and uncles and their children, who were frequent guests at Spocott. Sophie was the focal point of the family, and no one was more focused on keeping a family connected than her. Sophie's mother had died when she was only six, but her two sisters, Addie and Mary Ann, were married with numerous children. John had come from a family of twelve, with two dying young. Two of his brothers were killed during the Civil War, and two more died before George was born. There were, however, numerous cousins on this side of the family. At any given point in time, Spocott was crowded with relatives of all ages. John had enlarged the Spocott house after the Civil War to accommodate a growing family.

George's parents were highly educated and well versed in many subjects. While Sophie had been sent by her father to be schooled in an exclusive private school near Baltimore, John was largely self-taught and a compulsive reader. George claimed to have known his alphabet by age three, and since family conversations were highly academic, his unofficial schooling began early. He was home schooled initially but always surrounded by books, a somewhat rare commodity in isolated Dorchester County. George's father had built the only local school several years earlier, but with so many children and grandchildren in the home and other children living on and near the property, a cousin, Clare Chaplain, was hired in 1883 as both governess and teacher for what literally became a school within a home for the first few years of George's education. When George began to attend his father's Castle Haven School in 1886, he was pulled back home after just one day as his parents felt he was sickly. In 1887, he returned to the school and was able to complete all the pre-high school classes in just three years. As he would say, he was advanced compared to most of the students, and primarily used the school time to just read. Throughout all this George read everything he could get his hands on, being particularly drawn to history. The continuing cloud of the Civil War accentuated his interest in history, and this would become a major interest throughout his education.

George was one of three children that his parents would have in their second marriage. His two older brothers, Thomas Broome Radcliffe (1874-1954) and James Sewell Radcliffe (1875-1967), were considered healthy and were quickly integrated into the work regimen on the family farm while "sickly" George was given lesser tasks such as feeding the smaller animals on the property. This gave him additional time for reading, and George soon came to be viewed as the studious one of the three. His brothers would always joke that George sat inside and read while they did all the work. The inhabitants of Spocott operated as a completely self-sufficient community at the time, growing cotton and raising sheep for clothes, making their shoes, building structures and furniture with wood from the Spocott forests, forming nails and hardware in the family blacksmith shop, and growing all needed food and livestock. The experiences growing up on such a farm would have a lasting impact on George, and he would spend time at his beloved Spocott until the day he died.

His father, John, would live for the first twenty-four years of George's life and profoundly influence George's views and lifestyle. John was a kind but stern father with an amazing capacity for work. His life would see Spocott go from a farm which utilized slaves to one where Blacks and whites worked side-by-side as equals, at least to the extent that society would permit. While George would never acquire any of his father's remarkable mechanical and carpentry skills, he would develop his father's passion for history, desire to effect change through politics, and high moral character. George's mother, Sophie, would live through half of George's life, and she was the glue which melded the strong family fabric, which became George's trademark.

In many ways, George was raised by the Spocott community. Aunts, older siblings, and many of the Spocott workers became auxiliary parents, and he remained close to this larger family throughout his life. Especially important to him was Adaline Wheatley (1847–1929), the family cook, nurse, and confidante. Adaline, always a free Black, had married Columbus Wheatley, a former enslaved worker at Spocott, and George always referred to her as "Aunt Adaline." A remarkable cook, Adaline and her outdoor kitchen became a favorite retreat for young George, and he often thought of her as a second mother. George received more than his share of helpful advice and guidance from this wise and outspoken figure, and her influence on him was evident throughout his life. He would give the only eulogy at her funeral.

George quickly acquired a love for history and tradition in his childhood at Spocott. Surrounded by a large multi-generational family with strong Dorchester County roots, family stories and legends flowed, and young George soon came to know the ins and outs of his many ancestral families: Radcliffes, Travers, Keenes, LeComptes, Sewells, Beckwiths, Doves, and Broomes, to name a few. And no family get-together was complete without some retelling of history. One of George's favorite books was Dickens' *A Child's History of England*, and as a young child, he was said to have been able to name every English regent in order. He would also develop a passion for the history and traditions of Christmas, and the holiday and the year-long preparations for it would form the core of his happiest memories of childhood at Spocott. His mother was the impetus for this passion as she excelled in keeping the family and its traditions alive and well.

At age thirteen, he traveled into Cambridge to continue schooling at the Cambridge Seminary. Because the school was seven miles from Spocott, he stayed with relatives in Cambridge during the week. He completed his high school education in 1893 at the age of fifteen.

In October of 1893 he would take the entrance examinations to attend Johns Hopkins University in Baltimore, but with insufficient money to pay for college, he was unable to attend. While his family owned considerable land in Dorchester County, the family had never been wealthy. Even when John Anthony LeCompte Radcliffe was active in shipbuilding and farming, money was limited, with bartering being the preferred way to do business. While ship owners might have made their fortunes, shipbuilders were basically laborers. In one instance, John's ledger shows he and his brothers building a large schooner, yet, after expenses, John made only $182 for all his work on that ship.[1] The loss of slave labor after the War combined with John's age and his large family created difficult financial times. Evidence of this is found in a letter which Sophie sent out to family when George was in high school, asking for help getting her son a coat.

During the summer of 1893, George would spend his time at Spocott, reading and working on the property. That fall, Emerson Harrington, principal of the high school in Cambridge, asked his former student to be assistant principal. While George's assistance was needed at Spocott, he was much better suited to be a teacher than a farm laborer. In October of 1894, with the financial support of a relative, George finally entered Hopkins, getting his degree in three years, focusing on literature and history. He said that he was initially teased, partially because he was young for the class, but showing up the first day as the only one wearing shorts made an instant impression on the others. He joined the Kappa Alpha fraternity and made many friends with whom he would stay in contact for a lifetime. He graduated thirteenth in a class of fifty-one in 1897. One of the professors who made the greatest impression on him was a professor at Princeton University who gave a series of twenty-five lectures at Hopkins. George was impressed by the professor's knowledge and progressive ideas, both furthering George's love of history and instilling in him a desire to eventually teach. That professor was Woodrow Wilson.

At Hopkins, George's love of history led him to dig into two topics in particular: the history and traditions of Christmas around the world, and the Civil War. The former would continue throughout his life as George amassed one of the largest private collections of books on Christmas in the country. He never inventoried his collection but estimated having between one and two thousand volumes, plus many magazines and drawings. The latter interest would lead him to return to Hopkins in the fall of 1897 to get his doctoral degree in history. Money was still an issue with the family as his father was too old to work, and the farm was in rapid decline, but George was awarded a scholarship in economics for the next three years. His studies would be in politics, economics, and history.

With the Civil War still a vibrant part of his family's past, he decided to focus on Maryland's role in the Civil War. Of particular interest to him was why Maryland, a slave state, had not seceded from the Union, a move which would have left the northern capital, Washington, thoroughly entrenched in Confederate territory. The Maryland governor at this point in history was Thomas Holiday Hicks, by coincidence, also a Dorchester County native, and George was able to connect with Hicks' descendants to get many of the original documents related to their ancestor. Hopkins discouraged this as a research topic, as emotions connected with the Civil War were still boiling over in many areas of the state. George assured them he could remain completely impartial and set out for an objective review of the documents and previous research. He submitted his research for his doctoral degree in 1900, and at the lengthy oral defense of his research, he proved he had achieved his goal of impartiality as the reviewing professors stated they honestly could not see any bias or indication of his family's allegiance. George smiled, never indicating his views, but later he would say that he was still a "Rebel" at that point in his life. The University would publish his research in 1901, and the book, *Governor Thomas H. Hicks of Maryland and the Civil War*, republished many years later, is still used as a source on Maryland's entry into the Civil War. The main premise of his research was that Gov. Hicks avoided secession for Maryland by failing to call a session of the Maryland legislature at the point in 1861 when the state likely would have voted to secede.[2] Woodrow Wilson was one of two mentors assisting George with his research.

As a graduate student, George also pursued an athletic career, turning his love of running into a championship at the Penn Relays in 1898. While George hardly had the physique of an athlete, he could run, something he had always done on the farm at Spocott. He said that he always had an awkward walking gait, but he had a natural running stride and soon attracted the attention of the track coach, who quickly recruited him. George would become a key member of the Hopkins one-mile relay team which went undefeated in 1898. The gold watch he won for winning the Penn Relays became a treasured possession.

In the fall of 1900, Emerson Harrington would again call on George for a favor. The current high school principal had fallen ill, and the school needed a principal. George stepped in, acting both as administrator and teacher of Latin, a subject he had loved and excelled at in high school. Even though he was the building principal, he still taught every period in the day except one. He was extremely popular with the students since he was not much older than they, and the girls, smitten with him, often called him "Georgie." The next fall he received a teaching position at Baltimore City College, where he taught history and English. Well versed in both subjects, he had a significant impact on the students, as three years later the graduating class, which he had taught as freshmen, dedicated their yearbook to him. He would always remain close to them and attended their reunions until the year he died.

While George found that teaching fit him well, his passion for history was to take him to a higher level and a different career. His study of history had shown him that an understanding of law was key to most of the landmark moments in history, and he enrolled in the University of Maryland law school, also in Baltimore. He wanted to continue teaching, but finances dictated that he get through law school quickly, and he did all three years of the school in one year, getting his law degree and passing the

Maryland Bar examination in 1903. To pay his way through that year of school, he would both write and tutor, shared a boarding house with two remarkable individuals: Philip Lee Goldsborough—also from Dorchester County and a future U.S. Senator, who ironically George would replace in 1935—and Samuel King Dennis, who would become chief judge of the Baltimore Supreme Bench and, more importantly, George's closest friend in life.

With an amazing resume in 1903, he was eagerly sought by the American Bonding Company, a surety firm, and became their legal advisor, earning $40 per month. While a pittance, for a farm boy who never had seen much money, this was a fortune. By the next year, he was promoted to become the attorney in charge of the legal claims department, with a salary of $1,800 a year, and he would be an officer of the company for years to come. The knowledge and experience he gained in the insurance and financial worlds would serve him well in later years, and he would become the go-to person when a deal needed to be made. However, a personal relationship stemming from this work would later change his life.

The first quarter of George's life saw accomplishments enough for a lifetime for many individuals. By age twenty-five, he had acquired a college degree and a Ph.D. in history, had a book published, taught for a year, been principal of a high school, gotten a law degree, now had a job with perhaps the premier surety firm in Baltimore, and developed contacts that would open doors for him in the second quarter of his life. The "sickly" child was wasting no time.

His Early Career: 1904 - 1934

George was soon making a name for himself in the American Bond-ing Company, but at age twenty-six, he was also one of the most eligible bachelors in the area. That was how he was introduced to Mary McKim Marriott (1881–1963) of Baltimore. Her ancestors read like a *Who's Who* of Baltimore history as her Marriott, McKim, Hammond, and Wilson ancestors played a prominent role in nineteenth century Maryland. Mary had also made a name for herself, becoming an assistant editor of *Ladies Home Journal* prior to the age of twenty-one. George was immediately attracted to her for a number or reasons; she was intelligent and creative and had a passion for history equal to his. While a perfect fit in interests, they were as different as night and day in personality; while George was shy and reserved, Daisy—as George always called Mary—was impetuous and outgoing. A relatively short courtship would lead to their marriage on June 6, 1906. Daisy would be the love of his life until her death in 1963.

Sadly, tragedy struck Daisy several times the first few years of their marriage. In 1908 her brother Don—her only sibling—would commit suicide, probably partially influenced by his contracting syphilis. Her be-loved father, William Haddon Marriott, a prominent Baltimore architect, would become ill, finally passing in 1912. The two deaths rocked Daisy, and the next several years would see her struggling psychologically, trig-gering a few visits to an institution. George and Daisy lived in an apart-ment in Baltimore and visited Spocott whenever they could. During this period, the often-stubborn Daisy would frequently clash with George's brother Tom's wife Mae, and in 1914, George and Daisy built a house on the Spocott property, a home she named Windemere. Finally, in 1917, as she was beginning to get back on her feet, she would lose her first child, Mary McKim Radcliffe, six days after her birth. Daisy fell into depression, a condition which would occur periodically for the rest of her life. In 1919, their second child, George M. Radcliffe, was born, and Daisy turned all her efforts into raising him. Almost paranoid from the deaths of the previous decade, she would inflict much of her fear onto young George, keeping him out of school, believing him fragile and taking frequent "therapeutic trips" with him to Florida, Bermuda, and California. Throughout all of this, George L. Radcliffe kept working.

In 1912, the large American Bonding Company began planning to merge with the Fidelity and Deposit Company of Maryland, and while George opposed the merger, he soon fell in line to help facilitate the move. He was rewarded by being promoted to president of the American Bonding Company Baltimore firm, as well as vice-president of the now-parent company. Ironically, he would be charged with shutting down the American Bonding Company office, something which did not happen as its new president would use it to generate considerable business. He remained associated with the American Bonding Company into the 1930s when it largely faded out of the picture, and George stayed with the associated Fidelity and Deposit Company of Maryland for the rest of his life.

The job kept him a full-time resident of Baltimore, but he stayed connected to his beloved Spocott, corresponding regularly with his mother, and making frequent visits across the Chesapeake Bay by ferry. The farm had fallen on hard times after his father's death in 1901, and his mother soon went into debt, having to take frequent loans from family members. His two brothers had moved away from the area, and George had to make frequent trips to Spocott to help his aging mother keep the farm operating, and the buildings and property from deteriorating. George's position allowed him to constantly send cash to his mother, and soon he was able to start paying off these loans. Unable to drive, he would often walk long distances, avoiding public transportation, to save whatever money he had. In 1911, he also was able to buy back the section of the original Spocott grant which had left the family in the late eighteenth century. This was the first step in returning Spocott to its original stature.

His love of history led him to join the Maryland Historical Society in 1908, and by 1912, he had been appointed recording secretary of the organization. Although the organization had been in existence since 1844, it was still a small entity with limited membership, and was housed in a building shared with other groups. In one incident in 1910, George was to make a presentation to the Society on his PhD thesis only to have the speech cancelled because the topic was deemed too controversial because the Society was still struggling from animosity created by the Civil War so many years earlier. He would remain an officer of the organization for the next fifty-two years.

George kept his close association with Johns Hopkins, staying active in the Alumni Association and acting as its president from 1915 – 1919. In May of 1915, as alumni president, he oversaw the largest celebration to date held at Hopkins with the dedication of new buildings and a speech by President Wilson.[3] Also that year, he was put on a committee to plan a new military training course at Hopkins.[4] Plans were formed to add dormitories to the new Homewood campus, and George soon became chair of the dormitory committee with the goal of getting four dormitories constructed. The once shy college student was long gone, and George combined all his skills to begin mobilizing people. The plans were temporarily sidelined by the war but picked up momentum soon after. At one event in 1919, George raised $54,000 in one evening. Standing on a chair at an alumni dinner, he coaxed pledges from the different alumni classes, working the group up to where others were standing on chairs, shouting out pledges.[5] By 1920, the alumni had raised over $200,000 for one of the dorms, which would house 560 students, providing on-campus housing for the first time. George had been able to secure a donation from sixty percent of the men who had graduated from Hopkins. The dorms were to also serve as a war memorial for graduates who fell during the war.[67]

Although George at this time would have denied having any political aspirations, numerous circumstances were grooming him for public service. Dorchester County had produced a disproportionately large number of state political figures; even George's father, John, had briefly served in the Maryland Legislature. At Johns Hopkins, he had interacted with one of Hopkins' more illustrious figures, Woodrow Wilson, and when Wilson ran for President in 1912, George would get involved in the campaign in small ways. A former governor of Maryland, Edwin Warfield, became president of the Maryland Historical Society, and his former high school principal, Emerson Harrington, became governor in 1916. George was clearly in the shadow of political figures, and in fact, Harrington would appoint George to the Baltimore Liquor Board in 1916. George may have claimed to have no political aspirations, but the political world was beginning to close in on him.

The year 1917 would be one of several transformative ones in George's life. Personally, he and Mary would endure more tragedy as their first child Mary would only live for six days. With the United States entry into World War I, George, aged forty, was considered too old to enlist, but like so many, he felt the need to serve his country. He worked in a personnel capacity with the American Red Cross in Washington and was a key member of a committee that organized an *Over There* show to honor the men serving and to build patriotism. He served on the Maryland Council of Defense, both to help with fundraising and as chairman of the historical division, commissioned with amassing a complete record of every Marylander who fought in the war. George also volunteered for the *Dollar-a-Year Man* program in which he would receive a token dollar a year for lending assistance in some aspect of the war effort. With a choice of places to lend his legal expertise, he chose the Department of the Navy, partially because his father had been a shipbuilder, and it was here that he met someone who would change his life. The Under Secretary of the

Navy at that time was Franklin Roosevelt, and the two would develop a close friendship.[8]

By 1919, George was one of the busiest citizens in Maryland; his success as an organizer combined with his legal, banking, and insurance experience made him a prime candidate for numerous projects, and he would get even busier. In addition to his work with Hopkins, he was appointed treasurer of the Maryland League of Nations. Personally, he continued to find time to devote to Daisy, George, and his mother, whose health was deteriorating. His good friend, Emerson Harrington, called on him for assistance a third time, asking him to take over as Maryland Secretary of State. George's recordkeeping ability, business experience, and organizational skills made him a good fit for the position which now kept him running between Baltimore and Annapolis, with frequent trips to Dorchester County, through 1920.

George still had no serious political aspirations, but his numerous political connections were providing him statewide visibility. His friend, Franklin Roosevelt, however, clearly saw a political future for himself and was picked by the Democratic party as the vice-presidential nominee on Ohio Governor James Cox's Democratic ticket. Cox and Roosevelt lost significantly to Warren Harding and his running mate, Calvin Coolidge, and George saw the opportunity to grab Roosevelt for the Fidelity and Deposit Company. Van Lear Black—publisher, businessman, and Fidelity and Deposit officer—was also a close friend of Roosevelt, and George's suggestion met with immediate approval. Franklin Roosevelt accepted the position of vice president of the New York office of the Company. Although technically Roosevelt was subordinate to George, Franklin was given free rein to grow business for the firm in the New York area. The two friends would work together throughout the next eight years.

Roosevelt was diagnosed with polio shortly after accepting the position, and George would make many trips to New York and Warm Springs to visit him. In 1921, George was at Roosevelt's bedside at least once a week, and he was moved by his friend's strength as Franklin began to take charge of his situation. By the next year, the two were talking frequently about polio and what needed to be done to diminish its frequency and impact. These talks would evolve several years later into the National Foundation for Infantile Paralysis and the March of Dimes, organizations George would be heavily involved with for the remainder of his life.

The two friends took several business trips together, and, on at least one occasion, Roosevelt would visit Spocott. While Roosevelt dramatically increased business in the Fidelity and Deposit New York office, his methods did not always meet with the approval of the company's board. At one point, George was sent to New York by the Fidelity and Deposit executive committee to fire his friend, but in New York he was able to engineer the situation so that the company had to retain Roosevelt.[9] When New York governor, Al Smith, decided to run for president in 1928, Roosevelt was encouraged to run for Smith's vacated position as governor. George would strongly urge his friend to run, a favor Roosevelt would return in later years.

George increasingly found himself being drawn into the political world. He became involved in a succession of Democratic campaigns, and he would chair the inauguration committee for Maryland Governor Albert Ritchie in 1923, 1926, and 1930. Once again, his organization skills and attention to detail were making him a sought-after commodity. In hindsight, George was building a resume and reputation that would later make him a natural for political office.

In 1924, a chance meeting with Baltimore Mayor Howard Jackson launched George into the first of many historical preservation projects which would become a major focus of his life. In the summer of that year, the Baltimore Shot Tower, once supposedly the tallest structure in the country, was scheduled for demolition. Built in 1828 to make shot, the 234-foot-tall brick tower was enshrouded in history, and that was all that George needed to get involved. The cornerstone had been laid by Charles

Carroll of Carrollton, signer of the Declaration of Independence, and George's wife Mary's ancestor, John McKim, had been instrumental in getting it built. The Union Oil Company wanted more for it than the City of Baltimore wanted to pay, and George entered the mayor's office just as he was ready to sign the demolition order. George asked for time to raise funds and began an emergency letter writing and speaking campaign that would net the funds needed to save it. It still stands today almost a century later.

Later in the decade, George was the driving force behind raising funds for the Walter Hines Page School of International Relations at Johns Hopkins University. In the wake of World War I, George and others saw a need for the United States to take a more active role in developing the international connections and strategies which would prevent another war. George again unleashed his letter-writing skills and helped lay the groundwork for the school. He also insisted that the school admit women—one of many of his actions throughout the years which sought to further the rights of women.

He continued his close relationship with Roosevelt when he became New York governor, and when Franklin decided to run for president, George became a key part of his campaign. Roosevelt was hardly the choice of the insurance and banking communities that George was a part of, but with his Democratic roots and friendship with Roosevelt, George was eager to lead Maryland in getting Roosevelt elected. Roosevelt was not popular with the Maryland Democratic establishment, and initially it looked like Roosevelt would not carry the state. Maryland Democratic Senator Millard Tydings was also up for re-election, and with the Maryland Democratic Party somewhat disorganized, Governor Ritchie asked George to take charge of the Maryland Democratic campaign. With little party support, George would devote most of his time in 1932 to get Roosevelt the support he needed in Maryland. Both Roosevelt and Tydings carried Maryland handily. Somehow George continued working at his job and devoting time to the Historical Society and other civic projects. He was proving to those around him that he had the work ethic and stamina to hold two full-time jobs at one time.

This election would mark another turning point in George's life as now-President Roosevelt would turn to his old friend and business acquaintance for assistance. After Roosevelt's inauguration, rumors circulated that George was to get a Cabinet appointment. Many thought he would be appointed Under Secretary of the Treasury, but if he had been asked, he never let on. He told others that he wanted no appointment, with his work at the Fidelity and Deposit Company keeping him working overtime. In July, he received a phone call from the President asking him to fill a position in the newly formed Federal Emergency Administration of Public Works, later renamed the Public Works Administration (PWA). George, who was then acting president of the Fidelity and Deposit Company, declined, but Roosevelt persisted. George refused several more times, but with George's last refusal, Roosevelt asked him to meet at the White House the next day.

When George walked into the President's office that next morning, before he could even begin his long litany of reasons why he could not accept, the President thanked him for accepting the position, explaining that George's acceptance was a matter of "duty." As George would later recall, one could not say "no" to Franklin Roosevelt. George was appointed the Regional Advisor of Public Works for the Tenth Region, covering Maryland, Delaware, Virginia, West Virginia, North Carolina, Kentucky, and Tennessee, soliciting ideas and delegating funds for projects in the seven-state area: roads, bridges, electrification projects, rural development, etc. Although this was supposed to be a full-time job, Roosevelt agreed that George could retain his job with the Fidelity and Deposit Company. George then dramatically simplified his life and schedule by having Baltimore named as the regional Public Works headquarters, and he was able to use his Fidelity and Deposit office as the Public Works office, although he would spend considerable time on the road. As George would do many times in his life, he would work two full-time jobs.[10]

The appointment was not without controversy as several senators had identified other potential candidates. Maryland's Senator Tydings already had another Marylander in mind for the job and was surprised with Roosevelt's choice. Opponents immediately criticized Roosevelt for choosing an acquaintance over what were perceived as more qualified choices, and this initiated what would be an often-shaky relationship between George Radcliffe and Millard Tydings. The fact that Baltimore was chosen for the headquarters fed the controversy, but George quickly proved himself to be more than qualified for the job.[11]

Initially George would focus on the construction of two major bridges for the state of Maryland, and he had a personal connection to both. He was only too aware of how isolated the Delmarva Peninsula was, and three of the states he was responsible for were found within its boundaries. A bridge was needed across the Chesapeake Bay, and one was needed across the longest river on the peninsula, the Choptank. The Choptank River Bridge would be one of the first projects funded, and that bridge would be built and dedicated by 1935. Funding was always an issue for the costly Bay Bridge, and eventually the project was scrapped. George, however, would persist in later years while in the Senate, but the war would further postpone it for another decade.

George would only hold the PWA position for eighteen months, but he accomplished much during that period. Hospitals were built and revitalized, new schools were funded, sewage systems were upgraded—especially in the Chesapeake Bay region—a 600-mile road from Washington to the Great Smoky National Park was planned, naval ship development in Baltimore and the Hampton Roads area was invigorated, deepening of the Chesapeake and Delaware Canal was carried out, and dams and electrification projects were planned. The goal was not so much to employ the unemployed (which the Works Progress Administration, WPA, did with smaller projects) but to stimulate the economy with large projects.

George was determined to get projects moving as quickly as possible as each project would stimulate a local economy. He traveled frequently through all seven states, soliciting ideas. He set up a committee of volunteers and paid employees to administer the work, and the speed and efficiency with which he implemented projects attracted the attention of Roosevelt, who held up Region Ten as the model for other regions to follow. Within six months, George had developed a model advisory board and collected considerable data from every county in the seven-state area. With the board and extensive data, George and his associates could act quickly on requests, adjusting the Federal money to the unemployment in each area. George also quickly developed departments within his regional office with department heads reporting to him in daily meetings. These organizational accomplishments and his success in moving projects quickly set the stage for the next phase of George's life. He may not have sought attention, but he was getting it on local, state, and national levels.[12]

George's association with Franklin Roosevelt would add another item to his extremely busy agenda. Over the years he had not only gotten to know the man but also his disease. Numerous visits to see his friend in New York and Warm Springs had given George a more than ample opportunity to see how crippling a disease polio could be, and when a Birthday Ball was planned for the President's birthday in 1934 to raise funds for combatting the disease, George climbed on board, taking charge of the Baltimore celebration. Over the years, these Birthday Balls grew and eventually evolved into the March of Dimes Foundation, and George would oversee the Maryland portion of this for over thirty years. In 1932, he was elected vice president of the Maryland Historical Society, and this also would evolve into a major focus for the remainder of his life. His work with the PWA and the 1934 Birthday Ball not only cemented his already close friendship with Roosevelt, but it thrust him into both the state and national limelight, and later that year, everything would change.

THE POLITICAL YEARS: 1935 - 1947

The political arena in Maryland was growing uncomfortable in 1934 as Albert Ritchie was coming up on a possible fifth term as governor, and Baltimore Mayor Howard Jackson was also considering running. Many of the Democratic leaders felt that Ritchie would be unsuccessful in his bid for re-election, and Millard Tydings was afraid the governorship was going to fall into Republican hands. He, among others, began to ask George to run for governor, getting the standard Radcliffe response that he was way too busy with his other positions. In May of 1934, George was in the South for a two-week period inspecting the Smoky Mountain – Shenandoah Highway Project when he received an urgent telegram from Maryland officials to return. Franklin Roosevelt was now involved with the movement to get George to run for governor, and he would soon meet with George and Tydings at the White House. George once again got the supreme presidential squeeze combined with a vote of support from the State Central Committee, and he would soon succumb. The argument that won George over was that his running for governor might decrease the disharmony building in the Maryland Democratic establishment as animosity was building between the Ritchie and Jackson factions, and George was presented as a non-controversial alternative.

In June, George announced his candidacy for Maryland governor, with Tydings indicating that he could get Governor Ritchie to run for the Senate position being vacated by Republican Phillips Lee Goldsborough, who was now thinking of running for governor. Tydings, to appease Ritchie, even went so far as to say that he would resign if Ritchie were elected Senator making Ritchie the senior senator from Maryland; Tydings could then be appointed by the new governor, assuming it was

George, as the junior Maryland senator. However, by the next month, it was apparent that Ritchie was still going to run for governor, and George—out of friendship for him—bowed out of the gubernatorial campaign and was convinced to run for U.S. senator.[13] In that one month, he had assembled an impressive campaign committee, printed campaign brochures and buttons, and started to make the campaigning rounds. Without losing a step, all the campaign materials just had "Governor" replaced by "Senator," and the campaign steamed ahead. The man who never aspired to a political lifestyle tackled campaigning with the same gusto and organizational ability he had employed in all his ventures.

Things settled down after the crazy month of musical political offices, and George easily won the Democratic primary over William Maloy on Sept. 12, carrying every county and Baltimore City and getting double the vote total of his opponent. His Republican opponent would be former Senator Joseph I. France. The campaign was relatively mild compared to the political chaos early in the summer. George, of course, had his critics, and the primary point of attack was that he was just running as the friend of the president, a criticism that would carry on well after the general election.[14] George did little to distance himself from this line of criticism as he saw his friendship with Roosevelt as being a potential asset for Maryland. His record in Public Works, however, was a strong plus. His greatest selling point was simply his character and reputation for getting things done. As his campaign brochure stated:

> No man illustrates in his character and bearing the qualities which Marylanders like to associate with themselves—tolerance, open-mindedness, capacity for lasting friendships, hospitality—more completely than does Mr. Radcliffe. His fellow Marylanders have frequently proved their faith in his capacity for large affairs in the most practical manner in which men can prove that faith—by asking that it be used in their behalf and in be-

half of those whom they have served.[15]

On Nov. 6, 1934, George became the junior senator from Maryland, getting 264,279 votes to 197,643 for Dr. Joseph France. Ironically, Albert Richie lost his bid for a fifth term, losing to Harry Nice by a very slim margin.[16] In hindsight, Millard Tydings' plan for the Maryland Democratic Party was a wise one; if Ritchie had run for senate and George for governor, both would likely have been elected. Now Tydings would be regarded as the Maryland Democratic leader with George likely taking advice from him, but George had the ear of President Roosevelt, and that relationship would initially propel him up the political hierarchy. George stressed to all, however, that his relationship with Roosevelt was a personal, not political, one, although George had clearly run as a "New Deal" supporter.

On. Jan. 3, 1935, George was one of twelve new senators, all Democrats, sworn in; the freshman Senator from Missouri sworn in that same day was Harry Truman, and they would grow to be close friends. George was appointed to the Banking and Currency Committee, a logical appointment given his background in a surety company, as well as the Library and Patents Committees. It would be in his role on the Library Committee that he would form a friendship years later with Archibald MacLeish, Pulitzer Prize-winning poet, whom Roosevelt would appoint as Chief Librarian of the Library of Congress in 1939. Also sworn in that day was Joe Guffey from neighboring Pennsylvania, and he and George would work together closely on a variety of issues throughout George's two terms.

George would be a unique senator in several ways. He was the only U.S. senator to commute to Washington, although he did maintain an apartment at the Shoreham Hotel. He had a wife and fifteen-year-old son to return to, but he was still wearing many civic hats in addition to still being vice president of the Fidelity and Deposit Company. In fact, that first January, he was coordinating the second Presidential Birthday Ball in Baltimore because his personal interest with the Ball would never take a back seat to anything. He also was the only Ph.D. in the United States Senate, and his passion for historical research made him well suited to research issues and specific bills. In many ways he was equipped to be the professor of the Senate, more the academic than the fiery orator or the passionate advocate of a cause. Deliberate, well researched, and compromising would be his approach to all aspects of his Senate work.

The Social Security Act was the dominant legislative item that first year, and George would support it. His two years with what was now the PWA served him well as many pieces of legislation dealt with PWA projects. His interest in Chesapeake Bay preservation made him a leading advocate of Bay-related bills, and he continued his efforts to get a Chesapeake Bay Bridge funded. His history background would surface as he began what would be an almost two-decade fight to get the *USS Constellation*, thought to be one of the earliest US warships, returned to Baltimore. George, although now a national political figure, kept his focus on the state which had elected him. Maryland—and Baltimore in particular—never had a more adamant supporter in the United States Senate.

Surprising both critics and supporters in his first year in the Senate, George would prove to be his own man. Accused initially of being a "yes man" for the president, George would break ranks on several occasions. He was in favor of New Deal emergency legislation saying the economy needed to be strengthened as quickly as possible, and people needed to be put back to work. However, he would prove himself over the years to be a fiscal conservative and clearly opposed to unnecessary government intervention. He would state that as emergency situations abated, less government intervention was necessary. Siding with many Republicans, he supported the Neutrality Act of 1935 which, in the face of an increased potential for conflict in the world, prohibited transporting arms, ammunition, and the machinery of war to countries involved in a war.

But where George significantly broke ranks with the president was on the Public Utility Holding Company Bill, a bill aimed to control and eliminate public utility holding companies involved in interstate and foreign commerce. The bill would put all holding companies under the control of the Security and Exchange Commission (SEC). One aspect of the bill which came to be known as the "death sentence" provided for the elimination by the SEC of a holding company if it could not justify its existence economically within five years. George saw this as the government going beyond the necessary remediation to a place of unneeded involvement.

He was also a member of the Commerce Committee, and here he found his niche, the Special Committee to Investigate the Merchant Marine. A logical assignment considering his father had been a shipbuilder, here is where George would spend more than half of his time in the United States Senate, and he would chair the committee during his second term. In 1936, he took the lead in the Senate to secure passage of the Merchant Marine Act of 1936, which completely transformed the country's merchant marine fleet. His interest in the history of shipping led him to do significant research on the subject, resulting in a significant, but short, unpublished history of the United States Merchant Marine. While the country was nowhere near entering a war, especially with the growing isolationist movement, George still saw war as a possibility, and the deficient United States Merchant Marine could become the country's Achilles' Heel. He realized how unprepared the United States merchant fleet had been during World War I, with the Armistice signed before the first new merchant ship was launched. In 1936, George knew that the United States owned an inadequate fleet and had few shipyards—those were primarily on the East Coast, He realized that it would take time to create the infrastructure for an enlarged merchant fleet, and action was needed at that point in time. He was not going to let the mistakes in World War I be made again.[17]

The Merchant Marine Act of 1936 would provide subsidies for

U.S. ship construction as well as create a Merchant Marine Commission which would oversee the whole project. For George, this would remain his number one issue throughout his two terms, and the infrastructure would be in place and the first ships launched before the United States would enter World War II.

In 1936 Franklin Roosevelt was up for re-election, and George would once again head up the Maryland Democratic campaign. The more conservative Millard Tydings was not a Roosevelt supporter, and Roosevelt was certainly antagonizing the Southern Democratic base by pushing for what many perceived as too much government intervention in the lives of many. Prior to 1936, to receive the Democratic nomination, a candidate needed two-thirds of the convention delegates, but this changed that year to a simple majority. The more moderate Southern Democratic base, and that included many in Maryland, saw this as taking away whatever power and influence they had.[18] While George had some concerns about how far Roosevelt was willing to go, both his friendship and faith in the President made him a serious supporter of the President's re-election. He also credited Roosevelt with supporting many of the federal loans given to Baltimore institutions.

Albert Ritchie had died in early 1936, and factionalism was reigning supreme in the Maryland Democratic campaign. Tydings had opposed much of the New Deal legislation, and George was still being referred to as a "rubber stamp" for the President. When George saw few in Maryland rushing to support the President's re-election, he decided to take charge, even going so far as to pay the Maryland filing fee for Roosevelt, for which he was never reimbursed. He decided to remove himself as much as possible from the politicking and just work hard, with limited support, for the President's re-election. Ignoring criticism and the bait to jump into the political fight, he wisely stayed above the fray. It was also important for him to not get dragged into arguments with Tydings, as he did not want to damage the power and influence the Senator had for Maryland. Roosevelt would go on to win the state by an extremely comfortable margin.

For George, the 1936 election, while successful, seemed to be a baptism of fire, as several of the local Democratic Clubs criticized his chairmanship. The Trenton Democratic Club said that George's selection as chairman was "an indictment of the intelligence and wisdom of the Democratic leadership of Maryland."[19] George chose to just ignore the criticisms, and the election results vindicated his efforts.

Roosevelt's impressive sweep over Landon in the Maryland election by over 160,000 votes suddenly brought back support for George which had temporarily vanished. As Roosevelt's leading supporter in Maryland, George was asked to be the new Maryland Democratic boss. George's reaction to that was swift and predictable. "That sounds like a flight of someone's fancy. I have never had any aspirations to be a party boss, and I certainly have neither the taste nor the aptitude for such a position." And the news reported his predictable response, "The one-time schoolteacher turned financier has distinguished his political career by an aptitude for smoothing over factional differences rather than creating them."[20] The only part of that which George would question is that deep in his heart he was still that simple schoolteacher. As always, politics made him uncomfortable.

In 1937, George's relationship with Franklin Roosevelt suffered its first major fracture. The year began with the annual Birthday Ball, and George had managed to increase both the scope and the proceeds each year. However, in February, Roosevelt would release his Supreme Court reorganization plan, referred to as his attempt to "pack the Supreme Court." The court had overturned several of Roosevelt's New Deal measures, and the 1936 re-election emboldened him. His plan, which he hoped would make the court more liberal, would allow him to appoint a judge as an "assistant" for every judge aged seventy or older, up to six additional. Sen. Tydings immediately opposed the plan, but George refused to take a position. Roosevelt called his friend to the White House on several occasions, but George refused to support the plan. He told Roosevelt that he could not support the plan but thought there could be a less controversial compromise, suggesting that the matter should be referred to a committee of legal minds which could examine aspects of the court: Should there be a maximum age? Was nine the best number of justices? Were there matters the court should not deal with? Roosevelt agreed and sent George to explore. George's attempt at a compromise ended when it became clear that there was insufficient Senate support for the court plan. At that point, he voted against the plan, attracting considerable attention because of his well-known friendship and prior support of the President.[21]

In 1937, Roosevelt controversially nominated Sen. Hugo Black for the Supreme Court, not only because of Black's general support of the President, but because he had backed Roosevelt's attempt to pack the court. George would vote for the nomination, but shortly thereafter, all would learn that Black had once been a member of the Ku Klux Klan. There would be calls for his resignation, but since he had resigned his membership and otherwise seemed qualified, George and others would let the appointment stand. Criticism of George for this vote would surface again in his 1940 re-election bid.

George's friendship with Roosevelt survived the court issue, but the 1938 election derailed the relationship for a while. In that mid-term election, Roosevelt attempted to purge the Senate of the few conservative Democratic senators, mostly Southern, who often stood in the way of his legislation. George's Maryland cohort, Millard Tydings, was one of those senators. George was put in a difficult position, but in this election, as in 1936, maintaining party unity in the state was paramount to George. Tydings, running for his third term, not only asked George for his support but asked him to run his re-election campaign, which George readily agreed to, elevating peace in the party and state over his friendship with the President. Roosevelt, expecting George's support in finding a replacement candidate, was obviously upset, but George was also frustrated by Tydings, who, rather than thanking George, said that the move of support would probably benefit George more than himself. George was irritated by this comment, considering what he thought had been a gracious move on his part. "I told him that was the most graceless remark that I ever heard and advised him never to make a similar one to a person that had gone out on the limb for him."[22] George still worked tirelessly to get Tydings re-elected, but their relationship would begin to deteriorate. The relationship between George and Franklin Roosevelt hit rocky ground, and Franklin in retaliation withdrew support for his friend when George ran for re-election two years later.

George's involvement with the Maryland Historical Society was growing, and in 1939, he was elected its president with the goals of increasing membership, adding to the Society's already extensive holdings, and upgrading the programming. His connections in the Senate and federal government made him well suited for the latter. That same year the Presidential Birthday Balls came under the same criticism which George had personally dealt with, its close connection with Roosevelt. George was well experienced in combatting this issue, and the Balls now fell under the umbrella of the newly formed National Foundation for Infantile Paralysis, thus removing any perceived political connection. From the late 1930s leading up to the war, George had tapped into Hollywood for the Birthday Balls, bringing in star power each year, including Robert Taylor, Eleanor Powell, Mickey Rooney, and Olivia De Havilland.

With five years in the Senate under his belt, George was growing weary of the excessive politics, which he saw as impeding progress. He remarked on several occasions that the real Senate work happened in committees, not on the floor of the Senate. He commented on the propensity of certain senators to hold things up because they seemed more interesting in hearing themselves talk than working behind the scenes to get things done.

It will be a happy day for this country when our leaders will put their heads together and try to work in cooperation without so much criticism of one another. I don't decry criticism, but I think it can easily be carried to excess and the result is that its destructive qualities are over accentuated.[23]

While still calling himself a New Deal supporter, the banking and insurance man in him was starting to surface. With the Depression lifting, less emergency infusion of federal money was needed, in George's eyes. "Certainly, we must make material progress toward balancing the budget, eliminating certain emergency legislation, and reducing expenditures as far as it is feasible to do so at this time."[18] While wanting to avoid war at all costs, he saw continued build-up of the merchant marine and military forces as essential, referring to it not as preparation for war, but "insurance."

George was up for re-election in 1940, and he would face stiff competition in the primary from businessman Howard Bruce. Early in the campaign, several Democrats, including Bruce and Tydings, started a movement to gain support for George to run for mayor of Baltimore. When it became clear that this was just a move to vacate the Senate position so that Bruce could then be appointed, that plan fell apart, and pressure was now put on Tydings to support George, especially considering George's extraordinary support of his colleague in 1938. Tydings felt that George could not be re-elected because the Democratic machinery would likely support Bruce.

Millard Tydings did eventually support George in what would be a fierce campaign. Bruce argued that George had done nothing, with George replying that Bruce had actually supported everything he had done in the Senate. Bruce would repeatedly dredge up George's vote to confirm Hugo Black, but George would go on to win the primary by a sizeable margin. Although clearly breaking with Roosevelt on a couple of occasions, George did use his campaign as a referendum on the President, also up for re-election that year.

Tydings was clearly opposed to the re-election of the President, and George even had reservations, feeling that two terms should be the maximum for a president. The Republican candidate for Senator was Gov. Harry Nice, but the general campaign was relatively low-key. George went on to a resounding victory in November with a vote total almost double that of the Governor; and Roosevelt would carry Maryland.

George continued his commitment to keeping the country out of a war, saying:

> Today we are faced with the hideous realization that nations are far behind individuals in settling their disputes. For centuries individuals have settled their differences before juries and courts, but nations continue to fight over the slightest provocations. I am for world peace and shall stand firm to keep the United States out of the present conflict.[24]

The re-elected Senator began his second term on an optimistic note, even though things were deteriorating in Europe and in the Pacific, making his work to build up the Merchant Marine even more critical. The infrastructure was largely in place and merchant ships were under construction in multiple shipyards. By 1941, the U.S. had sixteen shipyards and had begun constructing economical cargo ships which came to be known as Liberty Ships. The first of these, logically named the *SS Patrick Henry*, was launched on Sept. 27, 1941, with George delivering a nationwide address for the occasion. His commitment to the merchant marine was also reversing his adamant pro-peace position as he now urged for repeal of the Neutrality Act which he previously supported. Always the historian, he compared Nazi aggression on the high seas to the action of the Barbary pirates which led to the formation of the United States Navy after the Revolution.

No nation in the world, which has ever prospered for any long period of time, has maintained steadily a policy of isolation . . . still is heard throughout the United States the voice of those who plead for peace at any cost, those who insist that we must restrict our activities to extremely narrow confines in the hope of avoiding friction. But they do not, they cannot, give us assurance that the policy of isolation they advocate could insure peace to us.[25]

Less than two months later, the United States was at war, and George's merchant marine sub-committee would now go into hyperdrive. He would later say that he introduced over one hundred bills related to the merchant marine in his term as chairman of that committee. In 1943 his only son, George, enlisted in the US Army Air Corps, bringing the war closer to home than he would have wanted. Young George served in the Pacific on Kwajalein Atoll in the Marshall Islands as an aircraft maintenance officer but would see no actual combat.

One somewhat surprising issue that George L. Radcliffe was involved with during his second term was the Equal Rights Amendment, guaranteeing equality for women. George, who had always been surrounded by strong women, was an advocate of equal rights, yet did not want women to be placed in physically dangerous work situations or to serve equally in the military. In 1939, he had even gone so far as to suggest that Susan B. Anthony be one of the faces on Mount Rushmore. He had long favored promoting women to higher positions; in 1921, he hired a woman to run the training school at the Fidelity and Deposit Company.[26] In 1945, he gave one of his rare speeches in front of the United States Senate and was able to get the amendment out of committee for a vote, getting a majority but not the necessary two-thirds. He continued to advocate for that amendment throughout his life.

One of the criticisms of George by his opponent in the 1946 election was that he was often not in Washington. This was likely true as he must have burned a rut in the roads between Baltimore and Washington, frequently being in both cities, and often twice, in the same day. With his positions as vice president and executive committee chairman of the Fidelity and Deposit Company, president of the Maryland Historical Society, and chairman of the Maryland Chapter of the National Foundation for Infantile Paralysis in Baltimore, and while still needing to be in Washington for Senate votes and committee meetings, it would be safe to say that he was overextended. Unable to drive himself, he hired a full-time chauffeur, Swain Foxwell, who was a lifelong friend. His schedule was nothing short of ridiculous, and he would later say that in his twelve years in the Senate, his expenses far outweighed his income.

During the war, he tripled the membership of the Maryland Historical Society, hired a director for the organization, planned expansion of the complex, and brought in a remarkable array of speakers. While some of the membership had urged George to cut back on Historical Society activities during the war, he was able to do exactly the opposite. In 1943, he used his Washington connections to schedule many of the country's military leaders for talks, bringing what was happening in Washington right to the people of Maryland. In 1945, he had two nationally recognized speakers: Gen. George Marshall and Vice President Harry Truman—two weeks before he took over as President. George and the Society were also given the job of assembling all of Maryland's war records for the current war as he had done for World War I.

His strained relationship with Roosevelt became a thing of the past as George would resume visiting the White House, often bringing terrapin (turtle) soup, which he knew the President liked. While George was becoming more fiscally conservative, he and Roosevelt stayed connected, with George enthusiastically supporting Roosevelt's re-election in 1944. After Roosevelt's death, the "terrapin soup train" would continue to stop at the White House as George would frequently visit President Truman, his Senate colleague and friend. The friendship and frequent White

House visits would continue even when George left the Senate, and the two remained close, writing frequently, until Harry Truman's death in 1972.

As a member of the Senate Banking and Currency Committee, George would become involved in developing the Bretton Woods Agreement, which in 1944 established an international monetary fund. In 1945, he offered an amendment which would serve as a directive in identifying trade restrictions. The agreement would stimulate and somewhat equalize trade in the post-war era; gold would be replaced by the US dollar as the global currency, and fixed exchange rates would be established between the dollar and other currencies. It would also create the World Bank and the International Monetary Fund. The agreement would make the United States the undisputed leader in the global economy.[27] George was interested in establishing international cooperation after the war, something he felt had not happened after World War I. With his continued interest in the Merchant Marine, he was looking for the establishment of significant world trade.

> The functioning of the bank and fund at the earliest possible moment in stimulating efforts to remove international trade and currency barriers will make a substantial and indispensable contribution toward the recovery of a world never before so enfeebled and prostrated.[28]

During this possibly busiest period for George in the U.S. Senate, he was falling out of favor with Maryland Democratic leaders. While he had never truly been a "party player," his more fiscally conservative measures were not setting well with leaders in Maryland. He suspected that both Millard Tydings and Governor Herbert O'Conor were plotting to get him out of the Senate, and this turned out to be political reality in 1946. George had filed for re-election late in 1945, but there was now a move to get him to run for governor, thus freeing up his Senate seat. Tydings denied this, but he also would not support George's bid for re-election.[29] There was also a move to get George to run for Baltimore mayor again. Finally, in 1946, Governor O'Conor announced his candidacy for George's position. George's advanced age, 68, was a concern for many, but he generally had been popular. It is quite likely that George would have lost any way in the primary election to O'Conor, a popular governor and party loyalist, but several issues in 1946 further complicated matters. George would oppose the maritime strike, wanting to keep his beloved Merchant Marine fully active. There was also a move after the war to institute price controls, especially on meat. George stalled on voicing his opinion as Democratic leaders in the State grew frustrated with him. He felt, as he did on many post-Depression issues, that things are best left to the market; unnecessary government intervention was not a solution. At the last minute, he ended up siding with the Republicans and voting against the controls. This would be the last straw for Democratic leaders in Maryland, and he would lose the primary to O'Conor.

He was admittedly shaken in losing as he had never lost an election before, but he quickly saw this as an opportunity to put all his time into his many other interests and responsibilities. He commented that he finally could take a vacation, but this was not to happen as George was to become even busier in 1947.

The Civic Years: 1947 - 1974

Retirement would be an inappropriate term for what happened when George L. Radcliffe left the Senate. He still was vice president of the Fidelity and Deposit Company, president of the Maryland Historical Society, and chairman of the Maryland Chapter of the National Foundation for Infantile Paralysis. He would remain so busy that one could wonder how he ever had time to be a U.S. Senator. Although he had lost some favor with the political establishment, he was still popular with the people and was sought after for a litany of organizations and speaking engagements. How ironic it was that the man who was considered a mediocre orator at best would probably give more speeches each year than he had in the Senate. He was never a dynamic speaker, but his knowledge of history, his impressive recollection of facts and anecdotes, and his ability to connect any event or organization to local history made him a frequent speaker.

His primary interest in the Senate, the Merchant Marine, continued to occupy some of his time. He followed the legislation carefully, and this remained the focus of his correspondence and frequent visits with President Truman. In 1948, he chaired Truman's re-election campaign in Maryland and would play a minor role in every election through 1960. Baltimore Mayor D'Alesandro appointed him chairman of the Citizen's Aviation Committee, the group which would assist the city in getting an international airport—Friendship Airport, now BWI-Thurgood Marshall Airport—dedicated in 1950.

Whatever the occasion or holiday—Maryland Day, Constitution Day, Defender's Day, or Flag Day—George would be involved, making speech after speech. Need a master of ceremonies? George was your man;

while once again not the best orator, George would leave them smiling with his warm approach, mastery of facts, a wonderful story, and his obvious love of Baltimore and Maryland.

George, as Maryland Historical Society president, would do more to promote Maryland history and the preservation of historical relics and documents than most anyone. He would help many of the Maryland counties develop their own historical societies and would speak often to many of these groups. As president, he was able to have the society acquire the original manuscript of the Star-Spangled Banner in 1954. Under his leadership and with his legal help, the society purchased the entire city block around its Baltimore center, allowing for the construction of a much larger complex in 1964. He stepped down as president in 1964 and was appointed chairman of the group until his death in 1974.

He focused considerable time and effort to commemorate Maryland's role in the Battle of Long Island during the American Revolution. In one of the most significant battles of the war, 400 Maryland troops had been able to hold off the British in 1776, allowing time for Washington and his army to get away, probably avoiding a quick end to the Revolution, although 256 of the Maryland troops were killed. In speaking about the battle, George said:

> ... in the hour purchased by Maryland blood, the bulk of the American army escaped to Brooklyn Heights within the fortified lines. Washington and his genius for organization, re-formed them and two days later evacuated them to Manhattan. Had the Marylanders failed, the cause of independence might well have ended. Washington himself later referred to that hour in the Battle of Brooklyn as 'more precious to American liberty than any other in its history.[30]

George was constantly in search of some history to uncover, some unsung hero to recognize, some historically significant structure or area to preserve. As president of the historical society and with the notoriety he had achieved over the years, he was well suited to put Maryland history on the front burner. In 1959, at age eighty-two, the history flame in him was still burning brightly, and Governor J. Millard Tawes asked him to be Maryland chairman of the Civil War Centennial Commission. Over the next few years, he oversaw re-enactments and traveled from Mobile to Vicksburg to Antietam to Gettysburg attending events and assisting other states. He used the Maryland historical roadside markers program, now under the control of the Maryland Historical Society, to commemorate significant events and Marylanders, including the first marker to recognize Harriett Tubman.

George was interested in the facts of Civil War history, not promoting one side versus another. If he still held any allegiance these many years later, no one could tell. He did not hesitate, however, to recognize the military brilliance of Lee, Jackson, and other Confederate generals as he had when he helped get the Lee-Jackson equestrian statue erected in Baltimore. To George, it was simply a matter of recognizing and remembering accurately a momentous period in American history. This was a fitting project for a man who over fifty years earlier had made his academic mark with his research and book on Maryland's commitment to the Union in 1861.

As chairman of the March of Dimes in Maryland, he oversaw each year's annual drive, always pushing to get funding to local agencies researching polio. He used his association with Johns Hopkins to funnel money to the research there, a forerunner of the work leading to the Salk vaccine. The development of this vaccine would lead to the oral vaccine in a few years, almost eradicating polio as a disease in this country. Ironically, the vaccine's success also made the organization's fund raising extremely difficult. While the March of Dimes would grow to cover birth defects and other crippling conditions, many perceived its mission complete with the advent of an effective vaccine. George had to work hard to maintain the interest of the public and was able to sustain effective fund raising throughout his long tenure as president, finally stepping down in 1968 at the age of ninety-one.

In 1950 and 1951, George continued his mission of historical preservation as he turned his focus to the Eastern Shore of Maryland. The Maryland Historical Society, in conjunction with the Society for Maryland Antiquities, undertook a comprehensive architectural survey of historic structures on the Eastern Shore built before 1800. Arthur Houghton, a prominent landowner, played a significant role and funded himself the restoration of one of the identified structures, St. Luke's Church. George secured funding for the survey which identified over fifty buildings, and this motivated him to roll his sleeves up and get to work.

At the same time, George was showing interest in Grace Episcopal Church on Taylor's Island, the church his grandfather had helped build years earlier. With the church needing work and with the survey identifying the Chapel of Ease, the original chapel on Taylor's Island, as one of the historic structures, George and local island residents set up a historical foundation to oversee the preservation of Taylor's Island history. Since his mother, Sophie, was born on Taylor's Island, this was also a personal journey for George. As president of the Grace Foundation, he oversaw the restoration of Grace Church and the moving and renovation of the Chapel of Ease to the Grace Church property. The Foundation also coordinated with the group restoring nearby Old Trinity Church, which George was also connected with. George got the Chrysler family to fund the renovation of Old Trinity, and the Grace Foundation gradually raised funds for its projects.

In 1962, he started the planning to celebrate the 300th birthday of his family home, Spocott. He loved parties and saw this as an opportunity to merge party and history. A small family party grew to a large family party of 100 guests. As word spread, members of his extended family asked to attend, and the invitation list grew to 200. The problem was that everyone claimed to be related to "Cousin George." Beloved by all in the County, the invitation list grew and grew until approximately 500 showed up for the event, complete with a major feast: oysters, fried chicken, and enough pies and desserts to sink the *Titanic*. Stories abounded, and the eighty-six-year-old Senator was in his glory. This could have been the culmination of a long life, but George was far from done.

The 1960s would present George with two major setbacks. His beloved wife, Mary McKim "Daisy" Marriott died in 1963 after four years of illness, during which she had often been hospitalized. He continued to live in his house in Baltimore, making frequent trips to Spocott Farm, and he still went to work each day at the Fidelity and Deposit Company. He kept an active routine, which included a workout at a local gym. In 1967, however, tragedy struck again. While working in his office one day, two men entered his office, threatening to harm him if he did not open the office safe. The eighty-nine-year-old refused, and he was beaten badly, breaking his hip, and even more significantly, damaging his spirit. The safe was intact, but the two men robbed him, stealing the gold watch he had won almost seventy years earlier at the Penn Relays. He was devastated to lose that watch, truly his prized possession. His hip gradually healed, but the loss of the watch left a piece of him missing. However, not long after, Johns Hopkins University honored one of its most illustrious graduates, presenting him with a duplicate gold watch. Not surprisingly, George L. Radcliffe was reborn.

In 1970, George's life would come full circle: he had moved from farm to county to state and then to country but now had returned to his father's farm. He was now ready for his final project. In 1888, when he was ten, his father's windmill had blown down in a winter storm. A young George had salvaged the steps and millstones from that mill, and eighty-two years later, it was time to rebuild it. Forming the Spocott Windmill Foundation, he found funding and hired a builder, master boatbuilder James Richardson, known to all as Captain Jim. Working from a model, he had constructed by rigorous trial and error, Jim and his crew built the two-story English post mill in the same location as the original. The mill was dedicated and presented to the Senator on his ninety-fifth birthday, August 22, 1972.

Less than two years later, George L. Radcliffe died, just short of his ninety-seventh birthday. He had outlived so many that he had known: Roosevelt, Truman, all his siblings, most of his cousins, and his long-time friend and chauffeur Swain Foxwell, who had died a few months earlier. George had lived long enough to hold his first great-grandchild and left behind younger generations who had come to know this legend. Praise came in from across the country, but friend and Maryland Historical Society colleague Sam Hopkins said it best:

> Senator Radcliffe thoroughly liked people. He was at ease with others regardless of place, background, or differences. He made them feel comfortable and enjoy being with him. A person full of infinite goodness and blessed with ability and good judgment, the Senator was instinctively turned to by people when they wanted a man in whom they could place their trust and from whom they would receive fair and wise help or advice. Individuals and groups, often those with conflicting views, turned to him for help in resolving their differences or accomplishing a task. He was a man of patience, quick to forgive and who could just not harbor a grudge. His very nature rebelled at man's cruelty to man. It was never for him to cause pain or mortification to others.
>
> It is an inspiration to look back on the life of Senator George L. Radcliffe. He lived a life in which a sense of the past was linked so beautifully with the realities of the present and an optimistic view for the future.[31]

Essays

———◆———

Early Influences

A Confluence of
Genes and Environment

The existence of each of us is a mathematical improbability since every one of our millions of ancestors had to survive to reproduce. If even one of them had died of a childhood disease, been killed in combat or by accident before reproducing, or chosen not to reproduce, the assemblage of DNA that makes a person could not have happened. George L. Radcliffe is descended from numerous lines, most tracing back to England, and these lines needed to make the voyage across the Atlantic and then survive in a young country with all its inherent dangers. Like so many Americans, he comes from "good stock."

His parents were John Anthony LeCompte Radcliffe (1818–1901) and Sophie Delilah Travers (1837–1927), both of Dorchester County, Maryland. So many of George's ancestors were early immigrants to Maryland, arriving in Dorchester County:

- Richard Ratcliff (1661–1721), 4th great-grandfather – arrived 1682
- William Warner (1654–1713), 4th great-grandfather – arrived 1689
- Stephen Gary (1624–1686), 5th great-grandfather – arrived 1650
- Sir Antoine LeCompte (1618–1673), 5th great-grandfather – arrived 1665
- Dr. Robert Winsmore (1630–1677), 5th great-grandfather
- William Beckwith (1571-1663), 5th great-grandfather – arrived in Jamestown 1608

- William Aip Travers (1640–1701), 5th great-grandfather – arrived 1665
- Capt. Henry Hooper (1605–1676), 6th great-grandfather – arrived 1651
- William Chapline (1625–1669), 6th great-grandfather – arrived 1651
- Richard Keene (1628–1675), 6th great-grandfather – arrived 1653
- Thomas Pattison (1630–1701), 6th great-grandfather – arrived 1635

His ancestors read like a *Who's Who* of early Dorchester County history. The first Radcliffe ancestor in America was Richard Ratcliff, who barely survived his voyage from England in 1682. As a twenty-one-year-old, he booked passage on the *Submission*, leaving from Liverpool, heading toward Philadelphia. A storm almost destroyed the ship, and as the log states:

> A great head (of) sea broke over the ship & staved the boat & took most part of it away, broke up the main hatches that were both nailed & corked & took them away that they were not seen where they went, broke the boat's mast & hyst that were lashed in the midship, broke the gunnell head in the midship & broke the forre shet & took several things of(f) the decks and severall things that were in the boat it cast betwixt decks.[1]

The 58-day voyage ended up in the Chesapeake Bay, landing at Choptank, Maryland.

Richard, a Quaker, settled in Talbot County, Maryland, where he joined the Third Haven Meeting House. His descendants would eventually move to Dorchester County. Richard's son, James, married Sarah Warner, daughter of immigrant William Warner, and granddaughter of Stephen Gary, also a Quaker. George L. Radcliffe, many years later, would grow up on Stephen Gary's farm.

Another ancestor, William Beckwith, had an equally hazardous voyage across the Atlantic. William was a tailor on board the *Phoenix*, one of the three ships of the first supply mission to Jamestown. Leaving England in October of 1607, the other two ships arrived safely in Jamestown in January of 1608, but these had lost sight of the *Phoenix*. Given up for lost, the *Phoenix* finally arrived in Jamestown three months later. Blown off course by a major storm, the ship had docked in the Caribbean for the winter.[2] Once in Jamestown, William then had to endure the trying early days of that colony.

Many of the earliest settlers to Dorchester County settled in the Neck District area, between the Choptank and Little Choptank Rivers, stretching west to the Chesapeake Bay. They were an unusual breed, many of them Quakers, and most fleeing difficult situations in their own native countries. They developed an independent spirit as they lived in a relatively isolated area with both the Choptank River and Chesapeake Bay separating them from most early settlers to Maryland. They were farmers, but also shipbuilders, needing some access to the rest of the state as well as markets for the goods and crops they produced. They worked hard to survive and prosper in this remote area. The area was good to them, as they were also surrounded by a virtual cornucopia of seafood and game. These early settlers dealt with considerable hardships on a regular basis: disease; cold winters; hot summers; and the dreaded mosquito, which could humble even the strongest individual. Such was the environment and ancestry that George Radcliffe was born into.

George's mother, Sophie, was the daughter of Thomas Broome Travers (1802–1875), a shipbuilder. Her mother, Mary Elizabeth Travers died at age twenty-three, leaving Thomas to raise Sophie and her two sisters by himself. George's father, John Anthony LeCompte Radcliffe, was the oldest child of James Sewell Radcliffe (1793–1851) and Margaret Harris (1798–1879). Both John and Sophie lost their first spouses; John lost Rebecca Sarah Beckwith in 1870, and Sophie's first husband, Andrew Jackson Robinson, died in 1869. Between the two of them, they had sixteen children, making their marriage in 1871 the original *Yours. Mine, and Ours.* They would go on to have three more children: Thomas Broome Radcliffe (1874–1954), James Sewell Radcliffe (1875–1967), and finally George Lovic Pierce Radcliffe (1877–1974). George would thus be the youngest of nineteen children. Add to that crowd his father's nine siblings, and George was the youngest in a huge family, all looking out for him and giving him advice.

There is no doubt that George's father was a dominant influence. Referred to as "Mr. Radcliffe" by even his wife at times, John was clearly the patriarch of this family. As the oldest sibling, the father of thirteen himself, and a leader in the community, John was the one all looked up to.

According to his son, George, and grandson, George M. Radcliffe, John was an extremely serious and well-read man. While there had been no school available for him to attend, he acquired quite a library, and no day passed without him spending some time reading. John obviously passed this passion on to his children, and George L. Radcliffe became quite the serious reader. As an indication of the advanced level of his reading, George, at the age of ten, was given a copy of *Plutarch's Lives of the Noble Greeks and Romans*, hardly a book a young child would

*John Anthony LeCompte Radcliffe
(1818-1901)
George's father*

choose to read. Spocott had its own family library, and this became the biggest part of young George's education.

John also had a physically imposing presence, "seeming to fill up a doorway", how many described his appearance. At age fourteen, he had rescued his crippled aunt Catherine LeCompte from a fire. Racing into the burning house, he lifted Catherine in her chair and carried both outside to safety. In ensuing years, John did not become the Gentleman Farmer, but worked side by side with all the laborers, whether in farming or shipbuilding, thus gaining the complete respect of all. When he eventually freed his slaves, most stayed with him on the property, and several spent the rest of their lives working with him at Spocott.

John was descended from a whole line of shipbuilders, an avocation almost a necessity for a farmer. Somewhat isolated from most population centers by the Bay, rivers, and a myriad of creeks, ships were needed to take crops to market. As the oldest sibling, John logically spent his early years in his father's shipyard in the Neck District of Dorchester County. At age twenty-five, he married Rebecca Beckwith, a distant cousin from a nearby farm. Their first daughter Rebecca would die in her first year, but the couple would go on to have nine more children. Tragically, four of these nine would die in their first year. Of the remaining five, two more would die in their twenties. Thus, John would bury seven of his ten children, and this was further compounded by Rebecca's

Sophie Delilah Travers Radcliffe
(1837-1927)
George's mother

death in 1870 at age forty-six. His religion, hard work, and passion for life would see him through these tragedies. He would soon marry Sophie Delilah Travers, widow of Andrew Robinson, who herself had a large family. She lived nearby and was also from a shipbuilding family, originally from nearby Taylor's Island. John, who had seen his family dwindle over the years, was once again the patriarch of a large family.

In May of 1846, the United States declared war on Mexico, initiated earlier largely by the United States' annexation of the Republic of Texas in 1845. On August 10, 1846, John was commissioned as a captain in the "Washington Blues" of the Dorchester Extra Battalion. He never served in combat, but trained with a local group. At about this time, he started working at the nearby Spocott Shipyard on the property settled in 1663 by his ancestor, Stephen Gary. We assume his commission ended with the conclusion of the war in 1848. He continued the shipbuilding at Spocott, and in June of 1849, bought the property. From this point until the outbreak of the Civil War, he and his two brothers, Nehemiah and William, would build two-masted schooners, one of which, as his son, George, would say, actually circumnavigated the globe. Spocott prospered with the farming, shipbuilding, and trading the three brothers engaged in. This Golden Age of Spocott was captured somewhat by James Michener, who partially based the Paxmore Family in his novel *Chesapeake* (1978) on the Spocott shipbuilding family and John Anthony LeCompte Radcliffe. Michener had several long conversations with Senator Radcliffe in the early planning stages of the book.[3]

The Civil War brought an end to the shipbuilding at Spocott as several members of the family would fight for the Confederacy, with two of John's brothers being killed during the war. John, despite his past military experience, abstained and put his shipbuilding skills into construction projects on the farm and in the local community. George L. Radcliffe was born well after the war and with his father a few years removed from his prime. However, the Spocott work ethic and community spirit were thriving.

John believed in the equality of all and had a genuine desire to help those in need. In 1872, John was appointed Trustee of the Poor for Dorchester County, and was also elected as a delegate to the Maryland legislature, where he helped push through the law requiring equal but separate education for Blacks and whites. As terrible as this was by to-day's standards, the law did get the first state funding for the education of Black people. This was quite a change for the one-time slave owner. For the remainder of his life, John had an "open house" policy at Spocott. Anyone showing up at the door was granted a meal and could stay overnight if needed. If the guest was willing to work, he could stay longer. George remembered one evening when the house was so crowded that even the visiting governor of Maryland had to sleep on the floor. A short biography of John Anthony LeCompte Radcliffe stated it well:

> John Anthony LeCompte Radcliffe was saturated with the traditions of his community, and his lifelong effort was to perpetuate and develop the best of these in harmony with the march of progress. He tried to give his children the advantages of opportunity similar to those which he had received and better whenever possible. Possibly the predominating characteristic of his life was the desire to be truly helpful to those around him. He was the last in his community to continue the old-fashioned hospitable but expensive method of keeping "open house" throughout the year to which his relatives and friends were at all times welcome. It is undoubtedly true that during his lifetime there was no place in Dorchester County where hospitality was so freely, so cordially, and so generously extended as at Spocot.[4]

This could have been written about John's son, George, as well since he regarded all in the community as a part of his family. In 1963, George hosted a 300th anniversary celebration for family at Spocott, complete with a feast fit for a king. As many as 500 showed up, friends and relatives; George obviously had a large "family."

George L. Radcliffe had another trait which he shared with his father: the power of reflection. George often spoke of the fact that his father arose every day at 4 a.m., spending considerable time before dawn in reflection. John was a deeply religious man, a practicing Methodist, and would spend time each morning mulling over books he had read, sermons he had heard, or political news he had become aware of. An avid reader of theology, history, and philosophy, he had much to reflect on, and unlike many, his views and beliefs evolved throughout his life. John went from owning slaves as a part of his father's shipbuilding operation early in his life to being somewhat of an abolitionist in later years. The serious outlook on life, the constant search for more information, and openness to new ideas was instilled in his son, George.

George's mother, Sophie, provided the love and support; George was her ninth child, and she was forty when he was born. Well experienced in motherhood and the ways of the world, her guidance and discipline set George on a course to success, and her focus on family would lay the groundwork for George's primary focus in life. In that bed of love and support, John planted the passion for learning, openness to new ideas, and a work ethic almost unmatched anywhere. With this solid genetic and environmental foundation, their youngest son would rise to almost unimagined heights.

Just a Farm Boy

George L. Radcliffe grew up in a unique part of the country on a farm which helped form his character, work ethic, and views in so many areas. The Eastern Shore of Maryland did not exist as humans were beginning to evolve and populate the planet. It was formed in the aftermath of the last glacial event from deposits eroded by the Susquehanna River as it carried melting glacial water to the Atlantic Ocean. Dorchester County is found on the Lower Shore, formed largely from silt as gravel and sand were deposited farther up the Shore. The large county is barely above sea level and will succumb eventually as global sea rise progresses. The county is isolated not only by the Chesapeake Bay to the west, but by the Choptank River to the north, and the Nanticoke River to the east. No area of the county is more than a quarter mile from a river or creek. This unique geography has shaped both the history and culture of the area, with farming, shipbuilding, and seafood harvesting the primary historical occupations. Its geological isolation created independent and resourceful people, often self-sufficient and resistant to change, yet remarkably adaptive, nonetheless. Michener described this area beautifully in his novel *Chesapeake* (1978), and ironically, he would meet several times with George Radcliffe when researching the novel:

> What a memorable place he discovered: a small plot of flat, open land... surrounded by tall and stately oaks and pines. In every direction save east he could see extensively, and his eyes leaped from one spectacular view to another: to the north a bewildering maze of headlands and bays, each its own exemplification of beauty; to the south a new definition of vast loneliness, for there lay the marshes, refuges for innumerable birds and fish and small animals;

the noble view lay to the west where the island glowed in sunlight, with the blue waters of the bay beyond. From this headland Pentaquod could see across the bay to the mysterious lands where the Potomacs ruled, but if he looked downward instead of out, he saw on all sides his river, peaceful and reassuring.[1]

The Native Americans had settled early in this area as they had easy access to water and fishing, extensive marshes where wildlife could be trapped, and rich soil which could be easily farmed. They had well-established communities when the first white settlers landed on the Eastern Shore in the mid-seventeenth century. In 1662, Stephen Gary ventured up the Little Choptank River, reaching the head of the river a short twelve miles from the Chesapeake Bay. He had settled on the western shore of the Bay in 1650, but, being a Quaker, he was under pressure to move. He was under good favor with both Charles II of England, and Lord Baltimore for his service in the Royalist army, fighting to return Charles to the throne after several years under Oliver Cromwell. Also, individuals who transported people to the New World were granted land for their service, and Gary had brought several important individuals across the Atlantic. While several early settlers to Dorchester County had settled on the much longer and wider Choptank River, Gary laid claim to an area on the more remote Little Choptank River. He had the land surveyed in 1662, and it was deeded to him in 1663.[2]

He settled on this small 250-acre peninsula bordered on both sides by the two creeks which formed the head of the Little Choptank. Just north of the property was a well-used Indian trail stretching from the Choptank Indian reservation just east of what is now Cambridge, west to the Bay through an area now called the Neck District. With the Choptank River to the north and the Little Choptank to the south, every place in the Neck District was close to navigable water. In years to come, this area would become a major shipbuilding center on the East Coast.

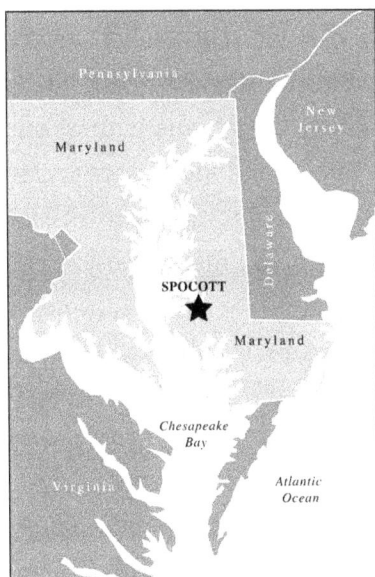

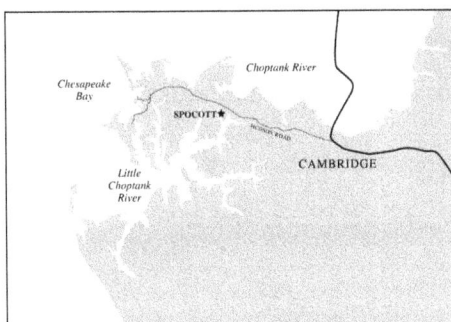

Location of Spocott in
Dorchester County, Maryland
Spocott is located in the Neck District
area, six miles west of Cambridge.

Gary named the property "Spocott," and many have speculated over the years as to the origin of the name. George's brothers told others that the name was likely derived from some Indian term, but George probably was on the right track when he claimed that the property was actually named "Specott," since the letters "e" and "o" were often inadvertently interchanged when copying documents. George traced the name Specott back to Gary's place of origin in Cornwall, England where there was a prominent Specott family in this area. Sir John Specott had fought in the Royalist army and probably knew Stephen Gary. George surmised that Specott might be the maiden name of either Gary's wife, Clare, or his mother.

Gary referred to Spocott as his home plantation, and it is likely that his family settled here in 1663. At that time Spocott was in a true wilderness area. Gary undoubtedly encountered many hardships: cold winters, hot summers, and enough mosquitoes to humble even the hardiest of settlers. While some considered the Native Americans a threat, Stephen Gary seemed to have made peace with them. Another of George's ancestors, Sir Antoine LeCompte, had settled a mile north of Spocott in 1659 and clearly had a different reaction to the Native Americans. He built a wall around his house, placed the windows above eye level, and hired local people to protect his home from the Native Americans, with whom he had some serious confrontations. The Choptank Indians were generally considered peaceful, yet history shows they could react if provoked.

Gary built his simple one-and-a-half story house near a tree referred to as the "Council Oak." Tradition has it that Native Americans occasionally met around this tree and that several unspecified historical events occurred under it. Whether factual or legend, the tree was imposing and was still standing in the 1930s. The Spocott property was likely heavily wooded when he settled there, with oaks and hickories dominating. Brackish marshes would have bordered the tidal creeks, and while the house was built near the creek named after Gary, the ground was high enough to be well above the high tide level. Stephen Gary had obviously been to the property before, as the deed refers to Gary's Creek, likely named from an earlier visit. The location he chose was no accident. Not only was the property surrounded by water, but the house was built where it was exposed to prevailing winds from northwest to south. In the summer, when mosquitoes were prolific, a breeze would keep the numbers down, yet the house was well protected from the major "northeasters," storms which would form off the ocean and pummel this area of the Eastern Shore with strong northeasterly winds over several days.

Gary had settled in an area where food was abundant, a fact that Native Americans had discovered long before. The shallow creek bottoms were covered with oysters and clams, and fish were abundant. The Native Americans had mastered the art of catching, cooking, and eating the bountiful blue crabs, and Gary undoubtedly acquired these skills early on. Hunting provided deer, turkey, and quail year-round, and in the fall and winter, waterfowl covered the area. The oaks and hickories provided huge quantities of nuts, which could easily last the winter. The surrounding forests provided all the building materials and fuel needed, especially as fields were gradually being cleared for agriculture. While disease, cold winters, and mosquitoes made life difficult, this was a virtual paradise for these early settlers.

Stephen Gary played a prominent role in early Dorchester County. In 1669, he was appointed one of the commissioners, tasked with keeping peace in the area. He would also serve as a justice and sheriff of Dorchester County. The property was deeded to his wife upon Stephen's death in 1686, and upon her death it was split between two of his daughters. George is descended through two lines from one of the daughters. Half of Spocott would pass out of the family in the eighteenth century, and George would buy it back in 1911, thus returning Spocott to the original 250 acres.

Almost 200 years after Gary's death, George L. Radcliffe would grow up in this paradise. Primitive by today's standards, Spocott was heaven to young George. Many changes had occurred since Gary's time, but the

Spocott Main House c. 1890
Spocott, where George was born, was built in stages with the left section built in 1663, the middle c. 1750, and the right section in 1868.

"Council Oak" still stood as a sentinel of earlier times. Much of the land had been cleared for farming, but the hedgerows that ran between the fields provided wonderful habitat for the bobwhite quails, whose "bob-white" calls dominated the farm on warm summer days. The oyster beds were still thriving, although no longer the major reefs which once existed, and the crabs were plentiful. George learned to collect oysters, catch hard crabs, and walk the shoreline to find those soft crabs which had just shed. While George was not much of a hunter, his two older brothers brought back a considerable amount for the family table. The oaks and hickories still filled the woods, but the family had planted walnut and pecan trees, and every autumn, he collected and stockpiled nuts for the long winters. Holly trees abounded everywhere, and these plus the plentiful bayberry provided both colorful and aromatic decorations for the winter holidays.

The original house still stood on the property and had been enlarged in the 1750s and again, by his father, just after the Civil War. With a dining room, living room, parlor, 7 bedrooms, and many porches, the house was still simple, yet comfortable. The outdoor kitchen was run by Adaline Wheatley who had married one of the previously enslaved workers after the Civil War, and there were numerous other outdoor buildings as a part of the working farm.

Life still provided its usual array of hardships as this was well before rural electrification and modern plumbing. An outhouse was situated a good distance from the house, and treks out to this on a cold winter night must have been challenging. Any idyllic images of a quaint outhouse would be completely erased when one realized that part of the outhouse routine was reaching into a barrel for a corn cob or two before entering. While horrifying to most today, this was normal routine in the late nineteenth century.

Young George was given the responsibility of maintaining the vegetable garden and feeding and managing the menagerie of chickens, turkeys, and goats. Every day began with feeding the animals and ended with either gardening or collecting firewood. He learned the routine and reward of hard work early on, and anyone in George's later years could easily start him reminiscing about these days on the farm. His brother Sewell would always interrupt these stories, saying that he and Tom did all the work while George sat inside reading away the day. George would always protest, but the twinkle in Sewell's eyes would tell all. He loved to tease his younger brother but cared for him dearly.

However, Spocott was no ordinary farm; it was a thriving community of families where everyone had their role, but all shared and worked together. The planting, cultivation, harvesting, and storage of grain crops involved all. Vegetables were grown, preserved, and stored. Adaline was the amazing cook for all of George's early years, and her husband Columbus was the master carpenter, always assisting George's father. Kemp Wilson managed the larger farm animals: horses, pigs, sheep, and cows. There was a farm manager at Spocott after George's father John passed in 1901. Boats and carts had to be maintained, and transportation by water was still the most efficient mode of transportation for going any distance. Adaline's outdoor kitchen was used in the summer when it was too warm to cook inside, and adjacent to that was her smokehouse for preserving meats. Her wood-fired oven was constantly in use preparing food for the large family. There was one building used for storing potatoes and coal. There was an icehouse where huge blocks of freshwater ice were stored, packed and insulated with straw; this lasted through the summer, and blocks were used in the dairy building where troughs below ground level could keep milk and butter "cool." A block of ice was placed in there periodically, but George still remembered the milk as usually lukewarm at best.

The farm had a blacksmith shop, and one individual would fill that role. John Anthony LeCompte Radcliffe had built most of these buildings, especially in the shipbuilding days before the Civil War. There were cottages used by the families of the Spocott workers, the carpentry shop

John used during the shipbuilding days, stables and barns for animals, and crop and seed storage, and in later years, equipment storage sheds. Spocott was in many ways a small town, and with a nearby windmill, store, and post office, it became the heart of the town of Lloyds.

Spocott was also a completely self-sufficient community. The farm provided all the food needed for the inhabitants. Butter was churned, grain was ground into meal, and Adaline could make biscuits, soups, pies, and entrees that made her a cook for the ages. The surrounding woods provided the lumber needed for the endless building projects and repairs, and the blacksmith shop could produce anything from a horseshoe to a nail. Wool from the Spocott sheep and the small amount of cotton grown supplied the essentials for clothing for the Spocott community. The Spocott residents even made their own shoes.

Holidays were a focal point in the community, a reward for all the hard work that led up to these events, as all came together to share and celebrate. Thanksgiving and Christmas followed the busy summer of planting and fall of harvesting and stockpiling for the long winter ahead, and they form the core of young George's fondest memories of childhood.[3]

Anyone who met and got to know George L. Radcliffe knew that in spirit he never left Spocott. He may have spent considerable time in Baltimore and Washington, but he was always the farm boy. In his later

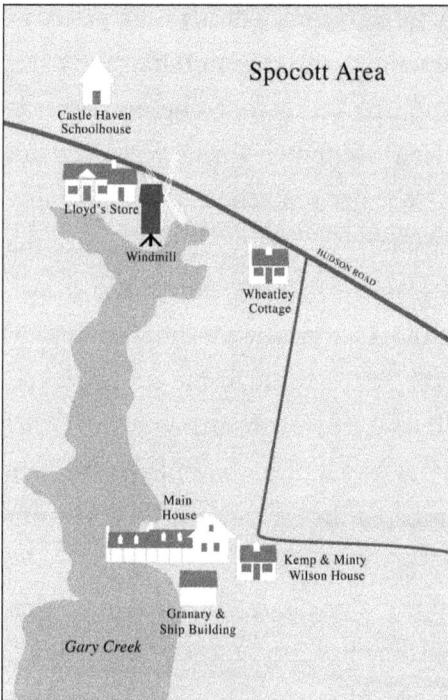

Spocott and Vicinity 1877

years, he rarely talked of his days in the U.S. Senate, the many years as an officer of the Fidelity and Deposit Company, or his years of service to the Maryland Historical Society. His stories were of eating Adaline Wheatley's biscuits, tending the family garden, swimming in Gary's Creek, ice skating around the perimeter of the property, huge family get-togethers on the spacious Spocott lawn, searching the woods for nice holly trees to replant in the Spocott lawn, playing with the children of the many workers, helping Kemp maintain the horses, and watching Columbus repair a shed. He literally could talk for hours, and anyone watching him was only too aware of the pure joy he took in reliving these moments. Many a family meal would stretch well into the evening as George told story after story with enough detail that one almost felt as if they had been present for the actual event. He rose to the height of political power but never forgot how the average person lived, working dawn to dusk to provide for a family. He may have interacted with presidents and heads of state, but the farm was where he relaxed and felt human again.

George learned other valuable lessons on that farm. A community is a well-oiled machine where the wishes of the individual are usually secondary to the good of the group. Each member of the Spocott community was valuable, contributing some skill that was essential for this machine to function. No one was more important than another; there was no place in such a community for egos. Spocott was never a wealthy farm and was almost sold off in the early twentieth century as the family really fell on hard times. But then, George learned many times over that money does not buy the real rewards that life has to offer. All birthdays were celebrated with much fanfare, but it was not the few presents that George remembered; it was the community uniting to share, relax, and laugh a lot. Hard work brought the biggest rewards.

For the first few years of his life, Spocott was also George's school. George was slightly younger than his brothers, Tom and Sewell, and some of his cousins were also living at Spocott. When George was young, the family hired Clare Chaplain, a distant cousin, as a governess, and she would be the teacher for the Spocott school. Learning for George was a twenty-four-hour-a-day venture; when he was not being schooled, he was surrounded by books, older siblings and cousins who were always "teaching" him, and two highly educated parents who made every dinnertime and family get-together an opportunity for sharing and learning. George claims that he knew his alphabet by age three. When Clare

Home School at Spocott c. 1883 Young George is sitting in the lap of his tutor, Clare Chaplain. His brother Tom is far right.

Chaplain moved on, John and Sophie sent George to the nearby school which John had built. George lasted one day at the little school before being pulled back home as his parents felt that he was too sickly. His mother continued his education, but the Spocott library became George's real teacher.

To hear George talk of those days on the Spocott Farm, one would think he had grown up in Oz. Money was always in short supply, but then in a self-sufficient community, what is money really needed for? We have a letter written to family members when George was fifteen asking

for help getting him a coat, as winter was approaching and he did not have one. The family was not poor, but Spocott was a working farm where a harsh winter or dry summer could create hardships for all. However, everything that young George needed to be a success in his life was sown into him in his years as a child at Spocott. He knew that hard work was what was expected every day and that every person has something valuable to contribute. He approached his work at the Fidelity and Deposit Company with this attitude, and this is how he operated in the Senate.

Even during the busiest periods of his life, he would always return periodically to the farm. The suit would disappear, and on would go the old clothes and well-worn hat. He would grab a hoe and head out onto the property, surveying the gardens, checking on the health of the trees, and examining the state of all the barns and outbuildings. Becoming that farm boy again kept him young at heart and gave him time to reflect, just as his father had done many years earlier.

The key to living a long life—and George did just that—is remaining a child at heart, to wake up each day excited to face the next adventure, to never stop dreaming, and to keep the word "impossible" out of one's vocabulary. George L. Radcliffe, the farm boy, lived each day to the fullest and never let problems sidetrack him. He never left Spocott in all his 97 years, and that childlike passion was infectious, drawing many others into his world. His brother Sewell, an amazing man himself, always said that his brother was living in the past and needed to move into the real world. I like to think he tackled the real world with the values of the past and the enthusiasm of a child. Spocott, in its over 350 years, has witnessed much history, and while others may have contributed more to it physically, no one embodied its spirit more than George L. Radcliffe. He still walks those well-beaten paths, and his spirit continues to infect the generations that still reside there.

The Mysterious Middle Name

George Lovic Pierce Radcliffe died at age ninety-six, and during all those years, he never knew where his middle name came from. Most thought the "L" in George L. Radcliffe stood for "LeCompte," the maiden name of his great-grandmother, Fannie LeCompte. Since George was the youngest of nineteen children from the combined marriages of his two parents, one can only imagine that they had run out of family names by the time he arrived. He was named after his uncle, George W.W. Radcliffe, who died during the Civil War, but no one ever told him exactly where "Lovic Pierce" came from. His father said that the name came from the author of a book he once read, but, to George, this seemed odd for a family which treasured and honored its ancestral roots with the naming of their children. As George said in 1963:

> When I came into the world, the obviously suitable names had been exhausted. I was named George after an uncle. About that time, my father read a book written by Lovic Pierce. It was doubtless a good book on some aspects of philosophy, and doubtless also he was a very good man, but that is no reason why I should have been saddled with his name. I had a right, I assume, to have discarded my middle name, but I held on to it too long to make a shift when the strong desire to do so developed.[1]

To understand George's roots, one needs to understand his father's background and views and what precipitated the somewhat mysterious naming of his son. George did spend some time trying to track down the origin of his middle name. His mother, who lived until George was almost fifty, was of little help. She knew no more than what George had been told. George talked of his father as a serious figure, one whom all, including his two wives, referred to as "Mr. Radcliffe" and George was hesitant to question his father about the source of the name. His time at Johns Hopkins and the start of his career put the question on the back burner, and only later in life did he start his search again. Unable to find any author named Lovic Pierce, he soon gave up. The name remained a family puzzle until shortly after George's death. In early 1976, his daughter-in-law, Augusta Boggs Radcliffe, an avid reader, was reading the fourth volume of John Jakes' eight-volume *Kent Family Chronicles*, written at the time of the American Bicentennial. In *The Furies*, Augusta ran across the following:

> Many at the Conference yearned for compromise, but the longing was frustrated by the vote. Lovick Pierce of Georgia has declared the southern Conferences will lodge a "manly, ministerial, and proper protest' concerning the Andrews affair. I have this very night heard talk of the form the protest will take: Separation. The sundering of the Church into two bodies, north and south.[2]

Knowing of the mystery, Augusta immediately showed this to her husband, George M. Radcliffe, and this rekindled the family fire to solve the long-standing mystery. George wrote to the publishing company, who forwarded the letter to Jakes, and in February of 1976, he received a letter from John Jakes, shedding some light on Pierce:

> Pyramid Books forwarded your interesting letter inquiring about Lovick Pierce of Georgia. I ran across a couple of brief references to him in Charles W. Ferguson's fascinating book *ORGANIZING TO BEAT THE DEVIL: METHODISTS AND THE MAKING OF AMERICA* (Doubleday, 1971).
>
> The first reference is in connection with the Method-

ist General Conference in 1844 – much as described in
THE FURIES. The second talks of Pierce's visit, in 1848,
to the Conference of the Northern branch of the church
– a branch from which his Conference had by then separated. One section states that "... Dr. Pierce was one of
the kindest and most agreeable of men in his personal
dealings ...." An obvious clue to your grandfather's admiration of him.[3]

Lovick Pierce (1785–1879) was a renowned Southern Methodist
minister who played a key role in the formation and early days of the
Methodist Episcopal Church, South. In 1805, he and his brother Red-
dick both applied for admission to the South Carolina Conference of
the Methodist Church. He was an active participant in many General
Conferences and was a key figure in the split of the Methodist Church in
1844. His son, George Foster Pierce, went on to even greater prominence
as bishop of the Church.[4]

Most references describe Lovick Pierce's almost impeccable character, a man who lived the life he preached. His son, in writing of his father,
gave evidence as to why George L. Radcliffe could not locate the source
of his middle name. Bishop Pierce said that his father "kept no diary, no
journal. There are no facts, or dates, or records outside of fragmentary
notices in the public print and the Conference minutes."[5] The bishop
said his father "lived in the present and scanned the future almost with a
prophet's eye. Current events, the prospects ahead, these were the staple
of his thoughts and the topics of his conversation."[6] Lovick was known
for his extraordinary speaking ability. His son remembered him, on several occasions, giving three 3-hour sermons in one day and still having the
voice and stamina to continue. No one ever heard him speak poorly of
another, as he lived his religion in every aspect of his life.[7] His son said:

> I have never known a more consistent, more painstak-
> ingly, Christian man. He was sometimes highly demon-

strative but commonly quiet; yet always tender, quick of feeling, and ready to respond to pathos, in word or scene or Providence. He was full of all generous sympathies. Charity, the bond of perfectness, girdled all his virtues. The law of kindness was upon his tongue. He spoke evil of no man.[8]

Lovick Pierce was an important figure in the Methodist Church during the War of 1812 and played an important role in many of the church conferences. He traveled considerably and was Georgia's representative to the 1840 General Conference in Baltimore, placing him just across the Chesapeake Bay from George's father. Slavery was becoming a divisive issue in the Methodist Church as it was in much of the country. Southern leaders were reacting to many of the abolitionist pleas from Northern Conferences, and Lovick was one of those interested foremost in preserving Church unity.

However, the issue of slavery came to a head in the Methodist Church in 1844. Bishop James O. Andrew, whom Lovick Pierce had supported from the beginning, became an unwilling owner of slaves

Rev. Lovick Pierce
(1785-1879)

as he had married a woman who had inherited slaves from her first husband. He disclaimed them but was legally unable to emancipate them. The General Conference, after much debate, voted that he should resign. Lovick supported the bishop, certainly not the same thing as supporting slavery. However, a year later, the Southern Conferences formed the

Methodist Episcopal Church, South, and Lovick Pierce remained an active part of the Southern church.[9]

This raises several questions:

1. How could John Anthony LeCompte Radcliffe have encountered Lovick Pierce and his teachings?

Clearly, there was no book, as young George had been told, and communication during this period of history was limited. John lived on the Eastern Shore of Maryland and was isolated geographically. Pierce was in Baltimore in 1840 for the Methodist General Conference and was in Baltimore for at least a month in 1867, allowing two possible occasions when George's father could have met him or at least heard him speak.[10] George's son's version that John heard one of Pierce's speeches in 1855 could also be correct, but there is no evidence to support that.

As a shipbuilder, John undoubtedly crossed the Chesapeake Bay to the Western Shore on occasions, where he could have heard Pierce speak. We know that as a Maryland legislature delegate in 1872, he spent considerable time on the Western Shore, giving ample opportunity for the two to meet. Pierce was ninety-two when George L. Radcliffe was born, yet in 1877 he was still speaking and writing his recollections. He was able to keep active into the 1870s.[11] Somehow, someway, Pierce impressed John enough to add Pierce's name as his son's middle name.

2. How do John Anthony LeCompte Radcliffe's and Lovick Pierce's views on slavery compare?

George L. Radcliffe's son, in a talk to the Dorchester Historical Society on September 5, 2007, proposed that John Anthony LeCompte Radcliffe had given his son the middle name of Lovic Pierce because of Pierce's abolitionist views. George claimed that his grandfather, John, had been moved to a more abolitionist point of view by a speech Lovick Pierce made in 1855,[12] but no record of this particular speech has been found. There is little doubt that John was an abolitionist, albeit a conflicted one. This date does, however, coincide with when John's views toward slavery were beginning to change. He did have enslaved workers at Spocott when he farmed and built ships, but something was altering John's view of slavery. He told his son that he released his enslaved workers at the beginning of the Civil War, but there is no record of this. He also made his abolitionist views known in his church, openly advocating that church members free their enslaved females.[13]

There is no question that John began his life pro-slavery as he even purchased a slave in 1841. He had come from a shipbuilding family, where slave labor was used. As John's records show, shipbuilding in this area was not a profitable venture, with records showing John and his two brothers splitting a little over $1500 profit to build a large two-masted schooner. They likely would have had no profit if not for the small amount of slave labor used. So, what caused a change in John's views? Family influence of any sort seems unlikely, and his Methodism seems the likely source. Lovick Pierce undoubtedly influenced him, whether to become more abolitionist in his views, or to just become more devout and caring of others.

What seems likely is that John connected with Lovick Pierce's complicated attitude toward slavery. As a Methodist, Lovick Pierce should have been, at least initially, anti-slavery. In 1844, he was sympathetic to Bishop Andrew's situation. Andrew was also anti-slavery but acquired slaves through a marriage. Pierce undoubtedly was more interested in preserving the Methodist Church just as he was later concerned with preserving the Union, thus opposing secession. Many Northern abolitionists lived in an economy where slaves were not needed, but Pierce lived in the South, where slave labor was an economic necessity to many.

Lovick Pierce's solution to the slavery question was to convert and educate the enslaved people, and he considered education as the first step to freedom. In many areas of the South, freeing a slave was illegal anyway. He clearly was a compassionate individual, and slavery would have seemed immoral in many ways, but he tried to deal with the situation at hand, not just to impose his views on the world around him. Sadly, this view prolonged slavery as it justified the pro-slavery views of many Southern Methodists. John Anthony LeCompte Radcliffe may have been similar in many ways. He genuinely cared for those who worked for him, both Black and white. He took an interest in them and provided for them better than most. Adaline, the Spocott cook, married Columbus Wheatley, previously one of John's enslaved workers, in 1868, and they were not just given any house; he gave them the home his brothers had lived in before the war. After the war he provided employment for any of his prior enslaved workers and made sure that all young children of these employees received an education, since there was no local school for Black children to attend. He also guaranteed employment for any of these children until they could get a job in the community. Before the war, he may have felt that caring for the enslaved was a better solution than freeing them. In fact, freedom for a slave in Dorchester County often left them in danger of being resold into slavery or, at the very least, cast into an unwelcome society with little or no chance of employment. Likely John, as did Pierce, saw slavery as the lesser of two evils, unfortunately not seeing how personally and morally crippling the institution was.

While neither Lovick Pierce nor John Anthony LeCompte Radcliffe would be politically correct by today's standards, they could be considered realists for their time. Although neither seemed to have been demonstrative in denouncing slavery, both cared for all around them and did what they could in the situation they found themselves in. Whether Lovick Pierce influenced John, or John just found in Pierce someone who thought and cared as he did, will probably never be known and is, in fact, unimportant. There clearly was a connection, one strong enough for John to use Pierce's name for his son's middle name.

3. What other aspects of Lovick Pierce could have made him an appealing figure to John Anthony LeCompte Radcliffe?

John was known for his impeccable character and extremely high moral standards. Pierce, almost a generation older, would have made a perfect role model for John. Lovick Pierce was of the highest possible character, more than up to the standards of a religious and proper man such as John Anthony LeCompte Radcliffe. In his obituary, Lovick was referred to "... as gentle as a woman, shrinking, sensitive, and timid. .... His sensibilities were unusually acute, and his aspirations of the highest and noblest kind. He had an exalted idea of the responsibilities of the lofty demands of his ministry and a painful sense of his deficiencies."[14] John's grandson, George, felt that this was the kind of individual his grandfather would have connected with.

John was a devout Methodist, and with much of his family rooted in support for the Confederacy, he would have related to the Southern branch of the Methodist Church, of which Lovick Pierce was a major force.

Lovick Pierce was opposed to secession, advocating strongly for preservation of the Union. In a letter in 1860, he said, "I pray daily that God may preserve this Union. Old as I am, if its fate depended on a battlefield, I would fight...."[15] John similarly wanted the Union preserved and chose not to fight while other family members did.

Pierce assisted his son in the creation of Wesleyan Female College, the first college in the world to exclusively grant degrees to females.[16] John Anthony LeCompte Radcliffe was also known to be in favor of the rights of women.

4. Why did John Anthony LeCompte Radcliffe never tell his son the source of his middle name?

In many ways, this is the most interesting question. John lived in an environment where being an abolitionist was societally frowned upon.

George L. Radcliffe told his son that his father had to leave his local church at least temporarily after advocating for the emancipation of female slaves in the 1850s. While 1877, the year of George's birth, was somewhat removed from the Civil War and the end of slavery, George did share with his son that Dorchester County was still heavily pro-segregation and that John's views would have not set well with many in the county.

Naming his son for a possibly abolitionist minister would have been a way to make a silent statement; naming one's child after a nationally known abolitionist would have been too obvious. However, one still would think that he would have shared this with George at some point in his life. While George admitted a nervousness to sometimes approach his father [John was sixty-nine when George was born], one would certainly think that George the student or George the professor would have done so. There is also the distant possibility that at this point in John's life, he had named so many children and used so many family names that he just grabbed a quick name simply out of convenience. This seems unlikely since family names up to this point seemed to have been well thought out, and John was well versed in his genealogy.

Clearly John's views changed from the 1840s until the time of the Civil War. He went from being a slave owner to one with certain abolitionist views. While John was deeply religious and would have found Pierce's teachings attractive, he certainly broke with his local church over slavery. He would never have been able to reject his religion, however, and access to a preacher such as Lovick Pierce would have been satisfying and necessary. John, as did Pierce, accepted slavery to an extent, but never looked on slaves as inferior or less valuable humans. Both were somewhat at a loss as how to deal with the issue of slavery.

Regardless of how John connected with Lovick Pierce, there is no question that all of this trickled down to George L. Radcliffe, even if he never learned the actual source of his name. George's father was definitely a key role model. A serious and imposing figure, John was nonetheless a caring person, opening his home up to all in need. John was a commissioner of the poor in Dorchester County and in 1872, as a Maryland legislator, helped get funding for the education of Blacks. George would often say that John cared deeply for everyone who worked for him, both Black and white, and was beloved and respected by all in the community.

George was aware of the family's Confederate roots but still began life with a belief in the value of all, somewhat atypical for the times. While George was not to become a Methodist himself, he was deeply spiritual. Like his father after his estrangement from the church, George valued his faith more than finding the need to regularly attend a church. While he often attended church, he never felt compelled to do so. George modelled his father's high moral character, and all who knew both, saw aspects of the father in the son. There is no question that Lovic Pierce had a significant impact on John Anthony LeCompte Radcliffe, both as a religious leader and a personal role model. Both wrestled with the issue of slavery and found a middle road that combined a belief in the value of all with the economic and political realities of the times.

THE RUNNER

George L. Radcliffe was the youngest of nineteen children, born to older parents; his father was sixty-nine, and his mother forty when George was born. Most of the children from his parents' first marriages were much older; the oldest was thirty-three years George's senior, and the youngest was seven years older than George. Throughout his entire childhood he played the role of the "little brother." His brothers, Tom and Sewell, were both "strapping young lads," as George would say, and he was clearly smaller, barely 140 pounds when he went off to college. He was always aware and self-conscious of his smaller size when he was a child.

One evening when George was still a pre-teen, an incident occurred which would change his life forever. He was in his room reading and could hear his parents talking in another room. Both parents were extremely bright and well-read, and their conversations were often quite serious as they debated historical, philosophical, and religious matters. George, a somewhat quiet child, was always the avid listener and would, years later, talk of all he had learned just by listening to his parents. However, this particular evening, their conversation was focused on him. They obviously never thought he could overhear the conversation as they discussed his health. While George was not a sickly child, his parents were concerned because he was both the youngest and still somewhat small for his age. They talked of their "sickly child," and both parents concluded that their youngest son would never live to see his twenty-first birthday.

This obviously devastated George, but he never brought the topic up with his parents. While most children might have gone into depression upon hearing this, it had the opposite effect on young George. Normally his two older brothers would do the more physical chores: chopping firewood, carrying coal, moving hay, etc. George had been assigned the job of feeding the chickens and turkeys. Of the three brothers at home, he was the avid reader and was most often found curled up with a book, consuming them faster than the family could track them down for him. The overheard conservation, however, startled him, and he decided that day that his parents' prognostication would not bear out. Realizing that feeding chickens would hardly bulk him up, he began to run—and he ran everywhere. His parents must have wondered what had gotten into their youngest as he ran from chore to chore and would often be seen running back and forth down the one-mile lane to Spocott.

George finished high school at age fifteen and decided to take a year off before going to college, partly for financial reasons and partly because he felt a year of work on the property would go a long way to negating his parents' dire prediction. And the running continued. He remembered finding the running effortless, and soon he was as happy jogging across the countryside as getting lost in the latest book.

At Hopkins, he not only discovered professors who inspired him and a library that he could get lost in, but the university had a gymnasium and a track. His daily ritual would include a workout in the gymnasium followed by many laps around the track. He also spent time hanging from the rings, not only to build muscle but to possibly add to his height. He claimed later that he had increased his height by an inch or two those years. The jogging was almost effortless for him, and he soon began increasing his speed. One day, he noticed someone watching him run. George later described this day:

George L. Radcliffe
Running at Spocott c. 1894

When I was at Hopkins, they used to tell me I had the ugliest walk and the best running stride of anyone on campus – a 'natural' stride. I didn't know what that was, and if it hadn't been for one of the coaches, I might never have known it.... Then one day while I was running, a man came up to me and said very excitedly, 'You do what I tell you, and you'll break records.' I thought he must be some kind of a lunatic, but as it turned out he was Bill Mackdermott, a well-known figure in local athletics and a man who really knew his running.[1]

This gentleman was the Hopkins track coach and noticed that George had a natural and almost effortless gait. Mackdermott also noted that for a person of George's height, his stride was remarkably long, measured later at seven-and-one-half feet. He asked George to report to track practice, and a new phase in George's life began.

George was able to run a 440 in fifty-four seconds and was soon added to one of the relay teams. In his final undergraduate year, he was a key member of his class mile relay team, having failed to make varsity, but he moved up to varsity during his graduate years. In the 1897-98 school year, the team won meet after meet, putting the Hopkins track team clearly on the national map. Even though he was a graduate student, George was the same age as the other three team members, all undergraduates.[2] He still weighed in at 146 pounds, but he had the physique of a runner. On May 1, 1898, the relay team won the Penn Relays, beating both St. Johns College and Columbian University from Washington in the finals with a time of 3:43 3/5, and this on a slow track.[3]

George ran the third lap of the relay and remembered that race well. The first and second Hopkins' runners had built up a nice lead, and George, in his excitement, fell flat on his face as he was grabbing the baton. The other runners passed him before he could get to his feet, and his teammates and coach moaned in agony. Regaining his composure,

George took off and by the end of his lap had not only passed the other runners but had built up a bigger lead than he had inherited. Hopkins easily won the event, and George's moment of seeming defeat ended in a feeling he never forgot. He was given a gold watch for this feat, and he treasured this throughout his life. He never bragged about winning elections or his many other achievements, but no person ever escaped his presence without that gold watch being pulled out. He recounted that race thousands of times to anyone who would give him the time. The relay team would be undefeated that year. That was the year George L. Radcliffe turned twenty-one!

Both of his parents were still alive at that point, and it must have been tempting for him to confront them with what he had overheard years earlier, but that was not in his character. His life was just beginning. He would continue his running, and he would never stop. He coached the

Johns Hopkins University Mile Relay Team
George is third from left.

Baltimore City College track team and assisted with the Hopkins team. However, he never thought of his running days as behind him. When he started working for the Fidelity and Deposit Company, he was instrumental in getting a gymnasium added to the top floor of the building. He also discovered that the building had a flat roof, large enough for running short laps. George was to work at that building his entire life and thus would always have access to a gym and a track. Rarely a day would pass when he was not running on the roof, riding a stationary bike, and working out. He returned to Spocott whenever he could and was frequently seen jogging down the lane and back.

While George worked in Baltimore, city residents were often greeted with a surprise. George was seen making the trek alone from his office building in downtown Baltimore north to his home in the northwestern area of the city, a distance of seven miles. Briefcase in hand, he would make this long walk, not of necessity, although he could not drive, but because he loved the exercise, fresh air, and the time to clear his head. His home in the Roland Park area of Baltimore had almost fifty steps leading up from the road to his front door, and he climbed these steps even into his nineties. He loved those walks from work through the city—his city—past museums, monuments, and historic homes. While always an Eastern Shoreman, he loved his adopted city of Baltimore, and no one loved walking those streets more than he did.

When he was elected to the Senate in 1934, this might have ended his days of working out, but the Senate had a gymnasium. His diary shows him busy every day, shuttling between Washington, Baltimore, New York, and Cambridge, but he always found a couple times each week to work out at the gym. He turned sixty during his first term in the Senate, but it was important to him to stay active. He noted the Senate gym was never heavily used, but he sought out the exercise, not the company. When he traveled, he would combine two of his hobbies, books and exercise, as he walked a city from one old bookstore to another.

George L. Radcliffe loved to dance. A frequent attendee at the Bachelor's Cotillion and other local dances, he rarely left the dance floor. His son used to say how popular he was with the young ladies, and his father's dance card would overflow quickly. On several occasions my parents, weary themselves, would have to drag George off the dance floor. One would have to look hard to find someone in their seventies and eighties with that much stamina.

In his later years, he would often return to Spocott where he would walk the property to inspect changes and the many ongoing projects. He would always walk with a hoe, both to steady himself on the uneven ground and to do a little work: weeding a garden, managing the small orchard, or filling in a hole. Physical activity was a mandatory part of every day.

In 1958, the *Baltimore Sun* did an article on him entitled "At 80, George L. Radcliffe is Still Running."[4] More than ten years past his days in the Senate, George still put in a full day of work, and most days included time exercising and running laps on top of the building. He would don his gym shorts and head up to the roof for a short jog. Some probably could have walked faster than he was jogging, but what was amazing was his mindset that he was not aging and could still adhere to a daily routine which included exercise.

By his ninetieth birthday, George was in excellent health, as active as ever. He referred to his annual doctor's visit as a chance to catch up with an old friend, Dr. Walter Baetjer. However, that year, tragedy would strike. He was alone in his office in downtown Baltimore, catching up on mail and his many projects, when two men entered his office. They ordered him to open a safe, containing mostly business records, but George refused, realizing that many of the document were confidential. The two immediately jumped him, knocking him to the ground. They took his wallet and the gold watch from the Penn Relays and beat him further, breaking his hip.

George would make a rare trip to the hospital and recuperate at his son's home, but his spirit would not heal so easily. What he could not get over was the loss of his prized watch. It was as if the thieves had taken a small part of his soul. As always, George was somewhat philosophical about the incident, but those close to him could see a change. Word eventually got to Hopkins of the incident and the loss of the watch, and on May 12, 1972, at the Hopkins Alumni Dinner at the Hunt Valley Inn, George was presented with a second watch, inscribed exactly as the first:

Johns Hopkins University
University of Maryland
St. Johns College
Columbian University
April 28, 1898

His son George, who was there with him, said, "I don't think I've ever seen him happier."[5] George L. Radcliffe was 94 at the time and still active. He had been associated one way or another with Johns Hopkins University for seventy-eight of its ninety-six years of existence but still considered the 1898 Penn Relays as a landmark moment in his life. Hopkins was honoring one its most valuable alumni, and George once again had his watch.

That "sickly" young child had lived seventy-five years past his twenty-first birthday, outliving virtually all his contemporaries and all but five of the students he had taught at City College in 1902. His most remarkable accomplishment may, in fact, have been that he lived as long as he did. He never smoked and might have a glass of port on occasions, yet he ate a breakfast with three eggs, bacon, and sausage every morning—hardly a low cholesterol diet. I think often of that ninety-year-old man putting on his gym shorts for a thirty-minute workout every day. That image captures the essence of who he was as much as anything—the "I can still do it" attitude. He undoubtedly had better genes than his parents realized, but that overheard conversation early in his life might have been as responsible for his long life as anything. Rarely has anyone approached each day with a more positive attitude. He may have dwelled in the wonderful stories of his past, but his life was always about the future; *what do I do next?* He may have known presidents, been chairman of so many entities, preserved so much history, and educated so many, but for those who knew him best, he was a

The Replacement Gold Watch
Presented to George L. Radcliffe by
Johns Hopkins University on May 12, 1972

remarkable individual with the ultimate positive outlook on life. His can-do attitude is what took him to the top. His parents inadvertently threw a challenge at him that evening early in his life, and he rose to the challenge. He always said that he would live to be 100, a feat never achieved by any ancestor of his. He could have and should have reached that age, were it not for an act of violence inflicted on him late in life. If there is a heaven and the Almighty does not have a good track up there, George L. Radcliffe has already corrected that. He is still donning those gym shorts each day and doing his laps. That aspect of him is still an inspiration to his family.

Teacher at Heart

University teachers must rule their students, not merely during the three or four years of university life but throughout their existence: not by what they know and inform (them) of, but by the spirit of the things they expound. And that spirit they cannot convey in any formal manner. They can convey it only atmospherically, by making their ideals tell in some way upon the whole spirit of the place.... The voices which do not penetrate beyond the doors of the classroom are lost, are ineffectual, are void of consequence and power.[1] *- Woodrow Wilson*

On June 6, 1955, George L. Radcliffe attended the fiftieth class reunion of the Baltimore City College (high school) Class of 1905. However, City College was not his alma mater, as he had graduated from Cambridge High School in 1893. George had taught history and English at City College to a class of freshman for one year only, yet he attended almost every reunion of that class and developed a close relationship with many of those former students. George was a teacher in public education for only two years (he also was principal of the Cambridge High School during the 1900 – 1901 school year) and while he would go on to an illustrious career in law, banking, and politics, he always remained a teacher at heart.

In 1971, he learned that I, his grandson, had decided to go into teaching. With both a father and grandfather being prominent lawyers, I expected a note of disappointment when my ninety-four-year-old grandfather approached me about my career choice. To my surprise, his reaction was quite the opposite. "You see, George, I'm a teacher, too." I knew he had taught for a year or two but then gone on to "much grander things"; however, I was taken back because he was using the present tense. We talked for a while as he shared his views on the profession. Being a young "wet behind the ears" adult, I remember thinking this was going to be an incredible waste of time. My grandfather had left the profession seventy years earlier; what could he possibly contribute of value regarding the profession today? As had happened many times previously, the elderly grandfather, whom I frequently thought of as having grown up in the Dark Ages, proved that he was far wiser than his grandson. He explained that teaching was a profession where one could not only change other lives but continue to grow oneself; it was just the logical progression of one's own education. He said that nothing he had done in life had been more rewarding than his brief tenure as a teacher, and, in fact, he still considered himself a teacher, just using non-traditional venues. Not only did he enjoy sharing knowledge but felt a keen responsibility to do so, saying each generation has the responsibility to lift the next generation a little higher. Learning to him was a lifelong quest, and an academic environment was where learning and growing were maximized. That day I realized that this renowned politician and civic leader was the strongest advocate for my career choice, and I felt empowered as a result.

At age 13, after a period of home-schooling, George L. Radcliffe was transported into Cambridge to attend the Cambridge Seminary (high school), graduating at age fifteen in 1893. The only boy in a class of six, George did develop strong friendships with those girls and many of the boys in the older classes. We have his report card from his sophomore year with no surprises shown. He obviously was well-behaved, as he was a somewhat shy child, but also because he grew up in a world of adults. Interestingly, the courses shown match his expertise in later years: history, literature, Latin, rhetoric, and declamation. Well into his nineties, George could recite Latin and English poems he had memorized in high school. While his relatively lower grades were in rhetoric and declamation, he would go on to a career of excelling in these areas. While younger than most of the boys in the school, he was probably well-qualified to become secretary of the school's Young Man's Beardless Association, although it is doubtful that he included that on his resume when he threw his hat into the political ring. Ironically, the high school's principal, Emerson Harrington, would become a close friend, and two decades later as governor of Maryland, would select his former student to be his secretary of state.

After finishing high school at age 15, George took a year off, both to help his aging father on the farm, and for financial reasons. With financial assistance from a family member, he entered Johns Hopkins University in the fall of 1894, and would complete his requirements for a Bachelor of Arts in three years. Hopkins opened in 1876 in downtown Baltimore and would not move to its current Homewood Campus until after George completed his graduate work. He was not only young when he entered Hopkins. but while he had grown to five foot nine, he still barely weighed 140 pounds. His first day at Hopkins was a nightmare for him as he was the only freshman to show up in shorts. Shy to begin with, he was quickly classified as the child of the class, a status that he would shortly lose since he had the mind of an adult. He would also quickly lose those shorts. Even at graduation, he would weigh in at only 146 pounds, but his running had developed an impressive athletic body for his size.

At Hopkins he worked under renowned professor and historian Herbert Baxter Adams. He was impressed with Adams' depth of knowledge but admitted that his lectures could often be dull. However, he also took some courses from and was mentored by one of Adams' former students, Woodrow Wilson. Wilson, like George, came to Johns Hopkins University to get his Ph.D. in 1883, just seven years after the university was founded, and quickly became discouraged with the heavy preponderance of lengthy, fact-laden lectures and an over-emphasis on memoriza-

CAMBRIDGE ✶ ACADEMY,

CAMBRIDGE, MD.

Report for _____

of _____

For month ending June 24th 1891

SCALE OF MERIT, AS APPLIED TO CONDUCT AND STUDIES.

	EXCELLENT: 4.50 to 5.00.	GOOD: 4.00 to 4.50.	TOLERABLE: 3.00 to 4.00.	BLAMEWORTHY: 0 to 3.00.

STUDIES.	1st Term. Av. Rec.	1st Term. Exam.	2nd Term. Gen. Av.	3rd Term. Gen. Av.	Final Average.
Latin	4.77	4.30	4.53	4.42	4.48
French					
Greek					
German					
Algebra	4.70	5.00	4.85	4.41	4.63
Geometry					
Astronomy					4.41
Rhetoric	4.98	4.26	4.62	4.20	
Arithmetic	4.90	5.00	4.95	4.38	5.67
Penmanship					
History	5.00	5.00	5.00	4.77	4.89
English Literature	5.00	4.67	4.83	4.86	4.85
Geography					
Chemistry					
Physics	—		—	4.94	4.84
Physiology					
Book-keeping					
Declamation and Composition	—	—	4.62	3.80	4.21
Spelling					
Observing Rules	—	—	5.00	4.99	5.00
No. school days					
No. days absent					
No. times tardy					

Remarks: George stands very high & gives promise of a bright future in his course at school.

Emerson C. Harrington, Principal.

George L. Radcliffe's 1891 Report Card

tion. Not at all a fan of Herbert Baxter Adams, Wilson struck out on his own, and in his second year he completed a book. In Jan. 1885, his book *Congressional Government* was published. He left Hopkins before officially getting his doctoral degree, but Hopkins still awarded him a Ph.D. in 1886.[2]

Woodrow Wilson was now a professor of history and political science at Princeton University, returning, however, to Hopkins every year for a series of lectures. In 1896 – 97, George's final undergraduate year, the professor gave a series of twenty-five lectures on comparative politics.[3] George, fascinated with history, found the lectures a refreshing change from the frequent drudgery of the traditional lectures at Hopkins. Laced with humor, anecdotes, and wonderful stories, the lectures really engaged the students, bringing often dull history facts to life. "Wilson was a great *teacher*, with spellbinding oratory, a ready smile, and a bottomless supply of funny stories. In these JHU courses he helped train an extraordinary cohort of future scholars and civic leaders...."[4] George would use Wilson's unique approach to teaching several years later in his brief teaching career.

George L. Radcliffe, 1901
Principal,
Cambridge Seminary
(High School)

In the fall of 1900, the principal of the Cambridge High School fell ill with typhoid fever, and George was available and a logical choice to step in for him. The temporary job became permanent, as the trustees selected him for the full-time position in December.[5] He would be both administrator and Latin teacher. Latin to him was a passion; it was as much history as language, and throughout his entire life, George would recite Latin passages and weave them into speeches. I remember marveling while I was in high school that he could recite passages from sixty years earlier while I was having trouble regurgitating something from the day before.

He was quite successful in that brief position as he was quickly recruited to teach at Baltimore City College the next year. That he had an impact in that first teaching role in Cambridge was never in question. The daughter of one of his students would comment in 1983 on the impact he had on her mother, saying that her mother had always wanted to be a Latin teacher after being a student in George's Latin class. Her mother remembered asking George for a topic for an essay, and he had suggested "Idle Thoughts of an Idle Maiden." She and her friends composed a little poem, which she recited enough over the years that the daughter could recite it word-for-word eighty-two years later, writing it down for George's family:

Teach us how to spell, Dear Georgie
Teach us how to sing
Teach us how to keep our hearts
From dangling on a string.
How we would adore thee
Could we but forget
"Seniors, please keep quiet,
Or you'll receive a demerit"

- By the senior class girls of Cambridge High School, 1901[6]

Beginning in September of 1901 he taught both English and history at Baltimore City College. and also coached their track team, a sensible task considering his illustrious track record while at Johns Hopkins University. Baltimore City College, one of the oldest public high schools in the country, was created in 1839 to provide white males a classical education. In 1865, it acquired the name "Baltimore City College" as it added a five-year track which led to a college degree. By 1901, when George was hired, the program was cut back to only a four-year track, but, as before, City College graduates could get into nearby Johns Hopkins University without an examination.[7] The link between City College and Hopkins made George a logical choice as teacher.

George taught only one year before moving on to law school the following year and would only teach one class of students, the City College freshmen. His effect on them was profound; three years later, in 1905, the class made him an honorary classmate and dedicated their literary magazine, *The Green Bag*, to him. That he would be selected for this honor from among four years of professors the students encountered, and that his impact would still be strong three years after his departure points to the fact that he significantly influenced these students in his brief tenure.

Those students would go to many illustrious careers, and most would remain in close contact with their former teacher. One member of the class went on to fame in Hollywood: Edward Everett Horton had a long career in theatre, radio, television, and film—often providing the voice of characters in cartoons. His career was a long one, with movies spanning six decades, earning him a star on the Hollywood Walk of Fame. He and George wrote each other over the years and would get together whenever Horton came to Baltimore. He always regarded George as his English teacher. "We used to harass teachers by taking seventeen-year locusts into class. But never into Radcliffe's class. We gave him respectful silence because he read things like Silas Marner and Ivanhoe."[8]

In reality, George continued to "teach" this class as he returned to one class reunion after another, making frequent speeches in which he continued to offer them advice. He wrote an article for the 1905 edition of The Green Bag in which he urged them to always think young as they went through life and to maintain the school spirit that they had. Titled "Lares and Penates," referring to the Roman household gods and the protectors of possessions, the article urged them to use school trophies and memorabilia to help keep their school spirit alive while leaving behind the immaturity of youth:

> Whatever the situation may be the spirit of his college days contains much of what is really essential in him. His crudity of thought and indefiniteness of purpose and plan are found to be impractical and insufficient. These are natural to youth and are among the many elements of a college man's make-up which should be left behind. He needs, however, to hold tenaciously to what college spirit has stood for – optimism, enthusiasm, freshness and wholesomeness of spirit, self-confidence and his college ideals.[9]

At their fortieth reunion, the class once again dedicated The Green Bag to him:

> To George L. Radcliffe
>
> Two score and four years ago we met as teacher and scholar. For two score and four years we have been friends. To the outside world you have been variously Teacher, Lawyer, Banker, and United States Senator. To us you have just been George, our classmate and our friend, and it is to our friend George L. Radcliffe that we, the Class of 1905 of the Baltimore City College affectionately dedicate this second edition of our Green Bag.[10]

They asked him for comments to include in the reunion brochure, and George came back to the very same point he made forty years prior, although he addressed his earlier article as a "lumbering article of dubious merit." Though a prominent U.S. Senator at this time, George showed that he had never developed an ego but had, through all the years, maintained that "spirit" he talked about in 1905. Although he had remained personally close to these students, he remained ever the teacher, but he still recognized that teachers gain as much as they give:

> The close friendships which have continued throughout the years between you members of the Class of 1905 and myself have been worthwhile to all of us. I hope and believe I have been of some value to you. You have surely helped me. On many a dark day and in many a trying situation, the thought of your abiding confidence in me and of your warm friendship has had a sustaining and stimulating effect upon me which at times I needed acutely.[11]

Even in his work with the Fidelity and Deposit Company, he would step into the role of teacher, offering a series of twenty-five lectures at Johns Hopkins University on "The Principles of Suretyship" during the 1920 – 1921 academic year.[12] While George avoided the limelight in the Senate and avoided speeches unless he had something of value to contribute, he loved to speak on matters of history, always pulling on his vast knowledge of Maryland, classical literature, Latin, and modern United States history. His speeches were epic and always seemed more like a college lecture than a speech. He always had a point to make and used the backdrop of history to make that point. In many public or social functions, he would be asked to "say a few words" and would soon launch into a lecture that included details, dates, anecdotes, and quotes. The family would always chuckle about his epic speeches and talks, sometimes thinking that senility had set in, but I came to realize that the teacher in him was burning strong. Although seventy years and more achievements than one could imagine had passed, he was still that young teacher interacting with that class, urging them on to greater academic heights and wanting to share the passion for learning and life that he had. In many ways, his resume should have listed "Teacher" first.

Returning to my conversation with my grandfather on choosing teaching as my career, I remember asking him why he had left the profession, choosing law instead. He explained that teaching was his passion but that teaching in this country had often become more of a job than a profession. I remember being startled by that comment as I considered the two terms synonymous. The idea of teachers' unions, teachers striking for better pay, and pay scales independent of actual achievement and competence struck a sour note with him. He wanted a profession where one could rise unobstructed and where excellence was valued. He did not want a nine-to-five job. To him, a job was something one did for pay, whereas a profession came from the heart. He then went on to explain how we are all teachers, laying the foundation for generations to come. Looking at his life, he educated many, and did so far better than many in the traditional teaching career.

George L. Radcliffe read constantly until the time of his death; there was always something new to learn. He never felt he was the master of a subject; to him that was when someone became "old." Few gave more speeches than he did throughout his life, and these were a learning process for him. He may have been the Pied Piper of local history in the Maryland area, but the many speeches, talks, and conversations were equally valuable to him as they forced him to clarify and expand his ideas. Most U.S. Senators, on leaving that office, would look at that service as their paramount achievement, but George just looked at this as another step, not a steppingstone to power, but a rung on the ladder of knowledge. George stayed a learner and teacher until his final days. He wanted to be remembered as a teacher and a lover of learning, not a politician. In many ways he lived up to Woodrow Wilson's ideal of what a teacher should be: "they must rule their students... throughout their existence ...by the spirit of the things they expound."

In June of 1974, George attended his final City College reunion; he passed away the following month. He addressed the few remaining students as he always did. In his usual modesty, he said, "The boys at City College helped educate me. I learned more from them than they did from me. Honor then not what I taught you but what you taught me."

Gustav J. Requardt, a successful engineer, and current President of the Class of 1905 at the reunion, then quickly responded, "You taught us decency. Thank God for you."[13]

Essays

The Historian

ONE FOOT IN THE PAST,
ONE IN THE FUTURE

It is impossible to understand George L. Radcliffe without looking at how deeply committed he was to the importance of history. Every move made, every speech delivered, and every cause supported had its roots in his passion for history. He was its poster child, a lifelong advocate of the importance of using history as the context for making decisions and planning for the future. That little boy who carried around his copy of Charles Dickens' *A Child's History of England* while reciting the dates of every English monarch grew up immersed in history. In the aftermath of the Civil War, he was surrounded by a family well-read and steeped in history. While most young children are read nursery rhymes and fairy tales, young George listened to stories of the Norman conquest of England in 1066, the futility of Napoleon's 1812 Russian Campaign, and Hannibal's crossing the Alps to invade Italy. It was no surprise that history would be the thread that connected all the events in the life of George L. Radcliffe.

While most viewed current events as the "here and now," George could only view them in the context of history. In a letter which he wrote to President Roosevelt in 1939, but decided not to send, he discussed this concept:

> During those days [graduate work at Johns Hopkins University] one of the ideas which became impressed in my mind was that history was a form of development—an incident in history is nothing more than a page in the middle of a book. It must be considered in connection with what has gone before, and it must be realized in all probability it is not the final page.[1]

It surprised no one that George ended up at Johns Hopkins University in the fall of 1894, where he would go on to major in history, and it was also no surprise that he pursued a Ph.D. in history. Teaching history was a logical career choice for the historian, but he quickly moved into a career in law. To George, law was history in action, and he wanted to be a participant in history and not just one who recounted stories of the past. George's father had been actively involved in the community and state, and George wanted to fuse his passion for history with a desire to contribute. Even after earning his degrees, he continued to read everything he could get his hands on, gradually building up an extensive library. In 1908 he joined the Maryland Historical Society, beginning a relationship which would last a lifetime. He would be an officer of the Society for sixty-three years, including president for almost thirty, and would oversee that organization's growth, making it one of the premier historical organizations in the country. George worked hard to bring in speakers with different historical points of view. Over the years he started attracting nationally renowned speakers such as Gen. George Marshall and Vice President Truman, and would start to increase the number of visitors, including involving schoolchildren in the 1950s. His tenure would see the Society expand considerably in the 1950s and acquire Francis Scott Key's manuscript of the Star-Spangled Banner in 1953.[2]

In fact, everything George did throughout his long life was steeped in history, whether in the U.S. Senate, the many civic groups he played key roles in, or on his own property. Whatever the topic, cause, or event, George found a way to weave history into it. As an extreme example of this, in 1948 in a talk in front of the Episcopal Pro-Cathedral in Baltimore, he turned a speech on faith into a history lesson on George Washington and his faith, even connecting it with the political happenings of the present day:

> I have spent some years as a student and teacher of history. My knowledge of history with the passing years

become more and more sketchy. I have retained, however, the habit of trying to fancy historical analogies. The accuracy of these comparisons cannot be proved. Nor can they be disproved.

So, I am going to chance a few guesses as to what Washington would have done in certain situations. These will not be deduced from brief comments by him, but rather upon what I believe to be his basic philosophy and his general trend of thought....

Can you imagine him marching side by side with Richard the Lionheart in full accord as to his policies? Like Richard the Lionheart, he might have utilized his tremendous physical strength in trying to batter open the gate at Acre, but my guess is he would have pursued other tactics. Had George Washington planned a crusade to recapture the Holy Land, he would have functioned in a practical, methodical manner. He would have had no sustaining faith in success until his painstaking and adequate methods had pointed out clearly the course to follow.

Had George Washington lived during the days of the Reformation, his faith in his own religion and his close adherence to it, would have never led him into advocating religious wars. Certainly, he would not have insisted that people following other religions should be burned at the stake merely because they did not share his concept of Christianity....

The clear-headed judgment of Washington would lead him to support a movement for the self-governing Jewish home in Palestine. The tremendous confidence which

Washington inspired in contemporaries would do much to persuade the nations of the world to accept his judgment as to what should be done in Palestine ...."[3]

George was as great an advocate of Maryland history as anyone. His life was one of bringing lesser-known events in Maryland history to light, recognizing key individuals, and ensuring that past heroes and political figures not be forgotten. He was largely behind the erection of historical road markers in the state, recognizing key historical figures and events. He spent many years trying to get a memorial erected for the 400 brave Marylanders who risked their lives at the Battle of Brooklyn (also called Battle of Long Island) on Aug. 27, 1776, giving George Washington the needed time to escape with his army. Through many speeches, letters, and visits to New York, George worked for a monument to recognize those valiant Marylanders.[4]

George was remarkably adept at connecting pieces of history. A bit of Maryland history which fascinated him was the conflict between Maryland and Pennsylvania over the placement of the Mason-Dixon Line. The North-South line between Maryland and what is now Delaware was to be placed at the midpoint between the Atlantic Ocean and the Chesapeake Bay. The controversy arose over whether Taylor's Island would be included as part of the mainland. William Penn won that argument, and the islands were included, thus moving the Mason-Dixon Line a couple miles to the west, shrinking Maryland by several square miles. To commemorate this event, George had a historic road marker placed on Taylor's Island on the property of the Grace Church and Chapel of Ease, which he was helping restore. This way he was able to connect two of the historical projects to which he was devoted. At the well-attended commemoration, Maryland Governor Millard Tawes referred to George as "the historian of all time as far as Maryland is concerned."[5]

Even in the U.S. Senate, history was behind his every action and vote. In sponsoring the Merchant Marine Act of 1936, he was trying to get the

U.S. to avoid the mistake it had made in World War I, when the country entered the war with a completely inadequate merchant marine and began the production of ships only after the war had already ended. George researched the history of the United States Merchant Marine, authoring an unpublished history of the service.[6] Once again, while connecting past and future, he also looked ahead to what would become of the ships after the war.

George also combined his love of history and family to become a remarkable genealogist. He came by this honestly as his parents were well versed on their families' origins. This interest was one thing which likely attracted him to Mary McKim Marriott, whose family was prominent in early Maryland history. George could rattle off his relationship to even the most distant relative, and he could trace the origin of every piece of family furniture, china, and silver. This was a lifelong pursuit, and he left behind enough notes and documents to fill a library. He came to be known as the family and community genealogist, and the countless letters he left behind showed that he helped literally hundreds unearth their family trees. He even spent time helping President Truman research some of his family roots.

Whenever Fidelity and Deposit Company business carried George to England, he would allow extra time to search for information on his English heritage. He knew that his fourth great-grandfather, Richard Radcliffe, had emigrated to this country in 1682 from Lancashire, England. The Radcliffes largely came from the town of Radcliffe, named after a red sandstone cliff across the river from the town. George visited the area and was able to uncover considerable information on the family. His ancestor, Stephen Gary, who had settled Spocott in 1663 had come from Cornwall, and George spent considerable time there researching that family. Rarely a day went by where George was not digging up information, researching old documents, or scribbling down what he knew of some remote part of his genealogy.[7]

That little boy who read about the battles and statesmen of history grew up to greatly influence history. One of my last memories of him was watching him read Dean Acheson's *Present at the Creation: My Years in the State Department*, which Acheson had sent him. George had worked with Acheson, Roosevelt's undersecretary of state, while in the Senate, and the two had become good friends. How fitting that George, at the end of his life, would be reading history in which he had played a role. Even when his physical health was failing, George remained mentally sharp and continued to read and tell the stories for which he had become famous. Every story would be a delightful mixture of anecdote, humor, and always a dose of history.

His brother, Sewell, always teased his little brother saying that he was stuck in the past. Sewell, the businessman early in his life and farmer for the second half, was not one to reminisce; while his brother would regale others with tales of long ago, Sewell would be more likely to talk about the latest Baltimore Oriole baseball game outcome or what price a bushel of corn was currently bringing. Watching the two talk was often comic relief as Sewell would try to drag his brother into the present while George always had one foot in the past. However, George also had one foot in the future because to him, the present was simply a bridge between past and future. Despite his passion for reminiscing, George did not live in the past, and while he loved to include history in his talks, these talks always had a modern-day purpose. As George so often said, history provides the context for evaluating the present and planning for the future, wisdom as true today as it ever was. In a newspaper interview in 1961, he spoke of history in reference to the Maryland Historical Society:

> When will people understand that the study of history is a practical thing, the use of the total experience of a nation. That is what I have always felt about history, since I got my doctorate at Johns Hopkins, since I taught history, and since I used it in the Senate. Now this

practical point of view is what we want for the Maryland Historical Society. We have new money now, and we are going to expand, always we hope with a realistic point of view. We don't want to be a bunch of old men debating how many swords some Civil War general carried into battle with him.[8]

"Born a Red-Hot Rebel"

In the final interview of his life in 1974, George L. Radcliffe was asked again how he would have sided in the Civil War, to which he responded, "I was born a red-hot Rebel."[1] To those who knew George, this comment came as a surprise since he clearly exhibited no bias during his life. He was a historian and always espoused that fact was more important than opinion; throughout his life, he would evolve from his origins in a "Rebel family" to view the world in a modern context. However, his family roots were heavily intertwined with the scars of the Civil War, so much so that it became a lifelong interest of his.

George was born twelve years after the conclusion of the Civil War, but the war still wove itself through many aspects of his life. The impact on his family and his wife's family, his passion for history, and his desire to preserve the record of the family's past can be seen in both the social and political aspects of his life. His family's Confederate leanings combined with his father's possible pacifist views must have created a degree of conflict, similar to what Maryland experienced at the outbreak of the war. Ironically, this conflict became his focus as he chose a Ph.D. research interest at Johns Hopkins.

Born in 1877, George was born into a Rebel family. Even though Maryland was a border state, it had been a slave state, and George's family had owned slaves at Spocott at one time. His mother's Travers family had also owned slaves on nearby Taylor's Island. When John Anthony Le-Compte Radcliffe had purchased Spocott in the late 1840s, he depended on a small amount of slave labor to build his ships and manage the family farm. While most of the enslaved people he owned were children from three families, there were adults from two of the families. The approaching Civil War split the Radcliffe family, with at least four of his brothers siding with the Confederacy. Nehemiah was killed fighting in Arkansas in 1862[2], George W.W. Radcliffe died in 1864 (causes unknown), and James also died in 1864, although we do not know if it was war-related. Another brother, William Harris Radcliffe, was a known Confederate sympathizer but could not fight due to injuries from an appendicitis attack. William was known by all to harbor Confederate spies and would openly ride into Cambridge with them. When stopped he would admit to accompanying a spy and apparently got away with it since the authorities never thought a person would be so brazen as to be truthful about such a subject.[3] George's father, John, chose not to fight in the war even though he had been a captain in the Mexican War, and George's mother had also harbored Confederate spies in her house during the Civil War.[4] With the possible exception of George's father, this was a solidly Confederate family.

Nehemiah Radcliffe
(1825-1862)
George's uncle who died in action
fighting for the Confederacy

William Harris Radcliffe
(1824-1902)
George's uncle who harbored
Confederate spies

George, in his childhood, lived largely in an adult world. His father's many siblings were a part of his life, and he was the youngest of nineteen children from his father's and mother's marriages. Many of his half-brothers and half-sisters were adults when he was born, and the youngest of these was seven years his senior. With the war in the recent memory of so many, the Civil War and its aftermath was a regular topic of conversation, and it is hardly surprising that the war would become a research interest of George while in the graduate program at Johns Hopkins.

The interesting question is what side George would have taken in the family debates which undoubtedly occurred. While John was likely an abolitionist and opposed to the war and most relatives committed to the Confederacy, there had to be considerable tension in the family. Evidence of this is shown by the breakup in the Spocott shipbuilding business just before the war. While John remained at Spocott, both William and Nehemiah, each a Southern sympathizer, ceased working with John. William moved to a nearby farm, while Nehemiah moved to Missouri where he died in the war.

One of the letters George preserved was a letter from the individual whose house in Missouri his Uncle Nehemiah died in:

> A gentleman from Schuyler Co., State of Mo. Named NH Radcliffe, formerly of MD, called at my house on his return trip from the Confederate Army in Arkansas. He was quite sick when he called, and I soon prevailed on him to send for medical aid.... I became very attached to him and he received every attention and comfort that one of my family could have had, he was a favorite of us all, he was a Mason, a Methodist, and doubtless a Christian as was evidenced by his constant and unremitting patience, fortitude, and resignation to the Divine will as he freely and frequently expressed.
>
> His disease was inflammatory rheumatism, and he was

sick some two weeks. He stopped at my house on the 23rd of May and died on the 6th of June [1862]. He belonged to Gen. Harris' Division, Col. Greene's Regiment, and was a private soldier. I have the consolation to know that everything was done to make him comfortable and happy while at my house.[5]

As with most of the Civil War fatalities, disease was more likely to kill than a bullet. While George obviously never knew Nehemiah, he was well aware that he had lost an uncle who was fighting for the Confederacy. While William never actively fought, relations between him and John were strained, but years later they would grow close again. George would get to know his Uncle William well, as William lived until 1902.

One question that fueled George's curiosity later became the topic of his research at Hopkins: why had Maryland not seceded from the Union? As a slave state, Maryland logically could have seceded. If Maryland had seceded, Washington, the Union capital, would have been deep in Southern territory, and the war certainly could have had a different outcome. The first blood spilled in the Civil War was in a riot in Baltimore on April 19, 1861, a week after the firing on Fort Sumter; that day Southern sympathizers fired on Federal troops marching through the city. Governor Thomas Holliday Hicks, also from Dorchester County and generally pro-South, moved the State legislature from pro-South Annapolis to pro-North Frederick where it voted not to secede. Hicks also decided not to convene a state convention, thus avoiding a secession vote, and Maryland remained neutral in the war. There was a prevailing feeling in Maryland, as in George's family, that cooler heads would prevail, and differences could be settled peacefully. George's research culminated in a Ph.D. dissertation, *Governor Thomas H. Hicks of Maryland and the Civil War*, completed in 1900 and published in 1901.[6]

George's relationship with and marriage to Mary McKim Marriott intensified his interest in the Civil War, as the war had also played a significant role in her family. Her mother was Aline Bracco (1859–1939), descended from a Talbot County, Maryland, family but raised in Tennessee. Details of her early life are sketchy, but she shared the following story with her son-in-law, George, in later years. While certain facts cannot be verified, George transcribed Aline's account word-by-word. The important point is that Aline carried this story with her throughout her life, and it clearly colored her views related to the Civil War. Her parents, John Bennett Bracco and Sarah Ann Elliott, were married in Tennessee in 1850, and her godfather was none other than General P.G.T. Beauregard, the Confederate commander at Fort Sumter when it was attacked in 1861. She had siblings, but their names are unknown.

The story Aline related to George took place in 1862. While Aline would have just been three, with likely no clear memory of the events, the full story must have come from her parents or her godfather. Apparently after some Union-Confederate confrontation in Tennessee, General Beauregard ended up hiding on the Bracco farm with a Major Collier. The Union troops pursued them and correctly surmised that he was hiding on the Bracco farm. The fact that the Bracco's had made Beauregard the godfather of Aline attests to his closeness to the family. The troops burned the house and barns, trying to flush the general out, and when that produced nothing, they set afire the thirteen large haystacks on the farm, figuring that he and Collier must be hiding in one of them. Twelve of the stacks were consumed with fire, but a thirteenth failed to light. Using bayonets, they rickstabbed this last stack before being summoned hurriedly to leave on a further mission. Ironically, this last stack was where the two Confederates were hiding. The major was wounded by a bayonet, but Beauregard escaped unharmed.[7] Even if aspects of the story are distorted, one can see why Aline was a Confederate sympathizer.

At approximately age ten, while Aline was visiting a cousin, her entire family—parents and siblings—succumbed to some disease, and the 1870 census shows her living in Talbot County, Maryland, with her grand-

mother and two aunts. However, Aline remembers spending
much of her remaining childhood with General Beauregard.
She remembers being remarkably close to him, and always
spoke fondly of him. He taught
her how to both shoot and ride
horseback. On one occasion, he
told her that she could have a sil-
ver-plated pistol if she could hit
a target with three out of four
shots while riding horseback;
she hit it with all 4 shots and
was given both the pistol and a
horse. She remained close to the
Beauregard family and was actually visiting Beauregard relatives
when she died in 1939. Her son-
in-law, George, gave her eulogy,
saying that "Baltimore lost a valiant figure of the Old South."[8]
Aline's segregationist views
were crystal clear to all.

Aline Bracco Marriott
(1859-1939)
George's mother-in-law and
goddaughter of Confederate
Gen. P. G. T. Beauregard
Pictured here with her grandson,
George M. Radcliffe

Mary Marriott had another Civil War connection. A cousin of hers,
Robert McKim, although much older, was killed in the war. Although
Mary and George obviously never knew this cousin, they were close to
the cousin's sister, Emilie McKim, until her death in 1924. Robert was
from Baltimore and had attended one year at the University of Virginia.
On returning home at the age of seventeen, he and a group of friends were
temporarily held over in Manassas, Virginia, where they encountered the

Confederate army passing through. They were apparently so impressed by the soldiers that they enlisted on the spot. In the ensuing months, he wrote his sister of the deplorable conditions ((forced marches, scarce food, and lack of a tent), yet he remained optimistic and enamored with a cause he could probably scarcely understand at that young age. He served with Stonewall Jackson, and in the First Battle of Winchester (Virginia) on May 25, 1862, he was killed instantly by a Federal sharpshooter. In this battle, Gen. Stonewall Jackson routed the Union army led by Gen. Nathanial Banks. Robert was one of 400 Confederate troops killed that day while Union losses exceeded 2,000.[9] His death clearly shook his older sister. In 1897 Emilie spoke to the Daughters of the Confederacy of Maryland, saying of her brother:

> His fate was one of those sad incidents of our Civil War, which is most painful to recall. How little availed the great sacrifices made by those gallant noble spirits who fought for principle and honore! The short life of this gallant boy was full of grace and beauty. His varied and intellectual gifts and his charming personality so endeared him to those who knew him that they cannot cease to cherish his memory and mourn his early death.[10]

With such a family background, Mary McKim Marriott would have had, at the very least, strong emotional ties to the Confederate cause. In marrying George in 1906, there clearly was a fusion of family backgrounds. Both had lost family in the Civil War, so history was personal. This was not just a political view, and Confederate sympathy at this time was more about family than political inclination. One of the things that united George and Mary was clearly a reverence for their family histories as well as a love of history itself. George had already received his degree in history and written a book, and Mary would later write the family history, which would read almost like an English history textbook. Their passion for history continued throughout their lives.

When George first became involved with the Maryland Historical Society, early in the 20th century, he said that the organization was still "fighting the Civil War." He was asked to give a talk on his dissertation topic to the Society, but it was deemed too controversial and canceled at the last minute. George was told that if he "attempted to make an address on the Civil War in the Maryland Historical Society, the former Confederate and Union soldiers present at the meeting would insist upon fighting again the issues of the war."[11]

George, as a member and later officer of the Maryland Historical Society, found this to be true. Whatever the topic being discussed in those early years, George said that the room would soon divide in two, with all taking sides with either the Union or Confederacy. He felt this contributed largely to the Society's inefficiency, and, in becoming an officer, he would try to create programs which "left the war behind."

In 1947, after leaving the U.S. Senate, George was put on a committee to organize the dedication in Baltimore of a privately funded equestrian statue of Robert E. Lee and Stonewall Jackson. At the dedication in 1948, George spoke, saying:

> These ... famous Virginians were men of peace, who endeavored by all honorable means to avoid bloodshed. When, however, recourse was had to the abitrament of arms, each one fought bravely and resourcefully on the field of battle to sustain the cause he believed to be the true one.
>
> Scholars may continue to differ as to where was the weight in the preponderance of John C. Calhoun, Daniel Webster, Henry Clay, Jefferson Davis, and others concerning the problem as to whether any state did or did not have the right to secede, but no one questions the sincerity of purpose of those who asserted their views in the controversy and fought for their adoption.[12]

While that statue in Baltimore was taken down in 2017, as many viewed it as a symbol of racism, George would likely have been horrified by this action. While Confederacy was in his blood, history was paramount. He viewed the statue as preserving history, and while he likely admired the two generals, he never viewed the statue as an attempt to memorialize a bygone era.

His passion for Civil War history came full circle in 1959 when Governor Milliard Tawes appointed him chairman of Maryland's Civil War Centennial Commission. Civil War emotions were starting to fade at this point as veterans of that war were deceased, and most offspring of these veterans had also passed. For most, there was no personal connection to the war. George sought to make these reenactments and commemorative events historical and never political. Some strong Confederate sentiment, however, still existed, and George's commission sought to commemorate both Union and Southern troops. It had to be amazing for him to be involved with a centennial of the war which killed members of his family, the culmination of a professional interest that had begun with a Ph.D. dissertation sixty years earlier.

George lived to see integration and the Civil Rights Act of 1964, but one does not discard family history. His book would be republished in later years, and I, as his grandson, discussed the war with him on many occasions. Never once did I get an inclination of his original Confederate roots. He lived in a world of facts, seeing opinion as often corrupting our pursuit of the facts. Born in a Confederate household to a father who was clearly torn in his views, George must have had conflicted views, much as did Governor Hicks in 1861. Today, we are far removed from personal impacts of the war and can thus view it with increased objectivity. In denouncing slavery and the war today, what we often lose sight of is that in the half century or so after the war, family often played as much a role in shaping views as political feelings. Those who grew up in the shadow of the Civil War still had bonds to family, and this was not going to disappear in their lifetime. George L. Radcliffe's life spanned the century after the war, from the emotions of the post-war period to viewing it strictly from the viewpoint of history. His background in historical research allowed him to appear neutral, even if steeped in the blood of the Confederacy.

Wood Fires, Dickens, and Bayberry

A young George L. Radcliffe—future author, teacher, lawyer, banker, senator, historian, and civic leader--aspired to none of these avocations; his dream was to one day be an unpaid volunteer worker for Santa at the North Pole. As a child, he was completely focused on Christmas holiday and traditions, and these formed his most vivid memories of those early days at Spocott. Combined with a growing passion for history, the history and traditions of Christmas were to become a focus for George throughout his entire life.

Yes, Kris Kringle was alive and well in Maryland during the nineteenth century. There was never a more passionate advocate of Christmas and all its traditions than George L. Radcliffe. Possessing possibly the largest private collection of Christmas books in the country, George carried the Christmas traditions from his childhood at Spocott throughout all his ninety-seven years, even imposing his views on the United States Senate in a remarkable speech. As a child, reading numerous Christmas books, Dickens' *A Christmas Carol* among them, and with an unusual passion for history instilled in him early on, the holiday became his favorite fixation, considerably more than a mere hobby. Every room in his house was littered with books, magazines, and prints covering every aspect of the holiday. His Christmas book collection was estimated to contain from 1000 – 2000 titles, encompassing everything from rare titles to modern treatises. No one ever knew the exact count because they were never all situated in one location. There were books in his office, his Washington apartment, his home on the Eastern Shore, and beside every chair in his home in Baltimore. Relaxing for him on any occasion meant picking up one of these volumes and getting temporarily lost in it.[1]

Sen. George L. Radcliffe and His Christmas Book Collection

In addition to all the Christmas volumes, he amassed literally hundreds of copies of magazines, mostly English, specializing in Christmas. These included *The Illustrated London News, Graphic, Holly Leaves*, and *Puck*. An entire room of his spacious Baltimore home was stacked high with issues of these colorful periodicals, loaded with stories, anecdotes, and traditions. None ever made it into the waste disposal system.

Christmas to George was not just a one-day celebration, a religious holiday, or a day for children to dream and receive gifts. It was a historical and cultural phenomenon. He looked far beyond the commercialization of Christmas, already occurring during the latter days of his life, seeing the holiday as representing the best of humanity:

> It was the religious side of Christmas which interested me, the tremendous effect the Christmas idea had on so many people. This was so especially in the Middle Ages. At Christmas, even today, business comes to an end, wars come to an end, litigation comes to an end. When things like that happen, no one can go back exactly to the way things were before.[2]

He spent considerable time researching the history and traditions of Christmas. One incident he loved to recount occurred in 1418 when the forces of King Henry V were besieging the City of Rouen in Normandy during the Hundred Years War. Throughout the latter half of that year, Henry's forces blockaded the city, depriving the citizens of supplies and, in many cases, food. By December, the starving people had resorted to eating cats, dogs, horse flesh, and rodents, but on Christmas Day, Henry allowed two priests to carry in enough food to give the citizens a good meal. Christmas trumped war![3]

But the roots of George's passion for the holiday clearly lay in those early Christmases of his childhood at Spocott. Although growing up in the most rural of settings, he was surrounded by books. His parents regaled him with stories of bygone days and read to him regularly. The ground was fertile for the seed that would germinate and grow into his love of history and Christmas. At that time Spocott was a self-sufficient community, and Christmas was completely home grown. The holiday might have been a one-day event, but George's preparation for it lasted 365 days. The open fire, tree, holly, bayberry, and a meal fit for a king were all integral parts of the elaborate holiday.

One could never walk into either his home in Baltimore or his house on the Spocott property without seeing a massive wood fire burning in the fireplace. Both homes had a fireplace in virtually every room, and these fires were often terrifying to a young child. The fireplace at his Baltimore home was large enough to encompass a small couch, and the fire burning within so large that flames often licked the mantlepiece; charred places on these mantles were a record of many cold, wintry nights spent huddled in front of a blazing fire.

George's son, George M., had vivid memories of these immense fires, commenting that he never understood why the house never burned down. He remembered one memorable evening when his father threw a large bag of trash onto an already huge fire. This predated plastic, and his father often incinerated the trash. This evening, however, was different. Within a couple moments, the first explosion occurred, with a burning projectile launching into the room. Before young George could get to the burning sphere, another explosion occurred with another fiery sphere launching into the room. Soon war had broken out in the living room with young George racing around the room, putting out small fires. The bag of trash had contained a dozen golf balls, now exploding. The house survived this particular open fire.

The other focal point of the Radcliffe Christmas was the Christmas tree, always a red cedar tree cut down on the Spocott property, and George always made sure one was also transported up to his Baltimore home. He remembered as a child spending most of the year walking the property, looking for that perfect tree. As the open fire heated the room, the aroma of cedar would soon permeate the house.

As one would expect, the tree was decorated with all-natural products: pine cones, vines, and popcorn. George grew the popcorn which he would pop and then string, making strands which he could then wrap around the tree. The excess popcorn grown was sold in Baltimore, supplying George with a little cash for one necessary addition to the tree. He had to purchase, for his childhood tree, three candy lions, inspired by Dickens' account of the Battle of Hastings in *A Child's History of England*: "And the three Norman lions kept watch o'er the field."[4]

In later years, George and Daisy added a terrifying twist to their Baltimore Christmas tree. They adorned their cedar tree with candles which they would light in the evening. If one has ever seen how quickly cedar ignites in a fireplace, one can understand why their son George viewed the spectacle with terror. Fortunately, when I saw my first Radcliffe tree, electricity had made its appearance, but it was still a wonder to behold: massive, highly decorated, and filling the house with the aroma of cedar.

Spocott was naturally populated with four plants, which formed the basis of George's Christmas experience. In addition to the red cedars, growing naturally on the property in large quantities were loblolly pines, American holly, bayberry, and mistletoe. The loblolly pine tree was self-pruning and thus inadequate for a Christmas tree, but boughs with cones were pruned and used for wreathes, mantle decorations, and wall hangings. American holly trees are evergreen trees with stiff, multi-pointed leaves, and the female trees had red berries. Visually appealing and associated with Christmas, these adorned every room. Northern bayberry (*Myrica pensylvanica*), which tolerates well the often salty Spocott soil, is not the most visually appealing plant, but its leaves are covered with a resin that emits an appealing aroma when crushed. The heat from the Spocott open fire would release the aroma, which would soon permeate the entire house.

George collected the bayberry for more than just the pleasant aroma. The small berries are coated with wax, which when removed, can be used to make candles and soap. Fifteen pounds of the berries will make a pound of wax. Boiled in water, the wax will float and can be collected. George spent considerable time collecting berries and melting them down to get the wax. He was especially proud of the fact that he made these candles in molds belonging to his great-grandfather Radcliffe. Of his candles, he said, "I hope my bayberry candles displayed more magic powers than evidence of skill and workmanship." He happily shared this craft with all his grandchildren.

Getting ready for the holidays as a child was time consuming, and there was still school and the many chores to do. Christmas, however, became a completely natural event with so much grown, made, and prepared. It was all about tradition. Not having bayberry candles or holly adorning mantles would be like Thanksgiving without a turkey or a birthday without a cake.

And, of course, what would Christmas be without mistletoe, a parasitic plant growing high in the trees throughout the Spocott property. Family members shot pieces of it down from the tops of trees and added it to the house in several places. Christmas meant bringing the outdoors indoors for the holiday season, a multisensory experience which imprinted on young George and stayed with him throughout his life.

The preparation of the Christmas meal was an all-family event: meat came from a slaughtered animal (a job relegated to one of his older brothers); meal was ground from farm-grown grain in his father's windmill; vegetables were grown and prepared; pies, fruit cake, bread, and rolls were baked; elaborate desserts were prepared; nuts from black walnut and pecan trees on the property were collected; bountiful seafood was harvested from the creek beside the house. Young George was eager to help his mother with the baking. As the youngest of all the children, he had fewer physical chores. He did feed and mind the chickens, turkeys, and small farm animals, but with no sisters in the house at that time, he was the one expected to help in the kitchen. Christmas to him became pies, pudding, custards, breads, and biscuits. His mother would start baking cakes right after Thanksgiving, but the real culinary wizard was the remarkable Adaline Wheatley, who was a third generation Spocott resident and worker. No meal was considered complete without her biscuits, soups, and pies.

The passion for Christmas and its traditions almost became an obsession when George was doing research for his doctoral degree at Johns Hopkins. His historical research into Maryland's role at the outset of the Civil War somehow often sidetracked into reading Christmas books and researching the history of the holiday. History plus the traditions turned an interest into a lifelong fixation. George moved to Baltimore when he went to work for the American Bonding Company as a lawyer in 1903, but he never strayed far from his childhood home, returning to Spocott whenever he could, always returning for the holiday. When he married Mary McKim Marriott in 1906, he found a willing accomplice, as she too was fascinated with history and traditions. Her artistic ability and remarkable writing skills combined with his historical knowledge to create a wonderful symbiosis. The Christmas traditions just continued to grow and mature.

One would think that the U.S. Senate would provide no venue for George's Christmas interests, but he found a unique way to combine the two. George was not known for his public speaking as he often felt senators spent too much time in the spotlight and too little time in committee work, but he made an exception to this in 1942. With the one-year anniversary of the Pearl Harbor attack and with the slow progress in the European theatre, he felt the need to put the times in a historical perspective, and that meant connecting events with the approaching Christmas season. He authored a speech called "Christmas and War" which he asked to deliver to the entire Senate body. He was granted time on the last day of the Senate session before recessing for the holiday.

The day took on a humorous twist as George was in his Senate office while the body was in session. He got word that the Senate was going to recess in fifteen minutes, and his office was a good distance from the Senate chamber. Sprinting out of the Senate office building and across to the Capitol, he literally burst into the Senate as Senator Alben Barkley, majority leader and future vice president, was about to drop the gavel to end the session. Seeing George racing and stumbling down the steps of the chamber, he paused, allowing George to give his speech.

One must chuckle trying to picture a group of tired Senators, dreaming of returning home for the holiday, but now having to listen to another speech. I imagine that not many heard the speech that day. It is a remarkable speech but probably more of a college lecture than Senate business. In it, George outlines the country's place in history from a historical perspective and shows how the upcoming Christmas season is a time for optimism and renewing the country's commitment to not just winning but to restoring humanity to the world. The speech is fascinating, philosophical, and uplifting but clearly did not go down in the annals of the U.S. Senate as one of its most memorable addresses. It was, however, vintage George L. Radcliffe. The 15-minute speech delivered on December 15, 1942, ended with:

> Today, in the carrying on of all the activities which the grim necessities of war demand, in the sadness which the dislocations and separations in family life resulting from the war have brought to us, and in sympathetic realizations of the hardships, strains, and tragedies of this war so cruelly thrust upon us, we shall do well to be mindful of the best which Christmas can teach us.

> Were the Axis to win, Christmas, with its much-prized significance, religious and otherwise, would cease to exist. Its doctrines of equality, fraternity, and freedom, which we with increasing might are trying to preserve against

the violent and vicious attacks of the Axis, would be lost to the world. Our basic institutions would be submerged.

It is indeed highly appropriate that the recent successes of the United Nations in their fight against heretofore adversaries should be occurring as the season of Christmas is approaching.

The gigantic struggle which we are making today for free institutions demonstrates that the spirit of Christmas did not perish from the earth. It is reincarnated in the spirit which today leads us to resist the arrogant iconoclastic pretensions of the Axis Powers. By the time next Christmas comes, we hope, although we cannot reckon upon so soon a happening, the world will again be at peace. Then may it be that when on Christmas Day in the Morning the bells on earth ring "Peace on Earth, Good Will to Men" their notes will be heard by a world freed forever from the hideous menace of the cruel and sinister ambitions of the Axis Powers.[5]

I never had the opportunity as a grandchild of George L. Radcliffe to experience a Spocott Christmas. However, growing up in a small row house in Baltimore near George's alma mater, Johns Hopkins University, I still experienced my grandfather's Christmas as he basically transported Spocott to Baltimore. Each year on Christmas Eve morning, a farm truck would arrive from Spocott. Loaded with cedar trees, pine boughs, holly sprigs, mistletoe, and bayberry, our house soon became an olfactory smorgasbord. It was a wonder that there was any vegetation left at Spocott after all that came off that truck. My grandfather would arrive with the truck, driven by Hamp Asplen, the beloved Spocott farmer, and Donald Newcomb, another Dorchester farmer and family friend. George L. Radcliffe never learned how to drive, but would—along with his chauffeur, Swain

George L. Radcliffe on December 25, 1973
Celebrating his 96th and Last Christmas

Foxwell—lead the two-vehicle procession from the Eastern Shore to Baltimore. Within an hour of the truck's arrival, we had both an indoor and outdoor tree, every piece of furniture well-adorned with holly, pine, and bayberry, and our simple house was transformed into an early Spocott. For our generation, Christmas began with the arrival of that truck, and my grandfather made sure that we were being treated to the Christmas of his childhood. And this man, who years earlier had helped his mother in the kitchen, made sure the truck always came packed with turkey, oysters, sweet potato and pumpkin pies, and Maryland beaten biscuits. Adaline Wheatley had long since passed, but he always stopped by the renowned Camper Sisters Bakery in Cambridge on the trip to Baltimore.[6]

George wrote and spoke often of Christmas, finding every excuse he could to make use of his extensive knowledge of the subject. Every holiday season he was asked to give a Christmas talk to several organizations. After his Senate career, he wrote an essay entitled "Heigh-ho, Sing Heigh-ho Unto the Green Holly" (quote from Shakespeare's "*As You Like It*", Act 2, Scene 7). It's interesting that he used a Shakespeare quote as he says in the essay, "I have a real grievance against Shakespeare because he wrote so seldom about Christmas!" The essay was published in a national magazine (unknown) but later included in one of his Christmas cards. (The full text is found in Appendix 2.) George's extensive knowledge of Christmas literature and traditions and his belief in the holiday's significance are quite evident in it:

> Usually, when I was a boy, I made my plans for Christmas in front of a blazing wood fire. The dancing flames of the gleaming brass andirons seemed to present fleeting glimpses of Christmas. What a fascinating succession of them! None more beautiful than the Christmas story in the Bible, quaint Christmas carols, hymns, and Milton's immortal poem on the Nativity written probably when he was a student.

> As a very small boy I accepted readily the story of Santa Claus, not knowing that it was a variation in name and theme of the deeds of Nicholas, Bishop of Myra. It was probably natural that for a while I shared the ambition of many children who have wanted to live at the North Pole as voluntary unpaid assistants to Santa Claus.

> When the wind was cold and howling, it was instinctive for me, when basking in the glow of a genial wood fire, to browse over tales of old Scandinavian, Germanic, and English customs, especially alluring when concerned with Christmas. It was easy to visualize Christmastide celebrations around roaring fires after long voyages over

bitter wintry seas. Maybe we glamorize the charm of the Viking Yuletide's tumultuous celebrations and of those held within "castle walls ... old in story." Certainly, they were spontaneous and colorful.[7]

George L. Radcliffe never sent out a store-bought Christmas card. Carrying on the traditions of his childhood, he designed his own cards, every year with a unique design and message. These cards were educational, packed with history and tidbits of information about the family property, the holiday, and the varied traditions. George, while a Christian, had many Jewish friends, but all received his cards, which transcended religious beliefs. Each contained a photo and a message, one even containing a 2000-word essay on

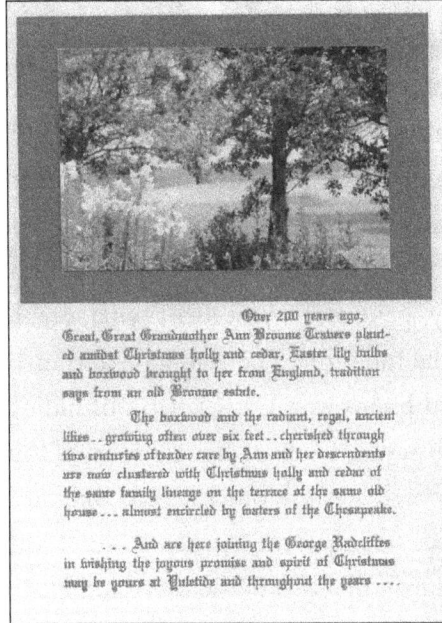

the historical significance of the holiday. They were truly collector items.

One of George L Radcliffe's Many Homemade Christmas Cards

George did go on to become author, teacher, lawyer, banker, senator, historian, and civic leader, but to those who knew him well, he did follow through on that early childhood aspiration. Santa Clause did have one special assistant living on the Eastern Shore of Maryland. No one was truer to Christmas than George.

SAVING A LION

L ike many, George L. Radcliffe was a collector, and his collecting was largely based around his two passions of Christmas and family history. His Baltimore home was literally a museum, filled to the brim with family portraits, china, documents, and letters; his Christmas book collection was extensive enough to fill a library. At the very end of his life when he had to move out of his home, his son George and his family spent over a year identifying, organizing, and moving the contents of the museum. The elaborate and involved move was further complicated by his wife Daisy's habit of hiding money in unusual places. In one instance, a box of Band-Aids was found to contain over $100, not just loosely stashed, but with each bill carefully inserted into a bandage wrapper. Much of the "museum" still exists today with many items and books donated, much to the Maryland Historical Society.

Two items trumped all in importance to George, and he would have parted with every possession before giving up either of these. There was the gold watch that he had won at the Penn Relays in 1898, running the mile relay for Johns Hopkins University. Equally valuable to him was a thirty-five-pound bronze statue of a lion, which sat on his desk throughout his long career. Many never knew the significance of that lion, but if one asked George about it, one would hear quite a story, a tale of another race, this one against time in the Baltimore Fire of 1904.

Early on the morning of Sunday, February 7, 1904, an explosion occurred in the Hurst Building (located near what is now the Royal Farms Arena).[1] New attorney George L. Radcliffe was at his office in the Equitable Building that Sunday afternoon as he frequently was early in his career. He heard the explosion but only later learned that a major fire was now progressing through that area of the city. The Equitable Building was on the corner of Calvert and Fayette Streets, some six or seven blocks from the Hurst Building, With the wind blowing from the southwest, the fire was headed in his direction. By early afternoon, it was apparent to George that the Equitable Building was in danger. He contacted James Bond, president of the company, and the two decided that, with the fire headed toward Calvert Street, the files related to claims needed to be moved. With the assistance of a Sgt. Ned Meehan, a former police officer and now company employee, they were able to obtain twelve carts. Meehan suggested that the files could be stored in his basement on Caroline Street, a safe distance away.

George and a couple other employees then began the Herculean task of moving all the company files. The office was on the second floor, and with the elevators out of commission, George and his assistants had to carry them down the stairway, load them on a cart on Calvert Street, and then head back up the stairs for another load. They continued this routine all through the afternoon and into the evening. Nine hours later, with the fire growing closer, the pace grew more frantic. This was where George acknowledged how valuable his track work had been as exhaustion was setting in. How many trips up and down a flight of steps can one make in almost nine hours? George estimated that he easily made several hundred trips, taking only a quick sandwich and coffee break. This would be the first and last coffee George ever consumed. As George stated years later:

> Every trip was a race against the approaching flames. I had done a lot of racing as a half- and quarter-miler on the Johns Hopkins track team, but this was the stiffest and most demanding race I had ever been in – and it certainly was the longest.[2]

Late in the evening, the Equitable Building caught fire, and an evacuation was ordered. Some files would have to be left behind. An exhausted

George made one last trip, and on the way out, he stopped by the president's office for a final check for valuables. That was when he saw the bronze statue of a lion on the president's desk. Sticking the thirty-five-pound statue under his arm, he struggled down the steps with the lion and the last of the files. As luck would have it, the last cart had just left. There were no trolleys running, and he was staying at a fraternity house sixteen blocks away. He was tempted to just leave it on the sidewalk, but in typical "George L. Radcliffe" fashion, he just could not do it. He had never quit while running a race, and he was not going to quit now.

Already near exhaustion from carrying files downstairs and loading them on carts all day long and into the night, he somehow found a little reserve. He made it a couple blocks but then had to put the statue down. As he later said, the lion seemed to grow to well over 100 pounds. Resting briefly and hoping to get a burst of energy, he soon realized it wasn't coming. Picking the lion up, he made it another couple blocks before having to rest again. At this point, an acquaintance, Dr. Herbert Harlan, happened by. He asked George what he was doing. George, exhausted and at a complete loss for words, could only utter, "I'm saving a lion." Dr. Harlan, initially not seeing the statue, burst into laughter, and George soon joined in. He imagined the sight that he must be presenting: a filthy, dirty, and completely disheveled man staggering along a dark street carrying a statue of a lion. This was the first moment in that hectic, stressful, and exhausting day that he breathed a sigh of relief. Picking up the lion, he made it the remaining blocks to the house.

A Lion In The Street

George L. Radcliffe with His Bronze Lion Rescued from the Baltimore Fire in 1904

A couple days later, he presented the lion to an astonished President Bond, and later at an executive committee meeting of the company, Bond awarded it to George. The statue remained in George's office his entire career as the ultimate conversation piece. After George's death, his son, George M. Radcliffe, retrieved the statue and placed it in the museum by the Spocott Windmill. Sadly, that was one of the items stolen when the museum was robbed several years later. The family guessed that the lion was probably melted down and sold, but the thieves never could have understood how priceless that statue was.

In his later years, Senator Radcliffe would spin a yarn for anyone willing to listen, and one could easily invest the better part of a day as George never tired of sharing a good story. The stories of that 1898 race and the Baltimore fire would always be part of his repertoire. The man who had met presidents and played a key role in history would much rather talk about a bronze lion. I heard his many stories more times than I could count, and each time he shared one, I would watch him closely; I had memorized every detail of the stories at that point. His face would light up, time would stop, and the two of us would be transported back in time. While it was hard for me to picture this older man carrying a thirty-five-pound statue a mile, watching him, I could see him reliving the moment in his mind. Even for all the money in the world, he would never have parted with this treasure, and it spoke volumes about this amazing, yet simple man.

"Fine Old Timbers"

In the late 1960s, the Radcliffe family joke revolved around a house and property named Cedar Grove. Senator George L. Radcliffe was marching through his nineties, slowed somewhat from a mugging by burglars in Baltimore, but as energetic and passionate about life as ever. However, the family was for the first time worrying slightly about his mental stability, as he had just decided to resurrect this ancestral home of the Beckwiths and home of George's father's first wife. George talked of the "fine old timbers" in the home, but the family could only see a house seemingly defying gravity and possessing the world's largest collection of snake skins hanging from every beam. With much of the roof gone, most windows broken long ago, and large sections of the walls missing, it was hard to tell the indoors from the outdoors in this home. My mother never got the nerve to enter the house, and I remember wishing that I was wearing a hard hat when I entered. Watching the first door I tried to open fall flat on the floor should have been clue enough for me to exit in a hurry. My sister soon stepped through the floor, and that sent us all outdoors quickly. My grandfather saw family history where the rest of us saw an accident waiting to happen. One good windstorm would surely collapse that collection of "fine old timbers," but George L. Radcliffe was determined to restore the old family home. The Radcliffe family did not need another house, and the family already had several rental dwellings. This restoration project was simply going to be an exercise in history as every potential carpenter laughed at the dilapidated structure, uttering only "tear it down."

As always, George L. Radcliffe would win the battle of wills, and Cedar Grove would rise from this pile of rubble. He was still the patriarch of the family, and even though his son George M. Radcliffe, a lawyer, presented as thorough a case for demolition as one could develop, his father prevailed, actually finding a carpenter who dared enter the building, the family fearing for his life. In hindsight, no one should have been surprised as George's whole life had been one historical reclamation project after another. Some individuals study history; George L. Radcliffe lived it, collected it, and practiced it like few have ever done. He did as much to preserve Maryland history as anyone else in the twentieth century, and these projects stand today as monuments to his passion. And it all began early in George's life.

In 1888, a ten-year-old boy surveyed the damage from a major winter storm which leveled telephone and telegraph wires, collapsed outbuildings, and left its footprint throughout the East Coast. One of the victims of this memorable storm had been the Spocott Windmill, built in 1850 by John Anthony LeCompte Radcliffe, who had recently purchased Spocott. George gazed at his father's collapsed mill and had a reaction quite atypical of such a young boy. Someday he would rebuild that mill. His father was seventy years of age and past his prime building years. John had built several mills in the county along with schooners and several buildings. His remaining energy was now invested in maintaining the farm. He would not rebuild the mill, but his youngest son vowed to do so. Young George retrieved the still intact steps leading to the second floor and the two heavy millstones. They would be stored in a barn and forgotten by all but George L. Radcliffe. In 1970, at the age of 93, he began planning the reconstruction of the mill, which would be dedicated on his 95th birthday, August 22, 1972. These two events form the bookends of a remarkable life dedicated to preserving history.

George earned his doctoral degree in history while at Johns Hopkins University. However, his father died just as he was completing his studies. His two brothers, Tom and Sewell, had moved north, leaving his mother Sophie alone to maintain the property. George, the youngest, had seen Spocott deteriorate over the last few years, and with his father now gone, there was little income to maintain the house and outbuildings. He poured every cent he could save into maintaining the property. Although he worked in Baltimore, he made frequent trips to the property to help his mother.

In 1911, he restored Spocott to the original 250 acres acquired by his ancestor Stephen Gary in 1663 by buying back the portion of the property which went out of the family when it was split between 2 daughters in the eighteenth century. Even with family money in short supply, he was committed to reuniting the original property of his ancestors. Over the next several decades he purchased other properties connected with his ancestors. In 1924 he bought the lot on which his father had built the Castle Haven School for the community in 1870, and then in 1930 moved the old school building to the Spocott property.

Moving His Father's School to Spocott, 1930

In 1925, he rescued his mother's family home from Taylor's Island. This Travers' home was in danger of ending up in the Bay as shoreline erosion was eating away at the western side of the island, and he had it dragged over one mile across the island by mules and transported up the Little Choptank River to become his home on the Spocott property. In 1932, George bought Cedar Grove, the home of his Beckwith ancestors. Many people collect coins, stamps, books, or political memorabilia. George collected family homes.

*Moving the Travers House
from Taylor's Island
to Spocott, 1925*

In 1924, the historic Baltimore Shot Tower, built in 1828, was owned by the Union Oil Company and faced almost certain demolition to make room for development. At an emergency meeting in Baltimore Mayor Jackson's office on July 21, 1924, George pleaded with the mayor to save the structure and was appointed chairman of the group to try to save it. His committee of seven included among others: Mayor Jackson; Sen. William Cabell Bruce; and Van Lear Black, Baltimore publisher, business-man, and aviation pioneer. There was not strong sentiment in the city to save the tower, and Mayor Jackson did not have the funds to purchase it. Demolition seemed imminent, and George was the perfect person to take on what seemed like a hopeless historical rescue. He was a seasoned lawyer, quite knowledgeable with property transaction resulting from his work with a surety firm, thoroughly versed in Baltimore history, and an officer in the Maryland Historical Society at that time.

Shot towers were a late eighteenth century invention for making shot more efficiently than using a mold. Molten lead was poured through a

The Phoenix (Baltimore)
Shot Tower, 1936

copper sieve at the top of a tall tower, and a spherical ball was formed as it fell, cooling and solidifying as it dropped, landing in water in the base which broke the fall, thus allowing the shot to keep its spherical shape.[1] Built shortly after the United States' second conflict with Great Britain, the tower put Baltimore in the lead in the manufacture of much-needed shot. The cornerstone had been laid by Charles Carroll of Carrollton, the last remaining signer of the Declaration of Independence. George also had a personal connection to the tower as his wife's great-great-grandfather, John McKim, Jr., had been a key figure in the Phoenix Shot Tower Company, which built the tower, and a major stockholder in the company. George was completely committed to the project.

The Baltimore Shot Tower (or Phoenix Shot Tower) was thought to have been the tallest shot tower in the country and possibly the tallest structure of any kind in the country when it was built. Standing at a little over 234 feet, it contained approximately 1.5 million bricks. With walls five-and-a-half-foot-thick at the base, it sat on a foundation with ten-foot-thick walls. Amazingly, it had been built without any scaffolding.

George had experience in politics at this stage in his life because of his tenure on the Baltimore Liquor Board the previous decade, and his brief service as Maryland Secretary of State, but saving the Shot Tower seemed initially to be a hopeless project. The Union Oil Company was eager to begin demolition and claimed the tower and property were worth $50,000, a price way beyond anyone's hope of collecting. The city had assessed it as $27,000, but the Union Oil Company would not agree to this price. Although the building was inspected and found to be in good condition, there was little interest in the city to save it. The mayor and the Union Oil Company were impatient but finally agreed to give George and his committee thirty days to raise $27,000, with the city agreeing to add something to that figure. September 4th was to be the do-or-die date.

Within three days, George had mailed out 3,000 letters in the hopes of obtaining enough subscribers to raise the sum. He and his committee approached every historic, patriotic, and artistic organization in hopes of generating the desperately needed enthusiasm and support for the property. As the committee soon found, August was the worst month to attempt such an initiative as so many key people were out of town on vacation. George and the committee were initially frustrated, with George saying, "It is unbelievable that the people of Baltimore are willing to allow the tower to be destroyed, both because of its unique value, and from an artistic standpoint." Undaunted, however, George spoke to numerous groups, wrote numerous letters daily, made several pleas on the radio, and wrote every political official he could. He even contacted Henry Ford, who had recently visited the city, with Ford saying that the Shot Tower and Johns Hopkins Hospital were the only two places he wanted to visit when in Baltimore.[2]

Interest grew, but the September 4th deadline came with only $7,000 raised. It looked as if the tower was doomed, and the Union Oil Company began plans for demolition. The lawyer in George presented a case, showing that more time was needed because so many had been unavailable in August, and Mayor Jackson granted an extension until October 1st. Sadly, that deadline came, and still less than half the funds had been raised. The committee was able to stall for a few days, but on October 10th, the Mayor ordered the demolition to begin. However, George had one miracle left, and the next day, he was somehow able to get Union Oil to agree to sell the tower and a portion of the lot to his committee for the $27,000 figure.[3] With $15,000 raised at that point, he was able to get the remaining money by December 1st, with the city adding an additional $2,000. Over 1,000 individuals and organizations had contributed to the cause. The lot and tower were deeded to the committee and then deeded again to the city. If ever there was an example of George L. Radcliffe's ability to get things done, this surely ranks high among them. With virtually no time to organize, the committee was able to save the Shot Tower, which still stands today, almost 100 years later. Without George, Baltimore would have lost a valuable piece of its history. In characteristic George L. Radcliffe fashion, he credited his committee for the miracle work. And as he would do so often in his many ventures, every donor received a personal thank-you letter from him. Few today remember his role in saving the Shot Tower, and that is exactly what he would have wanted. Preservation was about saving history, never about personal recognition.[4]

The next several decades would see George move into the political limelight although his pension for historical preservation would still dominate in his continuing search for family history. From the 1920s on, he would search for any artifacts from his family's past. With his wife Mary, he also tracked down similar pieces from her significant ancestors. Rarely a week went by without some inquiry, records search, or personal correspondence. In 1924, his wife's cousin, Emilie McKim Reed, died; she was the granddaughter of John McKim, Jr., a prominent Baltimore shipper, one of the founders of the B&O Railroad, and a philanthropist.

She and George were close, both connected with the Maryland Historical Society, and George handled her estate, purchasing many portraits and considerable McKim furniture from the estate. Another of John McKim, Jr.'s descendants, Elizabeth McIlvain, unmarried, also sold George a number of pieces of McKim furniture. By the 1940s, he had acquired a considerable inventory of family heirlooms, also purchasing a portrait from the Marriott family. Records show him even buying several lots of letters, family silver, and china. As evidence of the extent to which he would go to recover family heirlooms, he traveled to Italy in 1945 to buy back a set of Marriott china. He was able to recover a significant stash of family heirlooms from a number of his and his wife's ancestors.

He also worked to preserve aspects of the Spocott property, moving and maintaining many of the outbuildings which had been a part of the early Spocott farm. In addition to moving the old schoolhouse his father had built, he moved the home of Adaline Wheatley, the beloved Spocott cook, as well as the home of Kemp and Minta Wilson, lifelong Spocott tenants and workers. He salvaged Adaline's outdoor kitchen and smokehouse, his father's shipbuilding office, a stable, the granary, the old dairy, and icehouse. His passion for preservation also extended to the natural world, and he had the trees on the Spocott property surveyed, ordering work done on those needing intervention. He was especially interested in the Council Oak, a red oak so named because tradition held that Native Americans had assembled around the tree on numerous occasions. Aged at over 400 years, the tree dominated the yard north of Spocott. Sadly, despite considerable efforts and funds invested, the tree succumbed and had to be removed in the 1930s. Historical preservation had its limits.

When George left the Senate early in 1947, he suddenly had the time to take his preservation to a new level, especially with his position as president of the Maryland Historical Society. Several miles north on the Eastern Shore, the Old Wye Episcopal Church was being renovated, largely through the efforts and financing of industrialist and philanthropist

Arthur Houghton, Jr. (1906–1990). Arthur connected with George and the Maryland Historical Society as well as with the Society of Maryland Antiquities, and a group met early in 1951 to plan a survey of Eastern Shore historical buildings. Using an architect, the group did a thorough assessment of structures built before 1800, including houses, churches, community buildings, and the last remaining windmill, the Honga Mill in Dorchester County. This Eastern Shore Survey became the springboard for considerable historical renovation which would occur in the next decades.

Personally, George now switched his focus specifically to two local projects covered in the survey: Old Trinity Church in Church Creek, and the Chapel of Ease on Taylor's Island. Old Trinity Church is one of the oldest Episcopal Churches in the country, built about 1690. Restored in 1853, the church had fallen into disrepair and was one of the priority projects highlighted in the Eastern Shore Survey. The Chapel of Ease was affiliated with Old Trinity, erected sometime after 1707 as a substitute church for those too far away from Old Trinity to travel, hence its name.[5] It was determined that $100,000 would be needed to restore the two buildings. George soon connected with Edgar and Bernice Garbisch; Bernice was the daughter of Walter P. Chrysler, the founder of Chrysler Corporation. Bernice and Edgar soon agreed to fund the restoration of Old Trinity as a memorial to her parents.[6] The restoration of the old church would take seven years, and in August of 1960, a ceremony was held to commemorate its reopening, even though it had stayed active for the small group of parishioners through all the work. Left to George L. Radcliffe, it was no surprise that the ceremony would become a massive event. Over 8,000 invitations were sent out, with over 3,000 attending the ceremony for a church which could barely hold 100 people.[7] George and the others behind the project wanted to involve as much of the community and state as possible, and their passion for the project and the history was infectious.

Concurrent with this project was the work on the Chapel of Ease. George helped found the Grace Foundation on Taylor's Island, his mother's birthplace. Over the years the Foundation restored the Grace Church, which his grandfather had built, and moved the Chapel of Ease to the site of the church. He was president of that foundation for the rest of his life, helping to preserve the history and culture of the island.

As all of this was transpiring in Dorchester County, George continued in his role as president of the Maryland Historical Society, continuing in this role until 1963, completing his tenure as president of the organization for twenty-five years and officer for fifty-two years. In this role, he was able to push for historical preservation at the highest level.

The *USS Constellation* became another of George L. Radcliffe's passions and pursuits, and he spent nearly twenty years trying to get the

USS Constellation, *1926*

historic vessel returned to Baltimore. This story has an unusual twist since all at the time were mistaken about the true identity of the ship. Everyone assumed this was one of the original six vessels authorized in 1794 and launched in 1797 along with the USS Constitution and four others. No one realized for the first half of the twentieth century that the original ship had been dismantled and a new one built in 1853–54 until renowned ship historian Howard Chappelle first pointed out the discrepancy.[8] George disputed Chappelle's claim, but this was one time where he got his history wrong.

The *Constellation* had ended up as a training vessel in Newport, Rhode Island, berthed there for the first part of the twentieth century, and George L. Radcliffe, along with Senator Millard Tydings and other local leaders, claimed, as early as 1935, that the ship belonged in Baltimore where it had been built. In 1941, the two senators introduced a bill in the Senate to have the ship restored and returned to Baltimore.[9] George had written a long article on the ship and mentioned it in many speeches he gave. In 1945, the Maryland Historical Society obtained records of the ship's construction in Baltimore in 1794–97, not realizing, of course, that this ship had been dismantled. In 1946, the ship was towed to Boston for repair and ultimately deemed too feeble to be repaired, and soon a political squabble erupted over who should end up with the ship. George and Maryland leaders felt the ship should end up in Baltimore since that was its origin. Senator J. Howard McGrath of Rhode Island argued that it should be returned to his state where it had resided for over fifty years. George had President Truman's ear even though he was no longer in the Senate, but McGrath was passionate in his arguments and often critical of George. In a speech in Baltimore where he noted that both Baltimore's Archbishop Keough and Rabbi Israel Goldman had come from Rhode Island, McGrath said, "There is something else you have been after, but we won't let you get away with it. George Radcliffe is largely responsible for it. You can have the archbishop and the rabbi, but please leave the

Constellation with us in Rhode Island."[10] The rivalry between the two continued, but George, as always, chose the high ground. In a speech given during the Baltimore Sesquicentennial celebration in 1947, George, in response to comments by McGrath a year earlier, said:

> The prophecy of Senator McGrath of Rhode Island that my efforts to persuade President Truman to return the *Constellation* to Baltimore will lead to Civil War between Rhode Island and Maryland is a most harassing one. He is wrong. We in Maryland again stand for peace. In 1860 and 1861 just before the Civil War began, no state was more active than Maryland in endeavoring to find a real basis for peace. In colonial days Rhode Island and Maryland were pioneers in advocating freedom of thought and tolerance—necessary qualities of a just peace.
>
> I am sure that if Rhode Island and Maryland were to start fighting each other, their spears and swords would automatically and immediately be turned into ploughshares and the other kinds of agricultural implements predicted in the Bible for the days of the Millennium.
>
> Would it not be much better for Rhode Island and Maryland to join forces in a Holy Cause? Why not Rhode Island aid us in getting back the *Constellation* built in 1797 in Baltimore, whose incorporation that year as a city we are now celebrating in our Sesquicentennial. In that way, Rhode Island could help us to get an ideal present on this, our 150th birthday. Then possibly we could help Rhode Island to secure some other ship or something very dear to that state.
>
> I offer this suggestion in the hope that it will avert hostilities and promote the peaceful and happy relations

between Rhode Island and Maryland which have existed for hundreds of years.[11]

George would win out in this rivalry, but his whole argument would be damaged by discoveries by Howard Chappelle which seemed to indicate that the *Constellation* was not the ship all thought it was. In an analysis of records and plans for the ship and comparing these to original records, Chappelle concluded that the 1797 frigate was a different ship from the present sloop of war. While the Navy and others refuted Chappelle's claims, George's reaction was "Astonishing! Mr. Chappelle is usually right, but he may have made a mistake this time. Show us the proof."[12]

Years later, Chappelle's records would prove him right, but George and others continued the fight for the ship they considered rightly theirs. In 1953, the Navy was still disputing Chappelle's claims but appeared ready to give up on the ship as it would take four-and-a-half million dollars to restore the ship. Representative Samuel Friedel had petitioned the Navy to turn the ship over to Baltimore, and George continued his fight in his role as Maryland Historical Society president.[13] George L. Radcliffe and Maryland would win out in 1955, and in August of that year, the ship would be floated down from Boston on dry dock in tow behind a diesel tug, and George, chairman of the welcoming committee, would lead the parade as the vessel was pulled into Baltimore.[14] In 1957, he would be part of a campaign to raise the two million dollars to renovate the vessel.[15] The question of identity of the ship was still being debated at the end of George's life; thus, George probably died before the issue was definitively resolved. Today, the ship on display in Baltimore Harbor is recognized as having been commissioned in 1855 by the National Park Service. Still, this second *Constellation* served in combat and played a major role in combatting the slave trade.[16] George L. Radcliffe may not have preserved the oldest ship in the U.S. Navy, but he certainly was a key figure in stopping the dismantling of a historic ship.

Beginning with his preservation of the stones and steps from his father's windmill in 1888, his whole life was about saving and preserving history. Had he accomplished nothing else in his life, he would have been remembered for this. There is no question, however, that the preservation nearest and dearest to his heart was his beloved Spocott. He had taken that property from one nearly sold as the family battled poverty to a successful farm with houses and outbuildings well-preserved. He would, however, do one final thing in the last year of his life. It was not enough that he had saved the property; he wanted it preserved in the future. In 1974, he and his son George donated a conservation easement on the property, preserving the property and buildings in perpetuity. They were one of the very first to deed an easement to the Maryland Environmental Trust. George L. Radcliffe's mission to preserve was now complete.

Essays

Key Individuals

The Little Woman

This day was another routine day for the Ocean City, Maryland, lifeguards—occasionally having to whistle in a child who had ventured out too far, keeping all a good distance from any obstacles in the water, and pretending to ignore the admiring teenage girls standing at the base of their elevated seat. Listening to the joyful screams of little children racing to and from the waves, the squeals of individuals immersing themselves in the cold water, and the almost monotonous breaking of waves, they always had to remain completely vigilant. This day they sighted something floating out well beyond the breakers, gradually drifting south with the current. What appeared to be a log at first suddenly assumed a human form as it drifted directly in front of them. Instinct and repeated drill kicked in as they sprinted to their lifeboat and rolled it down the beach into the water. Jumping in once they were in deep enough water, they rowed furiously, getting the boat past the breaking waves. As they rowed toward the body, there seemed to be no apparent sign of life, yet this body was floating face up. Getting close, they shouted, and the figure turned toward them. Relief suddenly set in as one exclaimed, "Oh, it's just the Little Woman."

Mary McKim Marriott Radcliffe, known to all as Daisy, was an impressive woman: attractive, strong, and a legendary swimmer. A regular visitor to Ocean City and a frequent long-distance swimmer, she had earned the nickname of "the Little Woman." Several times she had been seen floating on her back well beyond the breaking waves, once even while reading the newspaper. The fact that in her Baltimore home she put two potential burglars into the hospital had put the icing on this nickname, striking the first with a candlestick as he started to flee her home and slamming the front door on the arm of the other after chasing him down the stairs from the second floor. This was no ordinary woman, and she was the wife of Maryland's United States Senator, George L. Radcliffe.

Another noteworthy incident involving her was reported inaccurately by the Annapolis *Evening Capital* in April of 1938. The story reads:

> The rescue of a white collie dog, belonging to Mrs. Radcliffe, wife of Senator George L. Radcliffe (D-Md.), today delayed the Claiborne [to] Annapolis ferry steamer, *Gov. Albert C. Ritchie*, twenty minutes on its first morning trip to the Eastern Shore.
>
> The ferry boat had just pulled from the local dock when the dog, eluding its mistress, jumped into the harbor from the freight deck. The ferry stopped and a boat was lowered to save the swimming animal.
>
> Captain Merle Dawson, of the ferry, was in charge of the rescue party, which brought the dog, wet but none the worse for its experience, aboard the ferry.[1]

As her husband, George, and son, George M. Radcliffe, told the story on many occasions, this version left out a few details. They shared that Daisy loved her collies, and these usually traveled with her. On that April day, she boarded the ferry steamer and stood on the deck with the dog, watching as the ferry started to pull away from the dock. Lines were cast off, and the ferry started to gradually pull away. In her fascination with the ongoing process, she took her eyes off the dog. When the ship was a couple hundred yards offshore, the dog suddenly leaped through the railing into the water. She immediately spoke to the crew member beside her, but he said that there was nothing he could do. Assuring her that the dog could safely swim to shore and be picked up, he went back to doing his job.

Daisy then demanded to see the captain and was taken to see him. She ordered him to turn the ferry around, but the captain assured her the dog would be fine and explained to her that the time to turn the ferry around and to retrieve the dog would throw them seriously off schedule. With people waiting on the other side of the Bay, he had to remain on the tight schedule. This was after all the primary way that people crossed the Bay before there was a Chesapeake Bay Bridge (1953). He said that he would contact the dock and that they would hold the dog until she could make the return trip. His answer did not satisfy her, and she persisted, even when he tried to walk away from her. However, Daisy was not a person who would take "no" for an answer. She ran over to the railing, exclaiming that she would jump overboard if he did not turn the ferry around. She was well-known as a powerful swimmer, and those who knew her had no doubt she would do it. The captain still balked until she started to climb the railing. He caved and the ferry was ordered to reverse direction. The dog, seeing the ferry coming about, began now swimming toward the ship.

The frustrated captain, knowing that he was beaten, lowered a lifeboat, climbing into it himself. He and one of the crew members rowed toward the dog and managed to pull the wet collie into the lifeboat. Daisy and the dog were soon reunited to the cheers of the other passengers, and the ferry finally resumed its voyage, now far off its original schedule. She thanked the captain, soaking wet himself from pulling the dog into the boat, and he returned to his duties, humiliated and sure to be in hot water for falling far behind schedule.

Mary McKim Marriott was a force to be reckoned with. Born May 23, 1881, she was the daughter of Baltimore architect William Haddon Marriott (1849–1912) and Aline Bracco (1859-1939). Aline had been raised by her godfather Civil War General P.G.T. Beauregard after her entire family succumbed to a disease. Mary's family was well known in Baltimore society, but she often referred to them as being "poor as church mice." She frequently visited Maryland's Eastern Shore, where her mother had spent some time as a child, and on one visit in 1898, she en-

*Mary McKim Marriott
(1881-1963)*

countered a gentleman who said he would throw a "ball" for her where she could meet the "two most eligible bachelors in Cambridge." The first she found uninteresting, but she immediately connected with the second, George L. Radcliffe, then in the graduate program at Johns Hopkins University. In 1900 she was introduced to Baltimore society at the Bachelors' Cotillion, a societal "coming out" event started by her ancestors shortly after the War of 1812, but no other bachelor could compete with George.

She married George on June 6, 1906, although she was forty-five minutes late to the wedding. George waited patiently in front of the church, completely unphased because, as he said, "she had never been on time for anything." Later the family would encounter this trait of hers, and on one Thanksgiving, the 2:00 p.m. dinner finally made it to the table at 6:30 p.m. She was devoted to George until her death on May 29, 1963. This was a marriage of two immovable objects, both strong-willed and driven. In an age where a wife's place was often in the home and kitchen, Daisy rejected that stereotype quickly, becoming the assistant editor of *Ladies Home Journal* by age twenty-three. She would go on to champion causes at a national level, and her influence on her husband was profound. To understand many of George's causes and positions, one need look no further than his wife.

They say that opposites attract, and on the surface, Daisy and George seemed the ultimate mismatch. While her future husband had been raised on a working farm, Mary was raised in Baltimore society and went to all the prominent parties. Extremely creative and artistic, she was in many ways a mismatch for the shy, methodical, regimented historical researcher, and if opposites do attract, their marriage may have been Exhibit A. George was known for his ability to compromise and extend the conciliatory olive branch, while Daisy could be a bull in a china shop. She was initially opposed to their son's impending wedding in 1948, so much so that when her son, George, brought his future wife to the house for the first time, Daisy, carrying a shotgun, refused

*George and Daisy
at Windemere c. 1920*

to let them in the door. Daisy later, in protest, refused to attend their wedding. However, a closer look reveals many shared passions which lay the foundation for a strong marriage which lasted until Mary's death in 1963.

She more than matched George's passion for history, and her family roots were a treatise on Maryland history. Descended from the prominent Hammond, Marriott, Wilson, and McKim families, Daisy was both knowledgeable and proud of her roots. Her great-great-grandfather was John McKim, Jr. (1766–1842), prominent Baltimore shipping merchant, original B&O Railroad trustee, and War of 1812 financier. She was also descended from the prominent Baltimore Wilson shipping family and from Gen. William Hammond Marriott (1789–1851), who was a military officer, president of the Maryland Senate, and later Collector of Customs for Baltimore. The union of two proud and passionate genealogists seemed like a logical match. Their love of books, the arts, and history gave them much in common, if even quite different on the surface.

Mary McKim Marriott Radcliffe
Self-Portrait

After graduating from the Misses Halls School for Girls, Daisy enrolled in the Maryland Institute for Art and Design, serving as art editor of the school's *Paint, Plaster, and Pencil* in 1904. She initially worked as a laboratory artist at Johns Hopkins University. She submitted her first article to *Ladies Home Journal* at age nineteen, was contributing regularly by age twenty-one, and by age twenty-three, was an assistant editor of the magazine, which at that time had the largest circulation of any magazine in the country. She authored a regular monthly column, complete with her own drawings, which usually focused on homemaking tips, decorating ideas, and general advice. Painting was probably her dominant artistic passion, and her sketches and portraits adorned her house. Legend has it that she was displeased with a Rembrandt Peale portrait she possessed, leading her to repaint both the eyes and the placement of the hands. She felt that Peale had captured the subject incorrectly and felt she could do it better. The family still has her redo of the portrait. Her son, George M., claimed that she attempted once to paint a portrait of her husband, taking artistic license to paint him as she saw him. George L. Radcliffe, on seeing his portrait, could barely recognize himself and years later finally destroyed the portrait.

Both she and her husband, George, spent considerable hours of relaxation playing the piano in their home, and Daisy, who could also play the organ and banjo, composed several musical compositions. We do have many essays and several short books which she wrote. Her writing was flamboyant and colorful, and her amazing vocabulary and knowledge of history and culture are quite evident.

Daisy was an astute judge of people and transformed this skill into a fundraising mechanism. A lifelong supporter of many charities, she often volunteered at charity events as a fortune teller. She was extremely popular at these events as a palm reader since her "predictions" were often accurate. As she explained to her son George, she could size up a person with a conversation preceding the "reading" of their palm and could collect enough information to both amaze the subject and make a rather astute, albeit vague, prediction. How many knew that the wife of a US Senator was a fortune teller?

This quality and some unusual habits and beliefs undoubtedly led some to consider Daisy eccentric. She was at the very least an individual. Her pride in her Irish ancestry prompted her to wear green virtually every day of her life, and many cabinets and pieces of furniture in her home were soon painted green. Ironically after her death, her husband, George, would discover that her "Irish" ancestors had come from England. Her political and personal beliefs were extreme for this period, and she was never hesitant to give someone a completely honest opinion, even if not well received. This she apparently came by honestly as her bouts with her equally opinionated mother were epic, prompting her son George to remark that when these classic arguments started, all bailed out of the room quickly.

Tragedy would significantly intervene in Daisy's life after her marriage to George, and this would affect her in dramatic ways. She was one of two children and was devoted to both her father William, and brother, William Hammond "Don" Marriott (1885–1908). Although Don was successful in his early professional life, things began to turn dark about the time Daisy married George. In 1908, at Don's wedding ceremony, everyone showed up except the bride and groom, neither of whom apparently had ever planned on going through with the wedding. Things continued to spiral downhill, and a month later on March 15, 1908, Don took his life, inhaling chloroform in his boarding room in Baltimore after writing a one-line suicide note: "The game is not worth the candle."[2]

Don's death would have a dramatic impact on Daisy, and she began suffering periods of depression. Four years later she lost her father after a prolonged illness, which had ended his professional career. This second loss resulted in Daisy falling deeper into depression, and this was further intensified in 1917 when she lost her first child, Mary McKim, who died at birth.

During World War I, she volunteered in mothers' relief and baby clinics, and with the cooperation of the War Mothers of America, she sent postcards promoting peace to American soldiers in France. At the same time, she became actively involved in the Maryland suffrage movement. Early 1917 saw her both pregnant and becoming politically active; however, it is clear from letters that she was in personal turmoil. A letter from the chief psychiatrist at Johns Hopkins Hospital in March of 1917 shows that she was self-absorbed and clearly under immense stress.[3] Her psychological struggle was also being channeled into both her changing views and her increasing political and social involvement.

After the loss of her child, her increasing periods of depression forced her to retreat periodically to an institution for help. However, she soon became pregnant again, and in June of 1919, gave birth to her son, George Marriott Radcliffe (1919-2009). This gave her the personal focal point she needed, and young George became her happy obsession. Throughout the 1920s, she raised and homeschooled him, taking him wherever she traveled. Young George would later say that he was smothered and overprotected to an almost pathological extent, but that no mother loved a child more. Clearly, having seen her brother's demise and having her first child die at birth, Daisy became obsessed with the health of her son, often referring to him as sickly. Homeschooling was her way of further insuring that he would be healthy, and possibly less susceptible to childhood diseases.

Despite the periods of depression, her service work continued and was elevated to new heights. In addition to her active role in the Maryland women's movement, she became a prolific letter writer, reaching out to figures in both the Maryland and national women's movements. Her interest in women's health and child welfare led to her chairing the maternity committee of the National Congress of Mothers (which later became the national PTA)[4]. In this role, she corresponded with numerous national figures including Teddy Roosevelt, who invited her and a group from the congress to Oyster Bay to meet with him.[5] This never happened because he died shortly after the invitation. Daisy was beginning to get national attention.

Daisy became actively involved in promoting better conditions for mothers and infants. She saw that many expectant women were receiving substandard medical care and that there was a high rate of infant mortality from numerous childhood diseases. She was able to collect data to support her beliefs with the help of numerous organizations and Johns Hopkins University. She then helped to promote a series of lectures at the Johns Hopkins School of Hygiene, beginning in 1919. At that time, there was no stronger advocate for women's health and the protection of motherhood.

These interests, however, took on a slightly darker side, probably out of a combination of her relief work during the war, feelings still lingering from her brother's suicide, and the loss of her first child. Her ideas were expanding from the problems to what she saw as their causes. In her mind, the inferior status of women was compounded by overpopulation, and population control seemed to her to be the way to improve the lot of women and to promote better conditions for children.

Out of all these experiences, Daisy authored a brochure called *After the Carnage—Comes a Voice* in which she outlined, in her extremely colorful literary style, a plea for the elevated status of women, and for better protection of, and conditions for, mothers and young children. She had many copies of this printed and distributed throughout Maryland at her own expense, with some being sent to national figures. The brochure was a call to arms for mothers to get the respect long overdue them. The final few paragraphs clearly show the passion behind her beliefs:

> The mother Hour has Come – Through throes of mortal pain, through white lips of agony she is pleading through the ages.
>
> Soldiers of the World ...
>
> We have sent you forward to the Battlefront. We stand behind you, we the mothers.
>
> We pray that you deliver the World from its blindness and pain, that it may be safe for its motherhood, safe for the little babies.
>
> Over the carnage Comes a Voice . . . "inasmuch as ye did it unto one of the least of these, ye did it unto me."
>
> Mothers . . . Fathers of our Future
>
> A little Child shall lead you – The bugles are calling.[6]

Even if her approach was eccentric at times, her focus on the medical care of mothers and young children was valuable, especially for those times, and her vision of population control as a solution to many problems was far ahead of its time. Later in that decade her focus would extend to conditions in mental hospitals and juvenile facilities. With the cooperation of Baltimore and Maryland Departments of Education, the Juvenile Court, State Medical Commissioners, and the Public Works Administration, she made an exhaustive survey of the overcrowding in these facilities, presenting her results in 1937 to the Maryland legislature. As a result, funding of $2.75 million dollars from the state and PWA was made available to begin relieving this overcrowding.[7]

For the remainder of her life, she was devoted to many similar causes, but first and foremost came family. She was devoted to her only son, gradually accepted his marriage to Augusta Boggs, and completely spoiled her grandchildren with love and attention. She treasured her four grandchildren, and she introduced them to the arts, movies, genealogy, and history. For them, she authored a small book on their ancestry called *Our Adventuring Ancestors*, remarkably accurate considering she begins the story with eleventh century ancestors. It literally reads like a text of both English and early American history.

What is most significant here is the fact that the United States Senator from Maryland from 1935–1947 had no ordinary wife. Her influence on him was significant as his career shows an extraordinary attention to women's issues and their rights. With a wife involved with the women's suffrage movement, there is no surprise that George supported this movement early on. He recognized the historical importance of women, even before they had the right to vote, but he saw that right to vote as an inherent human right. As he stated on many occasions, "A woman is entitled to vote not necessarily because she would revolutionize the world, not even because without the vote her ideas would not have weight and force. I have always felt that she was entitled to the vote as a sheer matter of justice."[8] He was a popular speaker for women's groups, and his diaries show him frequently delivering an address on women's rights and their importance to these groups.

During World War I, many women began to rise in prominence as many men were obviously preoccupied in Europe. At that time, George L. Radcliffe was setting up a training school for his surety company. Despite the fact that there were many qualified males, to head up the school he chose a woman, Emily Dashiell, who had handled government supply contracts at Edgewood Arsenal during the war.[9] Even at this early point in his career, George sought the most qualified person for the job, and gender was not an issue. Not only did he have his wife's influence, but he applied the objectivity which had been a part of his historical research. If one needed to see the importance he placed on the women's movement, one need look no farther than his recommendation in 1939 that Susan B. Anthony be added to Mount Rushmore. His proposal died quickly as he was informed by the Interior department that the contract with Gutzon Borglum to sculpt the monument had only specified four figures: Washington, Jefferson, Lincoln, and Teddy Roosevelt.[10]

His interest in women's issues grew during World War II as he witnessed firsthand the critical role which women played on the home front. In 1944 at the Democratic National Convention, the Equal Rights Amendment was added to the campaign platform for the first time. At the time, this was primarily a Republican issue; they also added it to their platform as they had done in 1940. New Dealers had opposed an amendment, largely because of the opposition of labor groups, fearing the loss of jobs for their members. First Lady Eleanor Roosevelt was vocal in her opposition to an Equal Rights Amendment despite her many efforts to promote better working conditions for women. While supporting equal pay for women, she felt women should be protected and treated specially because of their differences. George felt this was not an issue since all, both men and women, should have adequate safeguards.

Sen. George L. Radcliffe often broke with his party, and in 1945 he introduced an Equal Rights Amendment in the Senate. Although more popular with Republicans, the measure was cosponsored by a bipartisan group of senators (twelve Democrats and ten Republicans). In a speech on May 3, 1945, he introduced the proposed constitutional amendment saying:

> I ask unanimous consent to introduce, on behalf of various senators and myself, a joint resolution calling for a constitutional amendment providing that the rights of men and women shall be coequal.

> I feel strongly that the adoption of this amendment would be a step forward and a wise one. Its adoption would cer-

tainly be one of the most important stages in the development of opportunities for women. Of course, I realize that for many years in countless indispensable ways
women have had many varied fields of usefulness which
they have utilized for the benefit of humanity. However,
ever-changing economic factors and processes have made
constantly more urgent the demand that women be giv-
en the right to exercise certain other privileges which have
so far in a measure been denied them. It may be that economic conditions of other days did not make imperative
that such rights and privileges exist in a full sense. Nevertheless, for many years, women have given unmistakable
and entirely convincing evidence that they are entitled to
equality of opportunity with men and that society in the
broad sense of the term would be greatly benefited by the
exercise of women of such rights.[11]

The amendment was the Alice Paul Amendment, advocated by
long-time woman advocate Alice Paul. Paul had changed the wording,
removing the word "women", simply stating that there would be no dis-
crimination based on sex. With both parties including this in their 1944
platforms, it stood a chance of passage. While previous attempts at an
Equal Rights Amendment failed to reach the Senate for a vote, the one
George introduced in 1945 made it to a vote in 1946.[12] However, in a
questionable scheduling move by Senate leadership, the Amendment
came up for a vote with no advanced warning on July 19, 1946. The day
happened to be one where twenty-three of the senators were away on
other business, virtually assuring the amendment could not pass. Sen.
Radcliffe had to make an impromptu speech since many of the backers
were away. He protested and tried to get it back to committee, but this
was blocked. The Amendment did get the vote of a majority present with
thirty-eight votes for and thirty-five against. The measure received more

Republican support with twenty-three Republican Senators voting for it while only fifteen Democrats voted in favor of the Amendment. Eighteen of the absent Senators were known to be in support, meaning he had been able to enlist the support of a significant majority of the Senate. Such is the nature of politics. George's efforts did not go unnoticed; an article by the National Women's Party attests to not only his efforts for this amendment but many other efforts:

> Senator Radcliffe (D) of Maryland led the debate for the proponents. His statement to the Senate was able, scholarly, and persuasive. One cannot speak in too warm praise of the admirable way in which he presented the arguments for the measure. As we listened to Senator Radcliffe from the gallery we thought with gratitude of the many times, beginning back in the days of the suffrage campaign, that he had lifted his voice in defense of justice for women.[13]

They may have been praising his voice, but the voice behind his was Mary Marriott Radcliffe. One can only imagine the conversations at that dinner table all those years. While I must believe George would have been a supporter of women as he respected and valued all, she was the strength in his voice. Ironically, that day, George knew his days in the Senate were numbered, as he had just lost the Democratic primary a month earlier. One must believe that if he had been reelected, he would have introduced that Amendment again. He did, in fact, after leaving the Senate, continue to give speeches in support of the Equal Rights Amendment.

It has been often said that behind every strong man is a strong woman. Mary Marriott Radcliffe had suffered considerably early in her life, and while some of her ideas may have been unusual, her passion and support of womanhood were unquestionable. Her influence on her husband was significant in so many ways. Quite different, they were bonded intimately. Their mutual love of family, genealogy, history, and the arts provided connecting points for a strong marriage to develop.

I remember visiting my grandmother in the hospital after her last stroke. I vividly remember that she had lost the ability to speak but still could clearly comprehend all that was going on around her. Like any child, I could never think of grandparents in romantic terms, but I sat in the room for a long while my grandfather sat beside her holding her hand. I remember watching how she gazed at him and how the love just flowed out of those eyes. I was so moved that I felt like an intruder, wondering if I needed to leave the room. If I had not known from past experiences how devoted they were to each other, those moments alone would have told the whole story. Our family possesses hundreds of letters between the two, often with more than one being written on a particular day. These also tell a story of the complete devotion the two had for each other. He outlived her by eleven years, staying productive as he had always been, but one could always see that something was missing with only one of the two bookends present.

George and Daisy in Baltimore, 1962
Their Last Christmas Together

"The Little Woman" was anything but a little woman: physically, spiritually, or personally. With George's job taking him frequently far from home, especially during his twelve years in the Senate, Daisy must have spent considerable time alone, but this was a marriage of two complete individuals. George L. Radcliffe was part of a package deal. While Daisy was often behind the scenes, choosing to stay out of the public limelight much of the time, in spirit, George never went anywhere without her.

The Judge

After getting his degree and his brief tenure as principal of the Cambridge High School, George L. Radcliffe moved back to Baltimore and shared a boarding house with two fellow Eastern Shoremen. All three would go on to historic careers. Among the three of them, there would be two United States Senators, one Maryland Governor, and a Chief Judge of the Baltimore Supreme Bench.[1] We can only imagine the conversations which must have occurred in that boarding house. George L. Radcliffe would become U.S. Senator, replacing his one-time roommate and fellow Dorchester Countian, Philip Lee Goldsborough (1865–1946). Goldsborough had already been Maryland comptroller, would become governor from 1912–1916, and would serve one term in the U.S. Senate from 1929–1935. The third roommate, Samuel King Dennis (1874–1953), was born in Worcester County, Maryland and was in the University of Maryland Law School at the same time as George. Sam would serve as Chief Judge of the Baltimore Supreme Bench from 1928–1944, becoming somewhat of a Baltimore celebrity. George and Sam Dennis would become close friends, and their lives would interact in so many ways. Both were from the Eastern Shore of Maryland, both went into law and politics, both would make invaluable contributions to the Maryland Historical Society, and they would remain civically active until the time of their deaths. Their friendship would grow deep, and George had no better friend or confidante than Sam Dennis. As a measure of their closeness, George asked Sam to be the godfather of his only son.

Sam Dennis, descended from several prominent Eastern Shore politicians, was born on his long-time family farm in Worcester County in 1874. Although he was raised on a farm, his family wanted him to attend

Princeton. He was sent to the Blair Academy in New Jersey to prepare for Princeton, but when he was seventeen, his father died, and Sam would have to forego Princeton to return to the 2,000-acre family farm, where he and his brothers would run the farm. His aspirations for a career in law would have to be put on hold.

When Sam was twenty-four, Congressman John Walter Smith would recruit Sam to be his secretary and aide, and Sam would leave the family farm. Smith (1845–1925) became Maryland Governor in 1900 and would also serve as U.S. Senator from 1908–1921. Sam served as Smith's aide and confidante until Smith passed in 1925, but during this period he pursued the career which had been put on hold years earlier. He earned his law degree from the University of Maryland in 1903 and was admitted to the Maryland Bar in 1904. It was during this period that he shared a boarding house with George L. Radcliffe.

In 1904, Sam became a member of the House of Delegates representing Worcester County, and in 1915, President Woodrow Wilson appointed him United States Attorney for Baltimore. In 1911, he married Helen

Judge Samuel K. Dennis
(1874-1953)

Gordon Moore. Sam often clashed with Maryland Governor Ritchie, and it came as a surprise when Ritchie appointed him as Chief Judge of the Supreme Bench of Baltimore. Some felt that Ritchie's appointment was an effort to remove Sam from the political landscape, and Sam served until 1944 when required to step down at age seventy.[2]

Sam Dennis also devoted considerable time to the fight against tuberculosis. The daughter of John Walter Smith had died from the disease, and Sam would help found the Maryland Tuberculosis Sanatorium in Sabillasville in Frederick County, Maryland. He would stay involved with that for many years as well as devoting time to the American Red Cross.

He was an officer with George at the Maryland Historical Society for years and was a key player in many society projects and functions. He served on the publications committee and as vice president, and wrote a brief history of the organization.[3]

One need only read George's brief diary of daily events to see how much he depended on Sam Dennis. At least once a week, his daily entry would end with "Long talk with Sam." With all the interactions George had while in the Senate, he clearly enjoyed and needed that weekly "long talk." George never revealed in the diary what the two talked about, but those talks undoubtedly ran the complete gamut from work to the politics of the day, and from Eastern Shore news to those childhood stories they both so loved. The two also rode to and from work together for years.[4]

It is clear from looking at George's diary and his frequent letters that he sought Sam's guidance at all the career crossroads in life. There is no doubt that Sam encouraged the more cautious George to accept opportunities, and Sam used his legendary wit and sense of humor to diffuse stressful points in George's life. His warmth and wit are captured in a thank-you letter he wrote:

> I must express to you other than my lame and halting
> oral declarations the appreciation I feel for your most

brotherly and fine solicitude. Certainly, no one could have been more generous in expressing their sympathy, and certainly no one could have felt more sympathy than you do. It is all very gratifying to me and places me under a further obligation to you, a debt which is like the debt of the English government in that it will never be paid as to corpus and only yields a little interest.[5]

A letter George wrote to Sam shortly before Sam's passing captures the closeness of the two friends:

I am finding it utterly impossible to find phraseology to express to you how deeply touched I am by what you have done in connection with the painting of my portrait and its presentation to the Maryland Historical Society. I am still totally in the dark as to who your associates were, but I know you were the moving spirit and that the plan would have never been conceived and carried out had it not been for you.

This is another illustration of the deep and affectionate interest which you have always taken in me and my affairs. I have been fortunate on being on very close terms with my brothers, but with no one of them, has my association been more intimate or more happy than with you. I shall always treasure as one of my greatest treasures in life your friendship. I am looking forward to our being together for many years, and I hope a part of that time will be on the Eastern Shore at Spocott and Windemere.

You have not only been a devoted friend to me, but you have also extended that intimate and helpful friendship to George and his family. Your status as godfather has been truly parental in nature. You had a big part in the job of raising him, and I believe he reflects credit on the joint supervision of you, Daisy, and myself. You have been a devoted friend and counselor to him in somber days as well as happy ones.[6]

Sadly, Sam would die a few months later. While I was too young to remember Sam, I always felt I knew him because my father, George M. Radcliffe, talked of him often as a son would speak of a father. Sam Dennis and his wife had no children, but he took an active interest in young George, becoming his godfather, cheerleader, and confidante.

George M. Radcliffe majored in engineering at Princeton and specialized in aeronautical engineering. He put this to practice in his 3 years of service in the Army Air Corps. However, getting out of the military in 1946, he made the switch to law, entering the University of Maryland Law School, as had Sam and his father. Young George often said that Sam Dennis was the person who influenced him to enter a career in law. In 1946, Sam had retired as judge but still had a private practice. He mentored young George, helping him get started in his law practice, ultimately passing all his law books on to him.

When Sam Dennis died suddenly from a heart attack in 1953, both Georges felt a real loss, and both were pallbearers at Sam's funeral. At a memorial service for him two months later, his good friend George L. Radcliffe gave the principal address:

> ... the main factors in his outstanding success were his integrity, ability, energy, painstaking industry, practical good judgment, and his indomitable willpower, together with a shrewd, keen, and delightful sense of humor.

> It was my good fortune throughout nearly all of my life to have had intimate associations with him, and I never had a closer or better friend.[7]

In many ways, the two friends led parallel lives, and their close friendship was thus no surprise:

- Both were born shortly after the Civil War on the Eastern Shore but moved to Baltimore to pursue their careers, ultimately ending up living just two blocks apart.

- Both were born on large family farms, growing up with a strong farm work ethic and a love of "getting dirty" and gardening.

- Both families were land rich but cash poor.

- Both grew up in large families.

- Both had fathers briefly in politics.

- Both married strong women, to whom they were devoted their entire lives.

- Both had an early association with Woodrow Wilson.

- Both found law more interesting than politics and chose that as their career, getting their law degrees from the University of Maryland in 1903.

- Both had a Maryland governor from their home county get them started in politics.

- Both were talked into accepting or running for higher position out of a sense of "duty" but were always happier practicing law.

- Both had statewide appeal because they were city dwellers with rural roots.

- Both had a love a history and were officers of the Maryland Historical Society.

- Both served as directors of the Fidelity and Deposit Company.

- Both were long-time members of the Maryland Club.

- Both loved to tell stories, especially of their early lives on the Eastern Shore.

- Both, through a political association, became connected to finding a cure for a disease.

- Both were known and respected for their remarkable honesty and lack of hypocrisy in their daily lives and actions.

- Both were congenial and social, having an army of close acquaintances.

- They were the key male role models in the life of George's son, George M. Radcliffe, who, not surprisingly, also became a lawyer.

- Both, despite their remarkable reputations, wanted all to call them by their first name.

Despite all of this, they were vastly different people and obviously complemented each other well. George was inwardly shy and reflective while Sam was quite blunt and outspoken. George never made enemies with his comments and dealings with people, yet his policies and positions certainly alienated some. Sam's bluntness may have offended some, but all who knew him saw a warm, caring person at his core. Sam could tell a joke while George, despite having a wonderful sense of humor, generally could not. While both considered themselves farm boys, Sam really was the farmer of the two. Sam was generally conservative while George tended to be liberal on issues, while remaining fiscally conservative whenever possible.

George was always deliberate when he spoke, almost to the point of being too methodical and boring. He tried hard to remain emotionless, using logic and carefully chosen words to get his point across. Sam Dennis may have been the polar opposite. Although well known for his fairness, he was never afraid to speak his mind. He had no hesitation as judge to issue the death penalty, when needed. They said he had memorized the pronouncement, "It is the sentence of this court that you be taken by the sheriff and be remanded to the custody of the warden of the Maryland Penitentiary, and there remain until a date is set, when, at a place herein before provided by law, you shall be hanged by the neck until you are dead." He was supposed to add the words "May God have mercy on your soul," but he refused to add these saying that he only had jurisdiction over their body, not their soul.

On one occasion, an older woman with an extensive past record had been found guilty of several offenses, and Judge Dennis sentenced her to one year in prison. The defense attorney spoke up, "Your honor, my client is sixty-four years old; do you know what this sentence means?" Sam quickly responded, "Yes, it means she will be sixty-five when she gets out."[8] Sam Dennis was colorful, a term never used to describe George L. Radcliffe.

Each of us is the sum total of all the people we have met and interacted with, and George L. Radcliffe was blessed to have crossed paths with so many significant individuals beginning with two very strong-willed parents, but none was as important to him as Sam Dennis, who not only influenced George's career, but became a rock in George's life. Everyone needs that wise person in their life who they can always turn to for advice and that perpetual cheerleader who lifts them up whenever needed. Sam more than filled those shoes. Sam Dennis' obituary read:

> Although an extremely dignified judge on the bench, his elevation to that position made no change to his manner or habits of thought. He was still "Sam" Dennis to his intimates, and his speech remained the same close to earth speech it had always been, interspersed with the uproarious stories he could recount in incomparable style. He had unshakeable loyalties and intense dislikes as well, and concealed neither, for he despised sham.[9]

Chimleys, Zinks, and Bull Turkles

George Lovic Pierce Radcliffe walked out of his home, Windemere, on the other side of the Spocott property, and to the shock and horror of his wife Daisy and son George, he climbed into the driver's side of his Lincoln. His wife Daisy walked immediately over to the car, asking what in the world he intended on doing. While the Lincoln was his car, he had never driven it. As a matter of fact, he had no driver's license. As the story was relayed by his son George, his father started the car, somehow got it into gear—although not without a lot of scraping and grinding—and headed down the road, saying he would be back in several minutes. While he planned on just driving dirt roads on the property, he wanted to get a feel for the car he had paid for but never driven. His wife Daisy was an accomplished, albeit adventurous, driver, holding what must surely be a Baltimore City traffic record--three collisions with a utility pole in one day! As her son once said, she "literally left her mark" everywhere she drove. But his father attempting to drive was an event that no one had seen coming.

Close to an hour passed with no sign of his father, and both young George and his mother were starting to worry. While his father had some-how started the car and headed out the lane, young George knew the property was only 250 acres. His father could have stopped at Spocott next door, but George knew his father was a busy man and did not have the time for a long visit. Just as he and his mother were about to send out a search party, they suddenly heard an engine rumbling in the distance and heaved a collective sigh of relief, knowing George Sr. was returning. But looking down the lane, young George saw a brown car heading down the lane, not his father's navy-blue Lincoln. Who could this be?

The car pulled off the road a good distance from the house, and George was shocked to see his father step out of the car. This was the Lincoln, no longer navy blue, but completely covered with mud. His father, as covered with mud as was the car, stormed across the lawn, muttering and mumbling every step of the way. The always calm and in control George Sr. was for once completely incomprehensible, and while young George laughed heartily and Daisy asked one question after another, George Sr. just mumbled away and stormed into the house. He never shared what had happened, and he never tried to drive that or any other car again! That task he left to a person who eventually became an honorary member of the family and a lifelong friend, J. Swain Foxwell.

George L. Radcliffe was a product of Dorchester County, and although he rose to the highest ranks both educationally and politically, he always remained a product of his roots. George was to go on to get both his Ph.D. and Law degrees, but he always remained the simple child who grew up surrounded by wildlife, marshes, and water. Nowhere was this more apparent than in his relationship with John Swain Foxwell (1895–1973), both his chauffeur and lifelong companion, known to all as Swain. I use the term "companion" rather than friend because while we might have multiple friends, a companion is a key person with whom we actually share our life. Swain was such a person.

Swain's and George's educational tracks ran in completely opposite directions. While George climbed to the pinnacle of the educational world, Swain dropped out of formal schooling at an early age to embark on a life as a waterman, catching crabs in the warmer months and tonging for oysters in colder weather. To meet him was to encounter a completely unrefined person in many ways. He came from a poorer part of Dorchester County where hard work rather than education was a ticket to success. He literally slaughtered the King's English, speaking of building a "far" in the "chimley," "warshing" dishes in the "zink," avoiding the "polices" while driving, and catching "bull turkles" to make snapper stew. Like all choosing the profession of waterman, he learned the value of hard work, whether getting up at 2:30 AM every morning or working 364 days a year. He might not have known what year Napoleon met his Waterloo, but he knew where the crabs would be biting at a specific time of year, when a storm was building in the distance, and how to rebuild an engine. Most significantly, Swain had a heart of gold, the most infectious grin ever, and a profound respect for all that was important. Both he and Sen. George L. Radcliffe were geniuses in their own way.

Swain could take a car apart and reassemble it, while George L. Radcliffe never even learned how to drive a car. George L. Radcliffe's son George remembers how Swain helped him get his first car. Swain bought a collection of metal, that one might have called a car, for virtually nothing, and after Swain made some inexpensive repairs, he sold it for enough profit for young George to buy a decent used car. George L. Radcliffe was born in 1877 and was in his forties before he saw a need for a car, still somewhat of a novelty. After the previously mentioned driving disaster, George was going to need a chauffeur, and Swain Foxwell, who was no longer working on the water, applied for the job. Thus began the relationship between two very different individuals, a relationship which would last a lifetime. Swain had a colorful background, even being arrested once during Prohibition for bootlegging. When in court, Swain had explained that the liquor was medicine for a sick friend, sick enough, Swain explained, that his friend would probably need a whole case of whiskey. The judge was not impressed, but George L. Radcliffe, several years later, was. The fact that he chose someone such as Swain speaks volumes about George's ability to see right to the core of a person.

Swain had moved to Baltimore and had several rental houses, which he maintained, but he was at Senator Radcliffe's beck and call. As the years passed, George relied on Swain more and more, and their relationship became as much one of companionship as one of employer and employee. Until their last days, however, Swain referred to George as "Senator." Although their relationship became incredibly close, Swain never wavered in the way he treated "the Senator". He may have come from a simple background, but he knew how to treat people and show the appropriate respect due an employer.

Swain was as colorful an individual as they come. One could pick him out of a crowd simply by his ear-to-ear grin and crowd-splitting laughter. If he had played Santa Clause each year, there would have been no non-believers. George M. Radcliffe, the Senator's son, knew him almost as a second father. He reminisced about the many times Swain "saved" him from his mother's sweet-free diet. George and Swain would secretly meet out behind a bush where Swain would present him with a box of candy to get the youngster by. Swain was never short of opinions, and many of his opinions would fly in the face of the politically correct world we live in today. But he had a heart of gold, and although he moved to Baltimore, he never left his South Dorchester roots. George M. Radcliffe remembers one trip from Washington to Baltimore with Swain and his father where Swain suddenly slammed on the brakes on a major highway, stopping traffic completely. He charged out of the car and ran back to pick up a "Bull Turkle" (snapping turtle) by the tail. Throwing it in the trunk of his Cadillac, he joyously exclaimed that he now had the ingredients for a great stew that night.

George M. Radcliffe recounted another story several years later when Swain, having just come out of the New System Bakery in the Hampden area of Baltimore, pulled out of his parallel parking spot right in front of a police car, barely avoiding a collision. When presented with a ticket, Swain went into a tirade, and the Senator had to intervene. Young George went into court to represent Swain and hoped to just walk out with just a small fine, but after the police officer testified, giving his side of the near collision and resulting argument, George M. expected the worst. Then Swain took the stand to tell his side of the story, repeatedly protesting that the officer "treated me rotten." He explained that in coming out of the bakery, he saw the police car coming up the street. Feeling so sorry for the hard day the officer must be having, he quickly pulled out of the parking place to give the officer the spot because he knew the officer would need and want "one of them great sticky buns." As it turned out, the officer was most unappreciative and just "treated me rotten." By the time he was done with this convoluted story, the entire courtroom, judge and all, was in stitches—that is, all except the police officer. The judge, wiping tears out of his eyes and finally gaining his composure, simply exclaimed "Not Guilty!"

Swain was always reciting his brand of poetry, none of which was going to win him the Pulitzer Prize. He had a verse or two for every situation, some verses his own and some he had picked up from his many colorful friends. He was always interjecting these into a conversation, whether appropriate or not. His favorite, which he cited often, was

> Beauty's only skin deep
> Ugly's to the bone
> Beauty slowly fades away
> But ugly holds its own.

Swain became a part of our Christmas tradition, and his Christmas Eve visit was the official kickoff for the holiday. He always had a wonderful story, and his laughter filled our house every time he visited. He drove George L. Radcliffe for longer than anyone can remember. In the later years, riding in the car with the two of them topped any amusement park ride. "The Senator" always sat in the back, befitting the roles they seemed to honor. The talk between the two was incessant, and frequently the conversations of one bore no resemblance to that of the other. Laughter, poetry, and stories abounded. I only got to be a spectator late in their lives when both were hard of hearing. They would shout back and forth at each other. Neither could hear what the other was saying, but that bothered no one. Swain spent much of the time looking backwards at George, terrifying any other passengers. To make matters worse, the speed of the car seemed to defy any posted limits. On one occasion, the car sped into town at a blistering twenty mph on a road posted at fifty mph, only to accelerate to forty mph when reaching town. My wife and I vividly remember spending one trip on the floor of the car, figuring this improved our chances of surviving the surely imminent crash. Who needed roller coasters?

In 1963, George L. Radcliffe threw a party to celebrate the 300th anniversary of the deeding of Spocott to his ancestor, Stephen Gary. He invited a couple hundred friends and relatives, but double the number invited actually showed up. One individual, unknown to all, appeared dressed in Native American attire. He introduced himself as a member of the Native American community representing his ancestors who like-

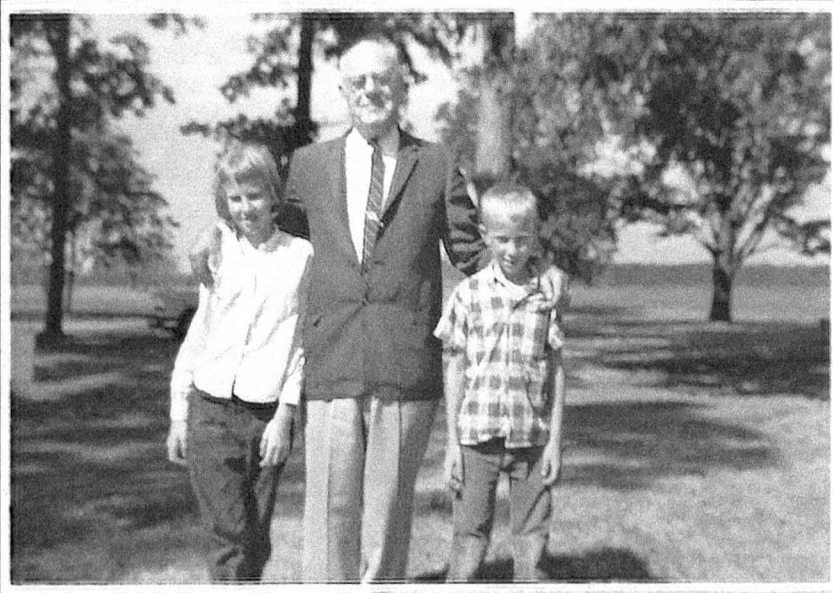

Swain Foxwell with Augusta and Bill Radcliffe
Two of George L. Radcliffe's Grandchildren
Summer 1962

ly made peace with Gary 300 years earlier. He mingled with the crowd, helped shuck oysters, and regaled the crowd with tales of a bygone time. Only toward the end of the party did anyone figure out that the Native American was none other than John Swain Foxwell.

But it was in the last few years of their lives that all realized that this fascinating companionship was so much more. Everyone knew that the two lives had become so intertwined that the death of one would surely lead to the death of the other. Swain was a good bit younger than the Senator, but by the late 1960s both were clearly starting to slip. George was mugged during a robbery in downtown Baltimore, and in addition to significant injuries, his spirit was deflated. Swain spent time with him every day, both in the hospital and when he returned home. He would go to George's house every evening, fix him dinner, and the two would talk the night away, with Swain often staying the whole night. They were so devoted to each other. Not only was time together part of a routine which had started years earlier, but the comfort they brought each other surpassed words. Swain eventually fell one day, and after a stroke, passed away in November of 1973. True to prediction, George was to die only a few months later.

The Radcliffe family made sure to carry George to Swain Foxwell's funeral, and everyone in the church knew the special loss he felt. The most unlikely of companions were separated for the first time, and George, even with the love of his supportive family, would never be the same. He had moved in with young George and his family after Swain's fall, and both families had seen the sadness in the two who could no longer get together to share their stories and comment on every issue under the sun. The two often had opposite positions on issues of the day, but that never mattered. It says much about George L. Radcliffe that, not only would he choose such a person as a companion, but that he would value his opinion. That encapsulated George in that he always sought out the opinions of all, not just those who sang the same political tune. But even more important, he saw right to the core of every person. While so many based their friendships on exteriors, George saw the substance of each person. Swain had only a fraction of the education which George had and possessed quite different views. George researched the most intricate details of every issue before forming an opinion while Swain often reacted emotionally. But George saw in Swain a genuine person, extremely intelligent despite his obvious lack of structured education, a totally warm and good-hearted individual. Their roots and core were the same, even if they had chosen completely different paths.

It seems rare today to see a friendship between two such individuals, so completely different in background, ideas, and language, but Senator George L. Radcliffe learned well from his parents. He knew not to judge people by what one sees on the surface. He learned early to look past skin color, religion, and background to see the core values upon which these superficial layers are laid. This lesson had been well taught by his father. George respected all, and in return, he was respected by all, even if they disagreed with him. If there is an afterlife, there are two old men residing there, telling stories and filling the heavens with genuine laughter. There is a crowd assembled around them, listening and marveling at how two such seemingly different people have found a common ground. To get into heaven, which they surely did, they would have had to be a package deal, a pair encompassing the best of humanity.

The Picture on the Dining Room Wall

In 1955, I visited my grandfather's boyhood home, Spocott, for the first time. Sitting in the dining room, I felt transported back in time. I had been told that the dining room was 350 years old, part of the house built by our early ancestor Stephen Gary. My grandfather had filled me with stories of this ancestral home: of Gary's making peace with the Native Americans around the historic Council Oak near the house, of the schooners his father built which traveled the globe, and of the unique self-sufficient community which inhabited the property for almost a century. The house even smelled old, and my mother, quite the city girl, found it hard to smile as she encountered mice, black snakes, and a seemingly endless army of flies in this old dwelling. The original beams defined the old ceiling, and the room was dominated by a massive fireplace, the source of many a winter meal. Dimly lit by several electric candles placed on the mantle and nearby cabinet, one could easily imagine early ancestors braving a brutal winter's day beside the fireplace in this room, or gathering for a Thanksgiving feast years ago. The room was adorned with relics of the past: pewter plates and candlesticks, an old clock on the mantle, a bride's ball used to carry fire to "jump start" a new dwelling's fireplace, molds for making bayberry candles, and artifacts related to the shipbuilding which had ceased almost 100 years prior.

What struck me the most, however, was that with all the history embedded in this home, there was only one picture hanging on the walls of this room, that of a young Black woman. To a young child who had been raised in an all-white world, the picture was puzzling. Why was there no picture of a family member? My great-grandfather's sword sat over the desk he used, but there was no picture of him. George's brothers, Tom and Sewell, had lived at Spocott most of their lives, but there were no pictures of them. As I was to find out, this picture was of no ordinary woman. Adaline Morris Wheatley, or "Aunt Adaline" as all had called her, kept watch over this room as she had for over sixty years. Born in 1847 a free Black, as were her parents and grandparents, she lived her entire life at Spocott, but as I was to find out, she had had a significant impact on the youngest of the children of John and Sophie Radcliffe.

Adaline Morris was born around 1847 to William and Mary Morris who, according to Adaline, had worked at Spocott, as had their parents. Adaline was the next to youngest of five girls1 and in ensuing years became a favorite of John Anthony LeCompte Radcliffe for her hard work and intelligence. Although she could not read or write, she became a vital part of the Spocott community, with her sharp wit and initiative. In 1868, she married Columbus Wheatley, a former Spocott enslaved worker. That both Columbus and Adaline were highly regarded is proven by the fact that they were given the main Spocott tenant house to live in. Here they raised their seven children, while working their entire lives at Spocott.

Adaline Morris Wheatley
(1847-1929)
Legendary Cook at Spocott

There is no record of Columbus Wheatley's birth. An 1860 census slave schedule shows he and his brother Augustus living at Spocott. They likely were part of the group of enslaved workers that John Anthony LeCompte Radcliffe acquired when he purchased Spocott in 1849. John, an abolitionist, claimed that he freed all the enslaved workers before the Civil War, but with no record of manumission, they likely were free to go but never formally freed.

After working at Spocott for the first part of the Civil War, Columbus joined the Union cause, enlisting in Company C of the 19th Regiment of the U.S. Colored Infantry at Camp Stanton in Benedict, MD on Christmas Day, 1863. On April 17, 1864, he transferred to the Navy as Landsman serving on the *USS Alleghany* stationed at Baltimore, MD, *USS Princeton* at Philadelphia, PA, and *USS New Hampshire* at Port Royal, SC.

Discharged on June 15, 1865, Columbus returned to Dorchester County where he briefly tried farming on his own. He was soon asked by John to return to Spocott, where he would spend the rest of his life as farmer and master craftsman. He was beloved for his eternally good nature, remarkable sense of humor, and classic stories, always highly exaggerated for comic effect. By the end of his life, his stories had completely rewritten the historical facts of the Civil War.

Adaline was the family cook, but over the years her duties expanded to include those of nurse and house manager. However, it was her relationship with young George that would be her real legacy. Sophie and John Radcliffe had been previously married and had lost spouses in 1869 and 1870, respectively. The two married each other in 1871, with Sophie bringing six children into the marriage, while John brought the five surviving of his ten children. They then added three of their own, with George being the youngest. George was thus born into a full house. Spocott was always full of children and grandchildren, and John further filled the house with his unusual open-door policy. His deep faith led him to leave his door open for all. Anyone appearing at the door would get a meal and bed for the night, staying longer if they agreed to do some work.[1]

It is easy to see how young George could have gotten lost in the shuffle, but Adaline was there to help fill the void. Her outdoor kitchen often had as many people in it as the main house because all would be greeted, not only with amazing foods and desserts, but with the original "Dear Abby." She was never at a loss for both counsel and comfort, and soon all in the community grew to call her "Aunt Adaline," clearly here a term of endearment. John was a stern, but loving, father who taught George the value of reading and hard work. Sophie was a wonderfully caring mother who managed to juggle the demands of the family. Adaline, however, became the glue holding all together in a vibrant and joyous household. In examining the letters of some who visited Spocott, Adaline is always mentioned. In writing a remembrance of Spocott, one frequent visitor wrote, "It was especially hard to leave Aunt Adaline. She called everyone 'Miss Nanny,' and I could hardly say goodbye. She was a dear, kind person, and when she died, something special went out of Spocott."[2]

All in the family grew to include Adaline and the other Wheatleys in increasing numbers of activities. One letter writer remembered playing croquet with her, but most remembrances were of that marvelous kitchen, where she worked "witchery in the kitchen." Adaline's recipes were included in the Delmarva Cooking Association's cookbook in the 1920s, with some of them circulated nationally, and her photo graced the cover of the association's brochure.[3] Her picture was also included in Swepson Earle's 1923 treatise, *The Chesapeake Bay Country*.[4] However, it was her caring and wisdom that endeared her to the Radcliffes, granting her a place of honor. Her picture, throughout the twentieth century, always hung prominently in the Spocott dining room, and no meal at Spocott passed without George L. Radcliffe recounting at least one Adaline story. In fact, George was as likely to talk about Adaline as about his mother or father.

When Adaline died in 1929, a couple years after his mother's death, George was profoundly affected. Her family had her buried at the local Black church and cemetery, but George, already a prominent lawyer and political figure, insisted on giving her eulogy at the service. In many ways, he had lost a second mother. Attendees at the funeral were moved, but not surprised, at the tenderness with which he remembered her at that service. She had largely shaped his childhood and had always filled the gap when his mother was not available. Later George paid for a large tombstone for her grave in Zoar A.M.E. Church Cemetery, near Morris Neck. The stone read "For 65 years devoted employee and friend of Mrs. John A. L. Radcliffe, whose sons Thomas B., J. Sewell, and George L. erect this." His affection for her was obvious to all in the community. George was to go on and become a United States senator, but he never forgot his roots.

Sen. George L. Radcliffe was born not long after slavery was abolished, grew up during the years of slow change in the relationship between the two races, and died shortly after local schools were integrated. He grew up in a white-centered world, went to segregated schools, went to an all-white college, worked at a firm which was undoubtedly all white, and served two terms in the US Senate, populated entirely by white males. However, he looked at the world a little differently than many of his peers. Although catapulted into affluent society functions by both his political status and his wife Mary's prominent family, he always remained a hard-working country boy. He never considered himself socially superior, and he respected all. His father ingrained this in him, teaching George to respect hard work and achievement, not privilege earned by birthright. He had been raised by a father who saw the value in all individuals and who had completely respected and cared for the Blacks who worked for him, whether enslaved or free. But it was George's relationship with Adaline which had the most profound impact. In her, he had a deeply caring figure who shared his father's work ethic. In this regard, George had two work role models, his father and Adaline. Despite the prejudice and segregation which limited George's exposure to the Black community, Adaline remained a part of him for his entire life.

George's relationship with Adaline and with the Black employees at Spocott gave him an unusual outlook on race relations in the country. Coming from a family of Confederate sympathizers, one which had owned slaves, would normally have set him on a segregationist pathway into the 20th Century, and it is clear from family letters that several distant family members considered Blacks inferior. While all at Spocott worked together, they lived separately, and the Black children could not attend the school or church which George attended. Children are born unbiased and segregationist views are learned. George certainly grew up in a segregationist world, but then there was Adaline, who seemed to bridge the gap between those two worlds.

It is clear from his letters that the relationship between the races interested him; he saw that there was something unnatural about the separation of the races. While many of his day thought Blacks intellectually inferior to whites, George knew Adaline to be an intellectual equal to all. A story he loved to tell illustrates this well.

He often talked of the day when Maryland Governor Emerson Harrington, also a Dorchester resident, was visiting Spocott. As did all guests, the governor first went in to speak to George's mother, Sophie, but after exchanging pleasantries, he went outside. A half-hour or so passed with no sign of the governor, and Sophie became concerned. It certainly would not look good to have something happen to the governor at Spocott; so, she called on George to go out and look for him. George immediately knew where the governor would likely be, as the aromas from Adaline's outdoor kitchen had drawn in many a guest. As George approached the small building, found between the main house and Gary's Creek, he could hear a voice he knew all too well. Adaline should have been a preacher, as she could launch into a sermon on any relevant point. While he knew her advice to be treasured by many, he did feel the need to go in and rescue the governor who, if he waited for a pause in the conversation, would never be able to get out of that kitchen.

Entering the kitchen, George could see the governor sitting in front of a veritable meal: Maryland beaten biscuits, cherry pie, terrapin soup. Adaline was well into a dissertation on how the governor should be running the state, including programs he should institute and ones which needed to be eliminated. George knew he had to get the governor out of there, but Governor Harrington was clearly enjoying himself, still working on that impromptu meal. Just then George noticed that the governor also had pencil and paper and was taking copious notes. The governor was actively seeking advice from this wise woman. Adaline sadly never learned to read or write, skills she deemed unnecessary for what she did. George's mother had taught all of Adaline's children to read, write, and do arithmetic, but Adaline did fine without it. Her wisdom, however, was for the ages.

George left the partially integrated property he grew up on to go live in a completely white world, one well steeped in racial prejudice, but he never forgot Adaline and the other Black workers at Spocott. He certainly would not have been an advocate for forced racial integration, but he saw all as equal in value.

Early in the 1960s, Senator George L. Radcliffe became involved with an unusual project. A group had petitioned the local historical society for funding for a marker honoring Harriett Tubman, the enslaved woman who had led many of her kin to freedom using the Underground Railroad. This was early in the Civil Rights Movement, and although small progress was being made, the local schools were still segregated and most citizens were, at the very least, uncomfortable with integration. The request was refused, but Senator Radcliffe, intimately connected with the historical society, decided to continue pursuing the matter. At that time, he was the chairman of the Maryland Civil War Centennial Committee, and he could see the potential marker falling under the umbrella of that committee since Tubman had served as a cook, nurse, and spy for the Union army. He was able to secure funding, and a state road marker was placed near her supposed birthplace. Tubman now had her first official recognition, although George admitted that he did think several other historical figures, including a Southern general, were more deserving. As always, in George's mind, history trumped everything.[5]

George must have seen a large part of Adaline in Harriet, but Tubman was different from Adaline, although they were somewhat contemporaries. Adaline chose a completely different path, one which would keep her out of the history books. She chose to stay with her family and employer and placed family over community service. To some, this might make her a weaker figure, but to George, it made her more special because to him, family ruled. In Adaline, George saw the power and strength of a Black woman, and he never forgot this. There is no doubt that, in finding funding for the Tubman marker, George was at least partly honoring that miracle worker in the Spocott kitchen.

No one would ever say that George was socially progressive. With his love of history, he sometimes seemed to be more content looking back at the past than thinking forward. He was content to live and work in

Maryland State Road Marker Recognizing Harriett Tubman
Funded by George L. Radcliffe's Civil War Centennial Commission
Location: Greenbriar Road in Dorchester County, Maryland

his white-dominated world, but he was no segregationist. He certainly tolerated aspects of segregation, but he differed from many around him in that he saw Blacks as equals in intelligence and humanity. He accepted the inequality imposed by society, not because it was the way it should be, but because society was evolving, and he believed true integration of the races would take time. He clearly was torn throughout his life, trying to balance his Confederate roots and family history with his genuine caring for a remarkable Black woman. George knew the love, wisdom, and strength of a Black woman, and he carried that with him throughout his life. It is no wonder that Adaline's picture was the only one hanging on that dining room wall.

Essays

Politics

An Unusual Friendship

In the 1920s, George L. Radcliffe was visiting a friend in New York State. The two had been acquainted for several years and now worked for the same surety firm, one in the Baltimore office and the other in New York City. They came from different backgrounds, one growing up on a relatively poor family farm and the other from a wealthy and prominent family living on a large estate. One was nationally recognized while the other was probably only known by some individuals in his state. Their friendship stemmed from a mutual admiration and numerous shared interests. Both were well educated and proficient in history, economics, and the political world.

This particular day the two were at the home of the New York individual, and having just finished dinner with his family, they decided to visit the friend's mother who lived nearby on the large family property. The home was too far away to walk, so they would have to drive, but this posed a problem. The New York friend was physically disabled with minimal use of his legs, and George, although in his forties, could NOT drive! This certainly was not going to prevent the visit, as these two had both made careers of solving what seemed insurmountable problems. The friend said he would drive, even with little use of his legs, and off they went. As George L. Radcliffe later described the episode:

> He could use his arms, but he could not do very much
> with his legs, and so that was a drive. We bounced around.
> Nothing happened to us fortunately, but I wasn't sure
> where I was going to land before I got there.... I don't
> remember assisting him on that, but I can see [us] run-
> ning into ditches. We didn't run into anything before we

got there but I was in fear and trembling because I didn't know where I was going to land before we got through.[1]

This scene repeated itself on several occasions in Hyde Park, New York, and the driver was to become the thirty-second president of the United States.

At the beginning of World War I, George was too old to enlist but he wanted to get involved stateside in the war effort. He volunteered for the "Dollar-a-Year Man" program in which business executives volunteered for a token salary of one dollar per year to lend their expertise to the war effort. Given a choice of places to volunteer, George chose the Department of the Navy, a logical choice for him, since his father had been a shipbuilder. It was here that he befriended the Assistant Secretary of the Navy, Franklin Delano Roosevelt. While we don't know the details of any interactions they might have had, it seems quite likely they met on numerous occasions as George was also chairman of the historical division of the Maryland Council of Defense. Charged with putting together a history of Maryland's involvement in World War I, George was trying to record the names of every Marylander who had fought and died in the war.[2] The Department of the Navy was involved in this effort, and Secretary of the Navy Daniels was the principal speaker at a ceremony on January 13, 1920 in which a plaque was unveiled honoring "Maryland's 800," the first 800 Marylanders to answer the Navy's call for recruits for the recent war.[3] This project surely would have also connected the two. We know from George's stories that he and Roosevelt had met enough times before 1920 that a significant friendship had developed.[4]

Roosevelt was the Democratic vice-presidential candidate in the 1920 election, and after that unsuccessful run, Franklin came to work for George's Fidelity and Deposit Company and was appointed vice president of the New York office of the Baltimore-based company. Van Lear Black, prominent Baltimore figure, was chairman of the board of the Fidelity and Deposit Company and also knew Roosevelt, making Franklin a logical choice for the firm. George pushed Black to select Roosevelt for the position, and both George and Van Lear Black saw that Roosevelt could be a major asset for the New York office. Roosevelt, happy to get into private business after eight years of public service, also saw the position as a way to continue to build his political resume.

That summer, while vacationing, Roosevelt was diagnosed with infantile paralysis (polio), and this had a profound impact on George. He visited Roosevelt on many occasions, usually getting to see him at least once a week. Sitting by Franklin's bedside, George saw an individual initially struggling to come to terms with his disability. The two talked at great length, and George would later say how amazed he was by Franklin's determination to move on with his life. The two talked often of Franklin's disease, and Roosevelt vowed to devote part of his life to bringing infantile paralysis into public awareness. As their friendship grew, George was also inspired to help find a treatment and cure for the dreaded disease, and he would head up the Maryland March of Dimes for thirty-four years, beginning with that first Presidential Birthday Ball in 1934.[5]

Their friendship blossomed over their eight years of professional association, and George would often visit the New York office where he and Franklin would get together socially. Roosevelt would visit George at Spocott on at least one occasion,[6] and George made several visits to Hyde Park where his fondest memories were of what transpired after every dinner there. The Roosevelts had six children, losing the first, Franklin, Jr., in 1919. After each dinner, George remembered Franklin and the children retiring to a room where he would gather the children around him and read to them. These evenings left a positive impact on George who valued family and was a voracious reader himself. Eleanor frequently retired to a separate area where she went about her business. George spoke of Eleanor with great respect but never developed the personal bond with her that he did with Franklin. He felt that her causes took her away from the family too often, but then George himself was married to a woman immersed in causes.[7]

Franklin and George also took several business trips together including one long business trip through the Midwest in 1928. Their relationship was one of mutual admiration, and they complemented each other well. While Franklin clearly had strong political aspirations, George basically had none.[8] George was the historian and had little interest in any self-promotion, but there is no question that Roosevelt heavily combined politics with his work with Fidelity and Deposit. He brought with him many contacts developed as Assistant Secretary of the Navy and further honed his political prowess as political maneuvering often played an important role in acquiring bonds.[9] For George L. Radcliffe, who had developed a small amount of political expertise in his small roles as Baltimore liquor commissioner and Maryland secretary of state, this was probably a time to develop the political skills he would later need as U.S. Senator. George, however, still had no desire to enter the political arena.

With Roosevelt in charge in New York, that office did a record business. However, Roosevelt embarked on several projects which the extremely conservative Fidelity and Deposit Company found too liberal. At an executive meeting of its board, a majority felt that they needed to let Roosevelt go. George obviously opposed the move but was unable to sway the board. Finally, he asked them if he could personally share the news of the firing with Roosevelt, feeling that it would be inappropriate to make the move by letter or phone call.

George then headed to New York, but with an agenda different from what the board expected. He knew the increase in company business was largely the result of Roosevelt's efforts and was determined that the company would retain him. When he got to New York, he said nothing of the "firing" to Roosevelt but instead engaged FDR in a discussion of possible new Fidelity and Deposit projects. Knowing of the planned construction of the Triborough Bridge, George asked Roosevelt if the company could get the surety bond for the project. Roosevelt made a couple quick phone calls and secured a tentative OK for the surety bond, one of the largest the company had ever acquired. Returning to Baltimore, George told the board that he had not fired Roosevelt, explaining that it would be imprudent to fire the individual who had just issued such a large bond for the company. The board acquiesced, and Roosevelt remained in his position.[10]

As he had in 1924, on June 27, 1928, Roosevelt gave a speech in Houston, Texas nominating Alfred E. Smith at the Democratic National Convention, and this speech would change the direction of his life.

> America needs not only an administrator but a leader – a pathfinder, a blazer of the trail to the high road that will avoid the bottomless morass of crass materialism that has engulfed so many of the great civilizations of the past. It is the privilege of democracy not only to offer such a man but to offer him as the surest leader to victory. To stand upon the ramparts and die for our principles is heroic. To sally forth to battle and win for our principles is something more than heroic. We offer one who has the will to win—who not only deserves respect but commands it. Victory is his habit—the happy warrior—ALFRED E. SMITH.[11]

George was hardly surprised at the quality of the speech; on many occasions he often remarked on Roosevelt's amazing speaking ability. "He had one of the best voices I have ever heard. He could go into Madison Square Gardens and make a speech there without apparently raising his voice to be heard. His voice had extraordinary carrying effects, I guess you might say."[12] Another quality of Roosevelt that George admired was Franklin's remarkable memory. George's son, George M., witnessed this first-hand when he attended a dinner at the White House in his father's place. Young George had only met Roosevelt once, when a child of eight. Many years later, here he was walking into the White House as a last-minute replacement for his father who was out of town on business. Young

George entered the large room where a crowd was assembled, frightened as he not only knew no one, but was not even sure the president knew of the substitution. As young George recounted the story, the moment he entered the room, the president looked up from the group he was talking to and flashed a big grin. Crossing the room, Franklin warmly greeted George, knowing exactly who he was, even though young adult George looked markedly different from the child Franklin had met only once. George was flabbergasted at being recognized immediately and at Roosevelt's knowledge of the personal details of young George's life. He always remembered the warmth of the man and his amazing memory for details, and knew why his father so admired him.

As a direct result of this 1928 speech, Smith asked Roosevelt to run for governor of New York, and George strongly encouraged him to enter the race. George knew well Roosevelt's political aspirations, and while he didn't want to lose a person who had helped raise the status of the Fidelity and Deposit Company, he and others had known all along that this was a temporary job for the gifted New Yorker. In later years, George, with his typical modesty, would downplay his role in Roosevelt's decision.[13]

The two kept in close contact throughout Roosevelt's four years as governor of New York, and when Roosevelt first considered running for president, George would once again encourage him to run. George had worked closely with Gov. Albert Ritchie in Maryland and been chairman of his inauguration committee in 1924, 1927, and 1931. With Ritchie in his fourth term as Maryland governor, he had achieved a degree of national prominence. George had initially thought that he would back Ritchie for president, but when it became apparent that Ritchie would not make the cut, George threw his support behind Franklin Roosevelt and would go on to be Roosevelt's campaign manager in Maryland, devoting a tremendous amount of time and energy to the task. The man who really did not want to enter the political world now dove in headfirst.

Roosevelt was initially not popular in Maryland, and George had his work cut out for him, having to bring together many diverse factions in the Maryland Democratic Party. A week before the election, he was able to get Roosevelt to Baltimore for a major speech, and Roosevelt went on to carry the state by a huge margin, getting sixty-one percent of the vote.[14]

After the election, many suspected that President Roosevelt would appoint George to a cabinet-level position, and there were unconfirmed rumors that he was being considered for Assistant Secretary of the Treasury. However, on July 25, 1933, Roosevelt asked George to be a regional advisor for the Public Works Administration (PWA), handling the Tenth Region covering Maryland, West Virginia, Virginia, Kentucky, Tennessee, North Carolina, and Delaware. George was reluctant as he was extremely busy as vice president of his company, but as George said later, no one could say "no" to Franklin Roosevelt. As George relayed the story, Roosevelt called him one afternoon to offer him the position. George declined although Roosevelt persisted in asking him. Finally, Roosevelt asked him to come to the White House the next morning for a brunch. When George entered the White House room where Roosevelt was, Franklin introduced George to the assembled group as the new PWA regional administrator.

While the job was a full-time position, George wished to remain in his role at the Fidelity and Deposit Company, and he was able to do this, using his Fidelity office in Baltimore also as his PWA office.[15]

The first Maryland project that he was to get funded under the PWA was a bridge over the Choptank River, the longest river on the Eastern Shore and one which basically isolated George's native Dorchester County. George was a senator when the bridge was completed, and Roosevelt came over on the *Sequoia*, his presidential yacht, for the opening of the Bridge on October 26, 1935. Roosevelt wanted to be standing in the bow, waving to the crowd, as the *Sequoia* passed through the draw span; he never wanted to appear crippled or weak.[16] He asked George to stand beside him to help support him. As George recounted the story, the river was extremely choppy that day, and he could barely keep his balance as the waves rocked the yacht from side to side. For a person disabled by polio, standing under these conditions was an impossibility. George grabbed Roosevelt both by the arm and by his belt, trying desperately to keep them both upright. Roosevelt waved to the crowds while George fought to keep his balance as the boat pitched and rocked. George's wife Daisy, in the crowd that day, fussed at him later for not waving at her, and he had to explain the situation, saying that he didn't want to be the first person in history to throw a U.S. president overboard.[17]

When George was asked to run for governor and then senator in 1934, the President would return the favor from two years earlier, strongly encouraging George to run for office. George handily won the election and immediately attracted national attention. The press made note of the fact that he was Roosevelt's "old boss." While George laughed at being

Choptank River Bridge Dedication on October 27, 1935
Presidential Yacht USS Sequoia *Passing Through the Bridge*

referred to as Roosevelt's one-time employer, it probably was technically correct. Because of the relationship, most expected him to be Roosevelt's "spokesman" in the Senate.[18]

While George initially supported Roosevelt's New Deal legislation, his role as a "yes-man" for FDR would be short-lived. Despite their strong friendship, George always kept personal and professional life separate. The Social Security Act warranted a lot of time and attention that first year, and George fully supported that. However, a provision in the Public Utility Holding Company Bill—referred to as the "death sentence"—would provide for the elimination by the SEC of a holding company if it could not justify its existence economically within five years. George felt this was government overreach and opposed the bill, much to the dissatisfaction of the President.

In 1936, Franklin Roosevelt once again chose George to head up his Maryland campaign. George's organizational skills ruled the day, and Roosevelt won nationally by a landslide, carrying Maryland by a large margin. However, 1937 would see a major professional break between the two over Roosevelt's plan to make the Supreme Court much more favorable to his New Deal legislation.

Roosevelt wanted to enlarge the Court, adding one justice for every justice older than seventy years and six months and who had served at least ten years, The Court had struck down some of his New Deal legislation at the end of his first term, and increasing the Court up to 6 more judges could create a body more supportive of his legislation. George did not initially support the president in his attempt to "pack the Court." Roosevelt called him to the White House on several occasions, but George refused to commit to supporting the move, although he was able to temporarily appease the president by saying that he would work on a compromise. Roosevelt was receptive to this move, but the vote on the issue killed any further discussion. George, in the end, opposed his friend and voted against the issue.[19]

Portrait of
Franklin Delano Roosevelt
Given to George L. Radcliffe

Their professional relationship would suffer significant damage during the 1938 election campaign. After the Supreme Court defeat in 1937 and several other setbacks, FDR actively campaigned against several of the conservative Southern Democrats who frequently opposed him. One of these was George's colleague from Maryland, Millard Tydings, who was running for a third term in the Senate. In an unusual move, Tydings asked George to run his campaign. Although Tydings and George frequently disagreed on issues, there was mutual respect. George, even knowing this would anger Roosevelt, placed state loyalty above his friendship. Tydings won re-election, but this caused a major rift between the two one-time friends, and for the next several years, the relationship between George and Franklin would be cordial but personally cold. They met on business, but the closeness seemed to be gone. Roosevelt even opposed George's re-election to the Senate in 1940.

George continued to officially support Roosevelt, but their frequent personal meetings and letters largely came to an end. George initially was opposed to Roosevelt running for a third term, believing that no president should serve more than two terms. Despite this, he still officially supported his reelection, although most of George's time in 1940 was spent on getting himself reelected. Finally, George was summoned to the White House and, as he had several times in the past, carried with him a pot of terrapin soup, something he knew Franklin enjoyed. George later said the meeting started awkwardly, but soon the friendship trumped any political differences.[20] The warm letters between the two resumed. Roosevelt's last letter to George on April 7, 1945, began, "Thank you so much for your two letters of April third. I am delighted at the thought of getting some of that delicious terrapin."[21] Sadly, he did not get that last care package of soup as he died five days later at Warm Springs. George took comfort in the fact that friendship had prevailed in those last couple of years.

On the wall of George L. Radcliffe's childhood home, Spocott, is a portrait given to him from his long-time friend and colleague. The portrait of Roosevelt is a treasured item as it commemorates a remarkable friendship between two individuals whose paths were intertwined for almost thirty years. The friendship changed George in two significant ways. It paved the way for him to become a United States Senator, a path he doubtless would not have chosen had he not befriended Franklin Roosevelt. Knowing and caring for a man who struggled to overcome the tragic nature of infantile paralysis also led to George's long dedication to the March of Dimes, from that first Birthday Ball George organized in 1934 until he stepped down as Maryland chairman in 1968. The friendship that grew as George sat beside the bed-ridden Roosevelt in 1921 changed him profoundly. Their days working together for the Fidelity and Deposit Company strengthened that friendship even if politics would put a strain on it in later years. That George would continue his work with the March of Dimes for twenty-three years after the death of his friend is a testament to the impact that Roosevelt had on him. The portrait still hangs in a place of prominence at Spocott, a memory of a special friend and one who inspired George L. Radcliffe to reach even greater heights.

THE GENTLEMAN POLITICIAN

L ou Azrael, Baltimore newspaper columnist for fifty years and close acquaintance of George L. Radcliffe, in a tribute to George shortly after his death, wrote:

> Beneath [Radcliffe's surface] lay a man of great compe-
> tence and great, often deceptively quiet, determination.
> When he ran for the U.S. Senate in 1934, his primary
> opponent was Howard Bruce,[1] a multimillionaire bank-
> er and industrialist who was much better known in the
> state and who had organizational support.
>
> In some of his speeches Bruce downgraded Radcliffe as a
> man of no special ability. Therefore, when I was talking
> to Bruce one day, I asked [him] to explain why, if Rad-
> cliffe had no ability, he could have become the Executive
> Vice-President of the Fidelity and Deposit Company at
> an early age.
>
> Bruce answered, "Because he was so good at settling
> claims against the company. And he was good at that be-
> cause he can't make decisions. He talks so long, and hems
> and haws so much that he wears other people down."
>
> Bruce was wrong in thinking that Radcliffe couldn't
> make up his mind. The hemming and hawing was care-
> fully planned to accomplish his purpose.
>
> His analysis was born out in that political campaign.
> Bruce spent big money, waged a spectacular campaign
> while Radcliffe went quietly around the state, talked to

people in friendly fashion—and won.[2]

In November of 1934, the most unlikely of individuals was elected to the U.S. Senate from Maryland. George L. Radcliffe was anything but a typical politician. Ask anyone to describe him, and somewhere in their answer would be the word "gentleman." He would be a duck out of water in today's partisan politics, power struggles, and excessive lobbying. Politics in his day was still often a dog-eat-dog game with certain individuals wielding excessive power, but George went to Washington to serve. He avoided the power struggles and stayed the same person he had always been. He was deliberate and unswayable as he judged each issue on its merit. He never forgot why he had been sent to Washington. As the only senator to commute to work, he was able to stay somewhat removed from the corrupting Washington establishment.

> I was born within a hundred feet of salt water. My early experiences were in my father's shipyard. On his farms, working in our canning factory, mingling with the farmers, fishermen, and oystermen who were our neighbors and good friends. The lives of those who toil on farms, on the oyster bars, are open to me.

> My duty, my pleasure, and my ambition is to turn out a good, sincere, unostentatious, successful record of service to my constituents, whether they earn their living with a pen, a hoe, or a pin mall. They all look alike to me.[3]

George Lovic Pierce Radcliffe was a quiet, hard-working academic, as well as a shrewd negotiator, having made a career in the surety business of bringing two sides together. And when one is the youngest of nineteen children, one has to be a clever negotiator to win any discussion. What George did gain early in life was a respect for hard work and family. He made the four-mile round trip to school each day on foot, coming home to chores which kept him busy until well after dark on those cold winter days. On a working farm, hard work is expected of all, and his father was a magnificent role model. He was an older man when George was born, but John Anthony LeCompte Radcliffe still worked a long day, inspiring all around him with his efforts, and commanding their respect with his fair treatment of all.

While George was an unlikely politician, there was something about Dorchester County, Maryland, which groomed individuals for the political world. He would jokingly say that on the Eastern Shore, if a baby, after being born, first looked toward Annapolis, he would go into politics. One might think that Dorchester County would have been the last place in the world to launch a statewide politician since its population was small, and it was isolated on the Eastern Shore by the Choptank River to the north, the Nanticoke River to the East, and the Chesapeake Bay to the West. However, by 1920, Dorchester had generated six Maryland governors (John Henry 1797–1798, Charles Goldsborough 1819, Thomas Holliday Hicks 1858–1862, Henry Lloyd 1885–1888, Phillips Lee Goldsborough 1912–1916, and Emerson Harrington 1916–1920). There clearly was something special in those Dorchester marshes. George's father had also been a member of the Maryland legislature in 1872. Despite all of this, George, with his passion for reading and history, seemed destined for an academic career, but circumstances would alter that path.

As George advanced through the American Bonding Company and Fidelity and Deposit Company, he remained the simple country boy, staying modest to a fault. He was known for being incredibly nonjudgmental, enjoying the company of all, whether a prominent Baltimorean or the simplest of individuals. However, circumstance put George in the company of many with political ambition: Woodrow Wilson, who mentored George at Hopkins; Edwin Warfield, founder of the Fidelity and Deposit Company, Maryland governor, and president of the Maryland Historical Society; and his high school principal, Emerson Harrington, who became a governor of Maryland, and selected George to become Maryland Secretary of State. But it was his association with Franklin Roosevelt which really put George on the political pathway.

His whole life changed in 1932 when his friend Franklin Roosevelt ran for president of the United States. George headed up the campaign in Maryland, and when Roosevelt was elected, he soon tapped his old friend George for the position of public works administrator for the East Coast. He attacked the job as he had everything else in life, but 1934 brought pressure on George from both Roosevelt and the Maryland Democratic Party to run for higher office. With Governor Albert Ritchie considering running for the U.S. Senate instead of seeking a fifth term as governor, political leaders from the Eastern Shore produced a petition requesting George to run for governor. His reaction was hardly unexpected:

> That was awfully nice of them. I appreciate it very much. But—well, the fact is I have never run for any office, and I haven't any idea of doing it now.
>
> I mix around in politics a bit and have held one or two appointive offices. Of course, anyone would like to be governor of Maryland and would fight for the office if he thought he had a chance, I suppose, but I really have no intention of becoming a candidate.
>
> However, I'm glad they think that way about me in Dorchester County. That's where I'm going to live if I get a dollar or two together and am getting old and ready to retire.[4]

Despite wishing to stay out of politics, George was talked into running for governor, and organized his campaign. Governor Ritchie soon changed his mind, choosing instead to run for a fifth term as governor. Without hesitation, George withdrew from the race, not wanting to antagonize Ritchie, who George considered a friend. Keeping peace in the Democratic party was far more important to him than any political ambition.

Soon George was talked into running for the soon-to-be vacated senate seat and won that election, serving 2 terms. It is safe to say that George still had no political aspirations; he was simply following the lead of others who wanted him to serve. Without Roosevelt's urging, he never would have run for the office, and the fact that he was willing to step out of the gubernatorial election to maintain party harmony says much about his character.

The
MAN FOR
U. S. SENATOR
———
GEORGE L. RADCLIFFE

CLARENCE W. MILES
POLITICAL AGENT

*Campaign Brochure
for George L. Radcliffe's
1934 Senate Campaign*

Amazingly, George had no ego. No one ever heard him brag or toot his own horn, even though he had many reasons for doing so. His campaigns were marked by an absence of negativity, filled instead with only talk about what he felt was good for state and country. It was said that George never said an unkind word about anyone. In reviewing his personal diaries, to which he added short personal comments at the end of almost every day for years, one rarely finds a negative comment about an individual, and when there is one, he also added something positive about the person. These personal diaries show George actively looking for the best in all he dealt with. This most unlikely of candidates was elected U.S. senator from Maryland in November of 1934.

A national article late in 1934 touted the recently elected senator from Maryland as Roosevelt's new closest ally in the Senate since George had formerly been the "boss" of the president, but George had no intention of being Roosevelt's yes-man. George must not have taken Politics 101, as he immediately sought to do only what he thought best for the state and country. While he did side with Roosevelt on many key issues, George was not afraid to cross party lines, and his record shows that he voted each issue on its own merit, never on how his position aligned with Roosevelt and the Democratic Party.

Despite George sometimes not backing the New Deal legislation, Franklin Roosevelt again chose George in 1936 to head up his Maryland campaign. After the successful campaign, George was asked by the Maryland Democratic Party to be the Maryland party boss. With no hesitation whatsoever and finding the suggestion almost a joke, he replied, "That sounds like a flight of somebody's fancy. I have never had any aspirations to be a party boss, and I certainly have neither the taste nor the aptitude for such a position."[5] George showed that he was not seeking power; his role as senator was only about service to the people of Maryland and never as a rung on a ladder to be climbed.

George's relationship with the other Maryland senator, Millard Tydings, also shows George as a persistent peacemaker. The two often disagreed on issues as Tydings was far more conservative, yet they made an effective team. When Tydings was up for reelection in 1938, he asked George to manage his campaign, a task which consumed much of George's time in 1938. Tydings was one of the Democrats least favorable to Roosevelt's New Deal agenda, but George considered him both an important and competent senator. George readily agreed even though he knew this would anger the president. He considered his responsibility to the state which put him in office a higher priority than a close friendship.

His passion for history and his insatiable appetite for reading made him as well versed as any politician in Washington. He was the only U.S.

senator at that time with a Ph.D. He looked at his position in the Senate as a chance to serve, never a steppingstone in his career. He was one of the lesser-known senators during his two terms because he was far more likely to be seen behind the scenes in committee work than making a speech on the Senate floor. While some of his colleagues disagreed with a position he might have, he had no enemies and was generally liked by all. In his diary, he often refers to the verbosity and attention-grabbing antics of some of his colleagues. Looking at the Congressional Record, we can see he chose his words wisely and never felt obligated to ramble on for the press or his colleagues.

George reacted to criticism with self-control, sound arguments, and a touch of humor. His diary indicates that he did take criticism to heart, but in public he was the master of calm and self-control. He was rarely argumentative but more often reflective; it was important for him to lis-

George L. Radcliffe Radio Address, 1941

ten, and he knew argument would often exacerbate the situation. In one moment of criticism from a crowd at a small Democratic meeting, he simply said, "If anyone has the time and wants to do any of my work, I will be glad to point out a lot of it to be done."[6]

While clearly a Democrat, if one had asked him his political affiliation, he would have said he was a Marylander. More important than scoring political points with colleagues, he saw himself as Maryland's ambassador to the country. While he would never tout his accomplishments, he was an unabashed braggart when it came to his state and especially the Eastern Shore of Maryland. With Maryland next door to Washington, D.C., George was constantly inviting senators of both parties to one of his many clubs: Maryland Club, University Club, Baltimore Country Club. While political business may have been a small part of these luncheons and dinners, to George, this was first and foremost to show off the state: Maryland crabs, terrapin soup, Maryland beaten biscuits. Each Christmas, George would send each senator a yearly diary and agenda book from his firm with a Christmas card and note. He would also share later that in the Senate lunchroom he would often seek out a political adversary, and rather than making political points, George would focus the discussion on family, history, and traditions. He knew that the seed of compromise was most often sown in a bed of positive associations. Many were more politically savvy than he, but few were as pleasant and congenial.

One relationship which exemplifies his political nature was his lifetime relationship with Theodore McKeldin, leading Maryland Republican statesman for several decades. McKeldin, twenty-three years George's junior, was twice mayor of Baltimore and served two terms as governor in a state which was heavily Democratic. George had gotten to know him in Baltimore at the beginning of McKeldin's law career and had helped him get into law school.[7] They disagreed on many issues but were extremely close throughout their lives, never letting politics trump humanity. Their relationship should be held up as a poster for how political adversaries should behave and interact. McKelden was every bit the gentleman that George was, and the two corresponded personally often throughout their careers. Everything they did was enshrouded in respect. In 1956 McKeldin asked George to write the forward to his book, *Washington Bowed*, and George wrote:

> Governor McKelden is an instinctive and constructive historian. His research into history is for the love of the subject, and his findings are utilized wherever they fit into our times. No doubt he handled this present work with some special affection because of his nearness to the narrative's scene.[8]

The two were a mutual admiration society, frequently praising and recognizing the other despite political differences. In a 1956 letter to McKeldin, George wrote:

> Your kindness to me on so many occasions has touched me deeply. What you said at the Advertising Club about me, the certificate you presented me with accompanying citation, are among the many instances of your kind thoughts of me. I shall treasure the memory of what you have said and done.
>
> Though you and I do not always agree on some matters of policy, nothing has ever interfered with the warm friendship which has existed between us since you were a boy and your friendship I cherish most deeply.[9]

With George, friendship always trumped politics, and he was equally drawn to individuals with a divergent point of view. He sought anyone with good ideas, and eagerly joined in any discussion where ideas were being shared. One of his unlikely friends was H.L. Mencken, renowned Baltimore journalist and George's contemporary. Mencken read George's speeches and often critiqued his use of the English language; the two rarely agreed politically as Mencken was no fan of the New Deal. However, they enjoyed each other's company, and George, never one to take himself too seriously, clearly relished the ribbing that he was often subjected to. As George stated in a 1937 letter in which he was trying to get the Board of Governors of the Maryland Club to accept Mencken as a member:

> I have found his style very interesting, even for instance, in 1934 when he wrote a large article in *The Evening Sun* opposing my election to the United States Senate, the only office for which I had ever been a candidate, and also in that article he advocated the election of my rival. It is needless for me to add that I wasn't enthusiastic over his conclusions, but I enjoyed the style of his article. As far as I know Mr. Mencken has never changed his opinion of me politically. Mr. Mencken's attitude toward me in politics does not, of course, in any way disturb or lessen my friendship for him.[10]

George may have been one of the few U.S. senators to lose money in the position as he claimed to have spent more than double what he received as salary. He remained the gentleman politician throughout his twelve years in the Senate, serving his constituents. To him, every constituent was important, and he practiced what he preached. He claimed to have answered every person who ever wrote him, and his diaries indicate days in which he dictated as many as 300 letters, often working until after midnight to do this. It is ironic that this attention to detail might have cost him reelection in 1946, but George would not have wanted it any other way.

George never wanted to run for political office, but he did feel a responsibility to serve. While politicians today are wrapped in lobbyists, George based his decisions on his extensive reading and knowledge of history and economics. He did not need someone to tell him how to vote.

He also knew that ours was a country built upon a series of compromises; that was what democracy meant to him. He was a friend to all and on more than one occasion was referred to as a "Gentleman from the Eastern Shore." Samuel K. Dennis, a chief judge of the Supreme Bench of Baltimore, said of him "... nor is he partisan. He has an idea his services belong to everyone and anyone. Hence men of high and low degree, of all political affiliations, in business and in office alike find him approachable, amiable, infinitely kind and obliging."[11]

How badly could we use that wisdom, patience, and desire to reach a consensus today. But then would a George Radcliffe even be elected today? He did not come from money or society and gained all through hard work. That work ethic continued until the day he died. To George, politics was service and working to reach a consensus for action; we so desperately need that attitude today. He remained the gentleman throughout his career; that was what his parents had drilled into him. He often was described as an old-school politician, but civility, hard work, and attention to detail should never be old-school values. *Baltimore Sun* writer, John Dorsey, said it best:

> If the art of being a courtly gentleman has largely disappeared from the world, the few men who still practice it with any grace are made the more notable by the scarcity of the breed. George L. Radcliffe is one of the few.
>
> With his gentle humor, his inexhaustible catalogue of reminiscences and stories to enliven conversations, his easy hospitality and his unaffectedly gracious manner one feels in his presence as if taken back for a little while to a different and altogether more agreeable century.[12]

THE MERCHANT MARINE

Senator Radcliffe added a luster to the political picture as very few have ever done. He told me without any trace of boastfulness as to his personal prowess, that a few years before the outbreak of World War II he was appointed chairman of the congressional committee in charge of the building of the much-needed Merchant Marine. To expedite matters and to remove the accumulated dross of legal technicalities, it became necessary to put through Congress nearly 100 bills! This resulted in achieving the largest Merchant Marine not only in our history but in that of the whole world.

I doubt whether many persons, if any, are aware of this amazing accomplishment. This typical-of-him modesty made people unaware of the true greatness of the man, George, as he wanted to be known by his friends.

- Stanislav Rembski, 31 July 1974,
in remembrance of George L. Radcliffe[1]

George may have been a freshman senator when he was sworn in January 3, 1935, but, at the age of fifty-seven, he was no rookie. He was initially put on three Senate committees: Banking and Currency, Commerce, and Library. If experience is a criterion for Senate appointments, then they hit a homerun with George. Thirty years in the banking and insurance world clearly made Banking and Currency a fit, and he served on this committee his entire tenure in the Senate. Whoever thought to put renowned bookworm George L. Radcliffe on the Joint Library Committee deserves a major commendation. This committee largely oversees the Library of Congress, and George would develop a long friendship with its director from 1939–1944, Archibald MacLeish—poet, writer, and three-time recipient of the Pulitzer Prize. George clearly saw in MacLeish, as did Roosevelt, an intellectual, who could take the Library to greater heights. During his career, he also served terms on the Finance and Immigration Committees. However, the Commerce Committee is where George settled in and spent a major portion of his committee time.

The Commerce Committee had two subcommittees: Aviation, and Merchant Marine. George became the chairman of the Merchant Marine subcommittee, and his work there was his most valuable contribution to the U.S. Senate. This was the most logical appointment of all since his father, grandfather, and great-grandfather had all been shipbuilders. His father's two-masted schooners had traveled the oceans, with one purportedly circumnavigating the globe. George had assisted in his father's shipyard well after its heyday, and he knew shipbuilding could have logically been his legacy.

His comprehensive knowledge of history also made him a good fit for this committee, and early in his term, he wrote an extensive history (unpublished) of the U.S. Merchant Marine. He saw the many errors this country had made in the prior century. The United States had been particularly poorly prepared for World War I, and with the world already in turmoil in 1935, he noted that the country was largely dependent on foreign ships for transport.

In many talks, he espoused the value of using history as a basis for moving forward. While we might not want to risk experimenting with the future, the past is a track record we can often rely on. History is littered with instances of the dangers of not anticipating the future and not making necessary preparations. In World War I, by the time the shipbuilding program was initiated, it was too late; the war had ended. George was not going to see history repeat itself.

The average citizen often does not understand that battles and wars are frequently won behind the scenes. In 1812, Napoleon may have had one of the most massive armies ever assembled but failed completely in his invasion of Russia. While disease, terrain, and weather played key roles, his failure to plan supply logistics adequately was clearly a key factor in his failure. Not only did events play out longer than he planned, but the supply train could also not keep up with his troops.[2] (Ironically the Germans would basically make the same error in World War II.) George, from this and countless other moments in history, knew that the U.S. military efforts could only be as good as its ability to transport troops and supply them quickly and adequately. This is where the Merchant Marine is so critical. As George stated:

> After the Revolutionary War, and again after the War of 1812, we had an opportunity to control world shipping. At one time in the heyday of our clipper ships, we handled much of the interocean trade of other countries and about ninety percent of our own exports and imports, but we permitted this supremacy to slip away as we turned inward to the conquest of the Far West.
>
> At the beginning of the first World War, we were brought sharply to the realization that our foreign commerce was handled almost entirely by ships of other nations. In many cases, ships owned by American citizens were being sailed under foreign registry to avoid expenses and restrictions which would have been necessary under the American flag.
>
> Suddenly, most of these vessels ceased to carry our commodities. We had to have ships, and quickly. We built

2,000 bottoms or more, but not a single one of these new ships crossed the ocean before the Armistice. Nevertheless, they gave us the equipment for a dominant merchant fleet.

And what did we do with them? Nothing. We sold some ships for a few dollars a ton—ships that had cost as much as $200 a ton to build—and countless others were tied up in our harbors and allowed to rot. We know one reason this happened. It was impossible then—as it is impossible now—for Americans to build and operate ships cheaply as other nations, due to high labor costs and higher standards.[3]

No one wanted war in 1936, but the world was starting to become a turbulent place, and genuine peace had definitely not resulted from the end of World War I. Hitler was Fuhrer in Germany—which had left the League of Nations and violated the Treaty of Versailles; Mussolini and Italy had moved into Ethiopia; Japan had also left the League of Nations and was creating turmoil in Asia. In his position on the Merchant Marine subcommittee, George knew what had to be done but faced several obstacles. Economics made it unprofitable for the U.S. to build and operate ships, the infrastructure for shipbuilding was seriously inadequate, and few in Congress saw any urgency, with most thinking war unlikely. At that time, the country had only six shipyards, and it would take several years to get new yards up and running. George remembered what had happened in World War I, and he drafted the Merchant Marine Act of 1936 in the Senate with similar action occurring in the House. On June 29, the Senate approved the bill, and Roosevelt signed it into law the next day.

The Merchant Marine Act of 1936 would completely transform the United States Merchant Marine, and large-scale ship production was underway by the time the U.S. entered the war. While others were involved with the bill in the House, George would be recognized as a major architect. In his characteristic, humble way, he would take little credit, but his hard work surely was the reason the bill was able to rise above the complacency which existed at the time toward the Merchant Marine. He would later say that two-thirds of his hours in the Senate were devoted to the Merchant Marine subcommittee. His counterpart in the House, and probably even more significant overall, was Schuyler Otis Bland (1872–1950) from Virginia who was chairman of the Merchant Marine and Fisheries Committee for years.[4]

The 1936 bill, amended in 1938, cleared out many of the obstacles to ship construction. Probably most important, it created a United States Maritime Commission which would prioritize and oversee the increased production of ships. This full-time commission would report directly to Congress and be authorized to cut through some of the existing red tape. To deal with the fact that foreign countries could build ships more cheaply than the U.S., the U.S. could subsidize fifty percent of the cost of new ship construction. This had previously been done through many messy and sometimes corrupt ocean-mail contracts, and these were cancelled. To limit foreign involvement, foreigners working in construction and as crew on the ships themselves were limited with the Act stipulating that ninety percent of the workers must be American citizens.[5]

What was severely lacking in 1936 was the infrastructure to build ships. Even with the red tape removed and subsidies in place, there were only six shipyards in the U.S. Even more significant, the shipyards were concentrated on the Northeast coast, and George foresaw that shipbuilding would have to occur on the Atlantic, Pacific, and Gulf Coasts.[6] By 1941, the total had been increased to sixteen shipyards.[7] By 1943, the plan was to expand to seventy shipyards.[8] The 1936 act provided for the construction of 500 ships during the next ten years, but this rate would increase as we entered the war. When Great Britain entered the war in 1939, President Roosevelt dramatically increased the rate of production, and a new more economical design was used. In addition to regular construction, the nation started building what were basically prefabricated ships.

The first of these ships, the *Patrick Henry*, was launched in Baltimore on September 27, 1941. George, always a Marylander first, was especially proud to acknowledge in his national radio broadcast that this ship had been built by Bethlehem Steel in Baltimore.[9] Because of Patrick Henry's famous line in a speech, "Give me liberty or give me death," these ships came to be known as Liberty Ships. Over 2,700 were produced. When the president was reviewing the design, he referred to the ship as an "ugly duckling," and this became its nickname. By 1943, a faster ship was needed, and the new ships were called Victory Ships. Through the efforts of George's committee and the work of the Maritime Commission under Admiral Emory Land, the U.S. was able to produce some 5,500 vessels. George's dream of building a strong Merchant Marine was more than realized.[10]

In addition to the extensive shipbuilding, the entire US shipping industry needed to become more efficient. Under the direction of the Maritime Commission, shipowners worked with the Government to add cargo needed to supply naval and air bases and to help import the raw materials needed for the increased ship production and expanding industry. Ships carrying cargo abroad now never returned empty. This was done without impacting the basic military ship construction. By 1941, all the pieces were in place, and the United States was becoming the dominant sea power. The United States was also able to supply Great Britain with ships as that country was entering the war.[11]

Launching of the **Patrick Henry** *on September 2, 1941 in Baltimore, Maryland*

One of the reasons George felt he was successful with Merchant Marine bills was the lack of partisanship on his committee. George's career would see him resist partisanship, and he always sought to bridge differences with individuals. Almost unheard of in today's world, he had the proxy of all three Republican senators on his subcommittee.[12] Part of this nonpartisanship resulted from the urgency of the work being done, especially when war seemed imminent, but George's experience in deal-making in his Fidelity and Deposit work paid off on this committee.

As the war was winding down, George's work was not yet done. The question now arose of what to do with all these ships. While George did not want to see the same mistake made as happened after World War I, there still would be a surplus of ships. He advocated for shipping subsidies to keep many of these ships in operation as an insurance policy against a future war. He and others recommended keeping a significant number of active ships, with others kept in reserve. He wanted subsidies continued with at least fifty percent of foreign trade being done with American ships.[13] Keeping the shipbuilding infrastructure was key, but he and others felt that the post-war period would see an increase in foreign trade, thus justifying the ships.

Over his tenure on the subcommittee, George authored or introduced well over 100 bills related to the Merchant Marine. Leaving the Senate in 1947 obviously meant that he would no longer serve on the Merchant Marine subcommittee, but this hardly ended his involvement. He often spoke to groups concerning the importance of not letting the Merchant Marine lapse again as had been done after World War I. He used his friendship with Truman to reinforce the importance of keeping many of the ships, but more importantly to maintain the infrastructure necessary to build them. Most of his letters to the president carried a plug for the Merchant Marine. In 1954, fearing that the U.S. was again letting the Merchant Marine lapse, George wrote an editorial, once again giving the issue some historical context and ending with:

We have again slipped back into a situation which experience has shown to be extremely dangerous. Today we haven't enough up-to-date ships nor an adequate building program in operation. The sudden outbreak of a new war would expose us to grave dangers on the seas because of our lack of adequate shipping. It is inconceivable that our people do not realize the gravity of the situation.

An adequate shipbuilding program requires the doing of many things besides actual ship construction. We haven't a moment to lose. We should start building ships as quickly as possible and, in doing so, get the closest cooperation between government and industry.[14]

The editorial did get noticed by Helen Delich, at that time a local reporter with an interest in the Port of Baltimore. Helen Delich Bentley (1923–2016, R-MD, 2nd District) always had a maritime interest, and she corresponded with George on many occasions. She would later serve as chairman of the Federal Maritime Commission and on the House Committee on Merchant Marine and Fisheries. In later years she would praise George's efforts in the Senate to build up the Merchant Marine.

Years later, atypical of him, George would openly talk with pride of his efforts to build a substantial Merchant Marine. It was clear to all that this was the Senate accomplishment of which he was most proud. Although George would never come outright and say it, one of the reasons for Allied success in World War II was the fact that we had a strong Merchant Marine, and key to that was that the groundwork for this was laid over five years before the U.S. entered the war. As he often cited, history allows us to learn from mistakes and to not make the same mistake twice. Sadly, in the history of this great country, politics and too much of a focus on the here and now often blinds us to the past. George L. Radcliffe was a historian rather than a politician. He understood the need for politics, the practicality of getting ideas turned into action, but he never lost sight of the essential historical context. In recognition of George's work, the Maryland Historical Society would name its maritime museum after him. The son of shipbuilder John Anthony LeCompte Radcliffe may never have built a boat himself, but he certainly kept up the family business in a significant way.

Note: The full text of George L. Radcliffe's 1941 radio address on the Merchant Marine is found in Appendix 5.

A Friend from Missouri

On January 3, 1935, George L. Radcliffe was sworn in as the United States senator from Maryland. All eleven new senators sworn in that day were Democrats; Franklin Roosevelt's popularity was contagious. George would connect with this small group over the years. He and Joseph Guffey from Pennsylvania worked closely together for twelve years, communicated often, and got together socially on numerous occasions. He always kept in close contact with Indiana's Sherman Minton, whom President Truman would nominate as associate judge of the Supreme Court in 1949. However, it was the new senator from Missouri who became a lifelong friend. That senator would become the thirty-third president of the United States in 1945 upon the death of Franklin Roosevelt. Harry Truman was quite different from George L. Radcliffe, but there was a mutual respect which connected them over the years. George and Harry wrote each other often, and George visited Bess and Harry occasionally in Independence, Missouri.

One of their first social outings together—an event about which George and Truman often reminisced—was a 1937 hunting trip in Pennsylvania organized by that state's senator, Joe Guffey. Guffey was joined by a group of Democratic senators and Vice President John Nance Garner. George and Harry were both part of that group.[1] What is ironic is that George did not hunt. His older brother Sewell was quite the hunter, but if George had ever held a gun before, it would have been a rarity.

The hunt was apparently a dismal failure with only Vice Present Garner making a kill. Apparently, a story circulated that Garner had in fact shot a cow, obviously not true. As the group sat down for a post-hunt dinner with Garner's deer on the menu, a letter arrived from President Roosevelt to Garner and was read to the group:

Dear Jack,

I have read in the paper that tonight you and twenty-four members of the Senate are attending the funeral of my old friend Bessie. I knew her many years ago when I was hunting in Northern Pennsylvania. She was the pet of the camp and would always come when you whistled and eat out of your hand.

I am sorry indeed that Joe Guffey removed the tinkling little bell which was always worn around her neck. It makes me feel so chokey when I think about her untimely demise that I do not think I could attend the funeral service tonight even if I had been invited.

I understand fully, of course, that this unfortunate hunting accident was not your fault—and I am glad, too, that if Bessie had to go, you shot her instead of whistling her up and cutting her throat with a knife. Dear Bessie probably never knew what hit her.

Under all the unfortunate circumstances attending her death, I hope, nevertheless, that all of you will enjoy the wake.

- FDR[2]

George and Harry served on different committees in the Senate, but common interests connected them early on. Their friendship in many ways was an unlikely one. George was seven years older, but by 1935, both were well seasoned professionally. The younger Truman had served in World War I while George served stateside during the war. There is no reason that their paths would have crossed before 1935. They were different individuals in many ways; "give em Hell" Harry was known for his colorful language and no hesitancy to confront, while George was much more refined and never known to utter a profane word.

Hunting Party with George L. Radcliffe and Sen. Harry S. Truman
Left to right: Truman, Sen. Clyde Herring, Sen. Carl Hatch, Radcliffe,
Polish Ambassador Count Jerzy Potocki, Sen. Joseph Guffey, Col. William
Kaul, Vice-President John Nance Garner, Sen. Sherman Minton, and Sen.
James Murray on December 2, 1935

However, both had a love of history and music, fostered by their mothers, and both had grown up on farms. Both were Masons and also belonged to many organizations. However, the farm backgrounds and history are what certainly connected them. No one ever had a conversation with George L. Radcliffe without some reference to his growing up on the Spocott farm, and any mention of history would launch George into a story or anecdote. Their later letters show these common interests were more than enough foundation for a relationship. Truman was often referred to as the "common man," a title that would have fit George equally. While he was far more formally educated than Truman, George always considered himself first and foremost a simple farm boy. Both George and Harry came from slave-owning families and from areas of the country still ripe with racial prejudice, but both believed in the decency of every person.

No one escaped George's near obsession with his family history. In a conversation with Harry Truman at a dinner at the Maryland Club in March of 1945, they began discussing one of George's favorite subjects, genealogy, and Truman mentioned that he had heard that the first Truman ancestor may have settled in Maryland. That was all George needed to launch into an investigation of any Maryland Truman. When George had time after leaving the Senate, he was able to put together a complete set of records for the president in 1948.[3]

George supported Roosevelt's choice of Truman for the Democratic ticket in 1944, finding him more moderate than Henry Wallace, but he was virtually alone in the insurance industry in supporting the Roosevelt-Truman ticket. Shortly after the election, George invited Truman to speak at the Maryland Historical Society. He had mined his political connections in Washington to provide a steady stream of informative speakers throughout the war years. He now had an opportunity to get the vice president to speak, and with Truman's interest in history, he was a perfect choice. George was accomplishing two goals: securing a good speaker, and enlarging the base of the historical society. Truman spoke on March 27, 1945, on "Maryland's Historic Doctrine of Toleration as Applicable to Present Day International Problems."[4] Little did the two know that two weeks later Truman would be president of the United States.

Shortly after Truman assumed the presidency, George made a major radio address in which he threw desperately needed public support behind the new president:

> President Truman and I were sworn in as members of the
> United States Senate on the same day, January 3, 1935,
> and we soon came in close contact with each other. We

agree on many points. We remembered John Sharp William's description of the United States Senate as a "cave of the winds." Both President Truman and I expressed belief that the value of making set speeches in the Senate is grossly exaggerated; that while many speeches are explanatory or persuasive, slogans and catchphrases and especially denunciatory language may attract attention, but seldom are illuminating or convincing, in the Senate or out of it. Again and again, he regretted that people do not realize sufficiently that the operations of the Senate are really a vast business enterprise, and that hard work, industry, and clearness of vision are as essential in the United States Senate as in any other place in the world.

Frequently, during the presidential campaign of 1944, I said in my speeches that if Truman should ever become the president of the United States, he would serve the people well, and he is doing so. He is modest and delights in no illusions of grandeur. He has shown he can be quick to act, and yet act wisely. He is firm in the position he takes, and he is his own president.[5]

George had the president's ear these next two years, and he visited the White House often. His chairmanship of the Merchant Marine subcommittee was occupying much of his time, and with the war ending, downsizing the U.S. Merchant Marine was front and center. He kept this issue in front of the president with numerous letters and visits. After George left the Senate, he would still be a frequent visitor to the Senate and the White House. On April 1, 1947, he resumed a routine that he had carried out several times with Roosevelt. He showed up at the White House with a pot of terrapin soup, one of George's favorites.

George also got President Truman involved in two of his pet projects:

returning the *USS Constellation* to Baltimore, and erecting a memorial in Brooklyn to honor the brave Marylanders who died there in the Revolutionary War. George would write the president numerous times about these issues even after leaving the Senate.

In 1948, George chaired the Maryland Democratic Convention and led the delegation to the Democratic National Convention, making a pro-Truman speech which put the election in the proper historical context.[6] Shortly afterwards, Harry Truman would ask George to chair the Democratic campaign in Maryland. While the Southern Democrats that George sided with often had reservations about supporting the president, he enthusiastically took on the job. In responding to Truman's request on August 11, George wrote:

> My strong desire is to do exactly what you suggest because of our long friendship and also because I am eager to see you be reelected.
>
> At this moment some factors in Maryland may be favorable, others do not foot up that way just now. For instance, Maryland is quite Southern in its viewpoints. The Doctrine of States Rights, vague as it is in many respects, is deeply cherished in Maryland. There is much anxiety in regard to the communistic activities in this country and abroad, and too little realization of what the federal administration has already done to ferret out, and too little realization that many of the methods of the congressional investigating committee are un-American and unfair.[7]

While George often sided with the Southern Democrats, he did not in this election. Many of them were not pleased with Truman's civil rights positions, and with Strom Thurmond entering the race as a Dixiecrat, many would throw their support behind him. While George also opposed excess intervention by the federal government, he, as did Truman, wanted all treated with respect. Truman would also lose many of the liberal Democrats as Roosevelt's first vice president, Henry Wallace, was running as a Progressive. Despite George's efforts, Truman did not carry Maryland, although he won the presidency over Thomas Dewey in the famous election surprise. During the next four years, Truman would have to deal with the increasing threat of communism, the Korean War, and his unpopular firing of General Douglas MacArthur.

George would continue to be one of Truman's staunchest allies, and many of his letters to others express his support of and admiration for the president:

> I have confidence in his integrity, and I also believe that he has a natural framework of conservatism. He is in good spirits and doesn't show any vindictive attitude of mind because of the fight of the Democrats against him or because finances and practically all of big business lined up solidly against him."[8]

Truman left the presidency with a historically low popularity rating, but he never lost George's support. George wrote him, voicing his eternal support:

> I will risk whatever reputation I may have as a historian that the Truman administration will occupy a high niche for efficiency in history. What is being done today in the international field would have been impossible had it not been for the highly efficient and sound foundation which Roosevelt and you laid. The United Nations, the Marshall Plan, and the various other associations and combinations have been indispensable toward obtaining any real stabilization. Very few people now would dare make the assertion that you rushed headlong into the Korean War. All your critics realize and admit that you really

had no other course which you could follow with honor and safety.[9]

After the election, George was asked to be a trustee of the planned Harry S. Truman Library in Missouri. He helped to ensure the success of the project and was present at the library's dedication on July 6, 1957. This was the first of several trips to Independence, Missouri, to visit his old friend. The two wrote each other throughout the ensuing years until this last letter came from the ex-president in 1970:

> Dear George,
>
> I was delighted to hear from you and would like nothing more than to have a visit from you, but, to my regret, it is not possible to make an appointment this far in advance. I would suggest that you write sometime in July, and we will see what the situation is at that time.
>
> With best wishes as always,
>
> Sincerely yours,
>
> Harry Truman[10]

Sadly, this visit never happened, and from that point on George's letters were answered by Bess Truman. Harry Truman died in 1972. George was also failing at this point, and one old warrior would join the other in 1974. Two farm boys rose to the heights of power and influence and made a difference, each in his own way.

THE CONTRADICTION

In his 1900 defense of his Ph.D. dissertation on Maryland's entry into the Civil War, George L. Radcliffe told the reviewers they would never be able to discern whether he was a Northern or Southern sympathizer, and he was quite successful in doing this, a fact of which he was quite proud. Similarly, no one ever heard publicly how George felt about civil rights issues. Born shortly after the Civil War into a family with Confederate leanings, he lived to see significant civil rights legislation and Supreme Court decisions. Many in his generation retained old biases, but George never overtly exhibited any segregationist views. No family member or close friend ever heard him make a negative comment about any minority, but then rarely, if ever, did he have a negative word to say about anyone. He, as his father, believed in the value of all, regardless of their race, religion, or economic status, but his Senate record sometimes showed a voting pattern which contradicted these beliefs.

George grew up at Spocott in a racially mixed community. His father owned enslaved workers before the Civil War, and several of them continued to live and work on the property after the war. He remembered at least one of his relatives was upset with his playing with some of the Black children as a boy, but he enjoyed these children and also grew very close to Adaline Wheatley, the cook. George obviously had educational and work opportunities that were not available to most in the Black community, and he would move on to work in a predominantly white world.

We do know there were two groups for whom he strongly advocated throughout his life. He was a strong proponent of women's rights, sponsoring an equal rights amendment in his second term. As early as 1939, he worked for the Jewish right to a homeland in Palestine, making many speeches and attending numerous rallies. A 1946 rally poster billed him as "a champion of Jewish rights in Palestine." However, there is little evidence that he worked to improve conditions for minorities. Although he may have believed in the equality and value of all, he seemed at a loss for how to achieve true equality.

There was no question that he cared deeply for Adaline Wheatley and the other members of the Spocott community. His letters often affectionately mention these individuals, and he thought of them as family. His son, George M. Radcliffe, remembered the care that his father exhibited to these workers, and it was clear to all that George L. respected and did much to give them a good life. The best indicator of George L. Radcliffe's actual beliefs was probably found in his son, George M., a lawyer and lifelong advocate of racial justice and advancement. Young George was an officer in the Army Air Corps while his father was in his second term in the Senate and was known for his fair treatment of the Black soldiers under his command. He took an interest in them and earned the respect of all. If his father, George L., had been truly prejudiced in his thinking, it seems unlikely his son would have been so open about embracing minorities.

Adaline, almost a second mother to him, was special to George, often found in family photos, and a frequent companion on road trips that George's wife, Daisy, took. George would also find the funding for a marker commemorating Harriet Tubman, but sadly much of his political record falls far short of helping lift up the Adaline's of the world. It was as if when George left Spocott for Baltimore or Washington that he left the plight of Adaline and her race behind.

His letters to Black businessmen and college officials show that he had built up a number of strong relationships with these individuals, and on at least one occasion, we can see him writing a letter of recommendation for a Black associate. He spoke numerous times in front of minority audiences, and while he advocated for the economic advancement of Blacks, his words often lacked specifics and sometimes are more about history, his favorite topic. In a speech to the annual convention of the National Negro Business League in 1943, he said:

> It is clear to everyone that we will not avail ourselves properly of these opportunities if we do not show the proper sense of responsibility, that is, responsibility which leads us to handle fairly and squarely the questions that are rising nationally and internationally. Opportunities to see that all elements of our society, racial or otherwise, are given a fair chance to work out and operate to the best advantage of our country and ourselves. This means that the members of the colored race should have increased opportunities for useful endeavor. This means that the members of the colored race and the members of the white race should, working in close cooperation, take increased advantage of these opportunities for usefulness.[1]

In the Senate, his committee assignments involved him with commerce and finance, not social issues. He did get involved with issues in Maryland, and on matters with racial overtones, he usually tried to take a conciliatory position. In a 1942 controversy over the placement of Black housing in Anne Arundel County, Maryland, George gave in to pressure from white residents opposed to the proposed property. "It is self-evident that something must be done to provide adequate housing for migrant Negroes, but it does not help anybody to establish such a housing project in an area where public sentiment is so strongly against it."[2]

In 1937, George supported President Roosevelt's nomination of Senator Hugo Black for Associate Justice of the Supreme Court of the United States. When it was then revealed that Black had been a member of the Ku Klux Klan in Alabama, there was a move by many to vote against his nomination. Black claimed that he had left the Klan upon becoming senator in 1927. Although George ultimately did vote for Black, he made it clear that he would never support a Klan member for such a position:

I cannot imagine anyone joining such an organization as the Klan. The ideas of the Klan would unquestionably make a man unfit to sit on the Supreme Bench of the United States. Much depends on the present views of the man. Perhaps Senator Black did join the Klan years ago. I would want to know what his record has been since, and what his views are today.[3]

Convinced that Hugo Black was no longer a Klan member and that he was well qualified otherwise for the position, George, after considerable thought, voted for the appointment. This was a typical George L, Radcliffe approach to a problem: view each issue with an open mind, while withholding an opinion until carefully examining all the facts. Criticized by some in Maryland for his vote, George was willing to overlook Hugo Black's past. Ironically Justice Black would go on to be a major advocate of civil rights while on the court.

Throughout his two terms in the Senate, George tended to take a more conservative viewpoint regarding civil rights. In 1946, when he was running for a third term in the Senate, *The Baltimore Afro-American* supported his opponent, saying that George's voting record was "reactionary" and did nothing to advance the plight of the Afro-American community.[4]

His voting record often showed that he resisted what he deemed unnecessary government intervention, and in 1954, although no longer in the Senate, George expressed reservations about the Brown vs. Board of Education ruling. He claimed that several of his Black acquaintances felt, as did he, that forcing integration might negatively affect the advancement of Blacks as this federal intervention might undo some of the progress which had already been made.

During his time in the Senate, George worked closely with some of the southern Democrats. He corresponded often with Virginia senator Harry F. Byrd, Sr. (1887–1966), well-known for his opposition to racial desegregation. Although they respected each other, George never indicated any support for these views of Byrd's. While Byrd was very opposed to Truman's election in 1948, George ran Truman's Maryland campaign.

He also wrote often to an old Hopkins classmate of his, James McIlhany Thomson (1878–1959), a prominent newspaper publisher. James was an extreme conservative and a rabid anti-Communist, as he also saw communism as a door through which racial integration would enter. He and George did share an opposition to excessive governmental intervention, but George neither agreed with nor disapproved of Thomson's excessive views. When Thomson suggested Sen. Byrd as a presidential candidate, George certainly opposed that.

Never in George's letters to either Byrd or Thomson does he show any support for their racist views, yet neither does he criticize their positions. He more often launched into some historical dissertation or some bit of family news. It was George's nature to build bridges rather than criticize. His failure to take a stand against their racist positions is surprising. For someone who cared as deeply as he did for Adaline, why would he not stand up for her and criticize comments which were clearly to the detriment of Blacks. While always the peacemaker, George appeared to condone these racist views by tolerating them.

Interestingly enough, George's views matched those of President Roosevelt, who, although in favor of the advancement of Blacks, was hesitant to do anything which would lose him the support of southern Democrats. Although Roosevelt was doing little to advance their plight, Blacks clearly appreciated the economic gains all had made with the New Deal legislation. The southern Democrats, however, started to break with Roosevelt when they saw his proposed 1937 packing of the Supreme Court as a way for Roosevelt to gain more socially liberal court support. George, who often sided with southern Democrats, opposed the Supreme Court packing for more complicated reasons, but clearly his alignment with the southern Democrats was a factor.[5]

Basically, everything in his political life seemed aimed at keeping peace. He made his reputation in the insurance world as a magnificent dealmaker and his company would always send him in to settle the most difficult cases. He was much less of an advocate unless the topic was his beloved history. His positions were not an acceptance of segregation but a belief that equality of races would ultimately result from gradual change. What George seemed to be opposed to was government interference. While this might seem to be an odd belief for a New Dealer, George's conservative background, honed by surety work, was at his core. His reputation as a New Dealer came early on from his association with Roosevelt and his belief that government should intervene in an emergency. He did not view race relations as needing this intervention.

His life seems a contradiction when examining his views toward race. In his personal life, he cared about Adaline and those remarkable Black workers at Spocott, but this caring did not seem to transfer to his business and political life. He was like many whites in that period—caring for the Blacks they knew but content to accept the status quo. He grew up and studied history which was slanted toward a white-centered world and attended white schools, churches, and social organizations. He may have wanted the best for Adaline and others of her race and certainly treated them kindly, but largely failed to act to improve their lot. His conservatism from his insurance background and his opposition to excessive government intervention prohibited him from being a strong civil rights advocate, but his father's beliefs and George's love for Adaline, instilled in George a desire to see racial equality. He tolerated the often-racist world around him, having faith that time would create true equality. George L. Radcliffe was not a perfect man, and he would have been the first to tell one that. Throughout his life, he evolved slowly as the world changed around him. His heart was always in the right place, but his willingness to just let time bring the races together was not the plan this country needed.

The 1946 Election: His Only Defeat

Georgge L. Radcliffe only lost one election in his entire life; the man who had easily won election to the United States Senate in 1934 and soundly won reelection in 1940 in a hard-fought campaign was easily defeated in the Democratic primary in his bid for a third term in 1946, an election he initially thought he was going to win. Knowing the man and the way he approached his time in the Senate, it is actually not surprising that George lost. He took the defeat in stride, and the loss just marked the beginning of the next phase of his life.

George probably could have won the general election, but he was not expecting to go down to defeat in the Democratic primary. In June of 1946, he lost to Herbert O'Conor, governor of Maryland, by a significant vote, winning only a handful of counties, and losing Baltimore City by a large margin. Twelve years had not only changed the political landscape but changed the New Dealer and presidential ally. An examination of these changes reveals why George's defeat was almost inevitable.

Age

George L. Radcliffe turned sixty-nine in 1946 while his primary opponent, Herbert O'Conor, was forty-nine and a popular two-term governor. The average age of a U.S. senator at that time was fifty-nine,[1] and while George was hardly an antique, his older age was certainly an issue. His son, George, often cited his father's age as the primary reason for his defeat. Balancing this negative was his experience, and this was clearly used as an asset in the campaign.

Charisma Often Trumps Experience

No one ever referred to George L. Radcliffe as a colorful figure.

Warm, congenial, experienced, and diligent fit him better, and George never sought attention. He never condoned colleagues who sought the limelight and seemed to like to hear themselves talk. George felt he should only make a speech when it was absolutely essential. He did not shy from the public and was a frequent speaker for civic groups. His speeches were never fiery oratory, but charming talks interspersed with historical anecdotes or personal stories. After twelve years, many in Maryland were looking for a change, a younger and more charismatic candidate rather than the warm grandfatherly figure that some saw in George.

CHANGING POLITICAL ORIENTATION

All assumed in 1934 that, with his election to the Senate, George would be FDR's reliable New Deal supporter. As Roosevelt's close friend and former boss (although the two were both vice presidents of different offices of the Fidelity and Deposit Company of Maryland), the press painted him as Roosevelt's "yes man" in the Senate. Initially this appeared to be true as George supported the Social Security Act and many of the early "alphabet" programs put forth to help lift the country out of the Depression. However, George earned his wings in the financial world where he was clearly a fiscal conservative. He often said that his early years in the Senate involved a lot of necessary emergency legislation, but as the country moved past the Depression, there was a need for fiscal restraint. He also urged caution as he saw the potential for government overextending itself.

By George's second term, he was no longer the New Deal champion, often breaking party to vote with the Republicans on fiscal matters. Herbert O'Conor was considered a true New Dealer, and was thus more appealing to many of the state Democratic leaders. O'Conor had the support of labor, initially a strong part of George's support base. The Congress of Industrial Organizations (CIO), which had strongly supported Roosevelt, now supported O'Conor.

MARYLAND DEMOCRATIC PARTY POLITICS

As was his nature, George Radcliffe was not one to dabble in back-room political wheeling and dealing. To him, extensive research was far more important than politicking. He accepted the role as a responsibility to serve rather than a way to achieve power. He had been asked early in his first term to play the role of Democratic party boss. As U.S. senator and close friend to the president, he was well-suited for such a role but wanted no part of it. He always voted a bill on its merits and not on what the party dictated. In 1940, fellow Maryland Senator Millard Tydings supported him, largely as payback for George supporting him and managing his campaign in 1938. However, after that, although there was clearly mutual respect between the two, Tydings was lukewarm in his support of George. Rumors began that Tydings had become closely allied with Governor O'Conor, and although Tydings would basically deny this, George clearly felt that political forces were beginning to align against him. In the 1946 election, Tydings remained neutral at best.[2]

In late 1945, Maryland Democratic leaders tried to draw George away from his position as senator, hoping to get what they termed a more "deserving Democrat." Because George had initially filed for governor in 1934, they thought they could convince him to run for that position, after luring O'Conor away from running for a third term by offering him a lucrative federal position. George felt that with his legislative experience and key roles on certain committees, the Senate was where he belonged.[3] Although nothing came out of all this political chess, it was clear that George would not have unified Democratic support in 1946. O'Conor, in fact, would not run for a third term and would challenge George in the June primary.

GEORGE WAS A GENTLEMAN.

The two-term Senator came under considerable criticism in the 1946 election, and many wondered why he did not turn more combative during that campaign. While attacking his opponent more aggressively likely would not have changed the outcome, this was not in his nature. George was a peacemaker, not a fighter. He could debate any point, but he never became personal in arguing with an opponent. He simply thought his record would speak for itself.

> People advise me 'to stand up and denounce' this and that. I am not by nature cruel; I shrink from causing people pain or mortification. I have no commission, no duty to denounce; and I doubt the sportsmanship of denouncing when protected by Senatorial immunity from suit for statements made in the Senate. Besides denouncing in lieu of consultation, consideration, and patience has caused the world enough hurt already. Vituperation [bitter and abusive language] is neither as legitimate or as convincing as my votes, which express my views impressively and often.[4]

HIS CUP RUNNETH OVER

George may have become more conservative by 1946, but O'Conor rarely used issues in attacking his opponent. His primary line of attack was citing George's frequent absence from the Senate. While this was clearly exaggerated, George was noticeably absent several days in May of 1946, and when Truman called the Senate to action on several labor issues, by chance, George was busy campaigning that day. O'Conor seized on this absence to drive home his point. "I am disappointed that when the nation's fate was hanging in the balance, Senator Radcliffe was not at his post of duty to uphold the courageous action of President Truman and to defend the integrity of the American free enterprise system."[5] George, in fact, had left his opinions with colleagues and was on call to return for any key vote.

By George's admission, O'Conor's charge had a small element of truth. Senator George Radcliffe's schedule was so full that he was often too busy to campaign. To compound matters, his Senate committee work involved more time than normal in early 1946, and he would only infrequently go out on the campaign trail. He was working on the development of several key pieces of legislation: a bill for the OPA (Office of Price Administration), an immigration bill, a farm loan bill, and a Federal Housing Administration bill, all particularly relevant to his constituents.[6] George was also an active vice president and attorney for the Fidelity and Deposit Company of Maryland, chairman of the executive committee for several organizations, president of the Maryland Historical Society, and Maryland chairman of the March of Dimes. He left most campaigning to friends and family, and he was able to make it only to a handful of Maryland's twenty-three counties.

THE FINAL NAIL IN THE COFFIN

As the election drew near, George still believed he could win. Although running against a popular governor, George thought his record would lead him to victory. He had, after all, won reelection in 1940, winning both the primary and general elections by a significant vote. However, early in 1946, he made several unpopular votes, including voting in favor of an anti-strike bill; labor was now definitely supporting his opponent. The local African American paper, *The Afro*, endorsed O'Conor,[7] and the polls were showing defeat was possible. He headed out for some last-minute campaigning, and as fate would have it, this would backfire. The OPA price control bill was being debated, and the House had passed a compromise. The Senate committee, with George absent, voted 3-3, and it was assumed that George would break the tie in favor of the Democratic-favored price controls.[8]

At the last minute, George rushed into the room and shocked all by voting against the measure, effectively killing it for the short-term. While George had been known to occasionally vote with the Republicans, no one suspected that he would side with them on this crucial issue. However, this was not inconsistent with how his views had evolved: less government interference, and more support of free enterprise. News of his vote quickly reached the state right before the election and likely sealed his fate.

———◆———

Turnout was low on election day, particularly in more rural areas where George always had strong support. George pointed out that many farmers were busy planting and did not have time to vote. O'Conor won by a significant margin and went on to win in the general election in a close race, a real contrast to George's almost 2-to-1 blowout of his Republican opponent in the 1940 election.

Letters to his friends and family show that he was surprised and briefly shaken by his loss, but he was too busy with other endeavors and his last six months in the Senate to focus on the loss for long. At age sixty-nine, this loss would have ended the career of many, but retirement was not in the cards for George L. Radcliffe, who would remain civically and politically active. Most of the lifetime achievements of which George was most proud would happen in these post-Senate years. He told all that he would take a long-overdue vacation, well-deserved since he had not taken a single vacation in the past twelve years. However, this was a man who could not sit for long, and that vacation would be a short one. He soon rolled up his sleeves and focused on the Fidelity and Deposit work, the Historical Society, the March of Dimes, and his numerous historical preservation projects. In 1947, the once-senator from Maryland became even busier, and he was now free to return to his real passions: history, family heritage, and his many civic causes.

Essays

Civic Responsibility

His Society

I am inclined to list him as the greatest chairman in Maryland history.

> - Maryland Governor Theodore McKeldin,
> speaking of George Radcliffe in 1955[1]

During the mid-twentieth century, if one needed something done in Maryland, the person to call on was George L. Radcliffe. With his extensive legal expertise, reputation as a dealmaker at his surety firm, financial experience, and reputation for hard work and attention to details, George, for half a century, was heavily sought after by organizations for leadership and guidance. His years of civic service began early in his career, and he was still volunteering and serving on committees in his late eighties, long after most of his peers had retired. It is difficult to say what led him to such levels of involvement: his education and experience initially, and later the desire of organizations to have a U.S. senator on one's board or committee. However, first and foremost, connecting George L. Radcliffe with an organization brought a masterful fundraiser, an unparalleled organizer, and one of the most congenial individuals a group could ever hope for. George organized campaigns, raised money for large capital projects, hosted dinners, increased the membership of numerous organizations, and was master of ceremonies for more dinners and events than the reader would ever have time to read about. This also explains why he seldom ate dinner at home for many years.

His diary reveals the extent of his involvement. On a typical day he might start in Washington, then drive to Baltimore for Fidelity and De-

posit business, then return to Washington for a Senate vote or committee meeting, and finally return one more time to Baltimore to speak at a
civic meeting, followed by attending another meeting after dinner. One
Christmas Eve, his schedule shows that he attended six Christmas parties
in support of his numerous civic affiliations. On one day, he was in Baltimore twice and Washington twice before ending up in New York City in
the evening. The man never took a vacation, and his chauffeur and friend,
Swain Foxwell, was one busy man.

George knew that his secretaries were the life blood of his work, and
he treasured them, always treating them as equals. Keeping track of his
mind-boggling schedule and the often 200 to 300 letters he would dictate
in a day was a Herculean task. During one stretch, he claimed he was sign-
ing 600 to 700 letters a day—and without a word processor or computer.
The fact that he treated these remarkable individuals well was proven by
their length of service with him. Dena Cohen, his Baltimore secretary for
more years than anyone could remember, was a jewel, and George cherished her. Many a day, she worked well past quitting time. Bertha Joseph,
his Washington secretary for his time in the Senate, was mentioned once
as a possible congresswoman, and went on to be a congressional liaison
officer and State Department official; keeping up with George L. Radcliffe for twelve years had trained her well.[2] These remarkable individuals
were advisors to him in many ways, and George made sure that they received the recognition they deserved.

What made George particularly successful in his leadership roles was
his extensive list of connections in many venues: his time at Johns Hopkins University and his numerous alumni responsibilities, his acquaintances at the clubs he belonged to, his Maryland and Washington political
connections, his many years with the Maryland Historical Society, and
the wide array of individuals he kept in close contact with via his extensive letter writing. George was a true people person, and his numerous acquaintances gave him an almost unlimited reservoir of talent to tap into;

this may have been the most remarkable thing about him. He knew he could call on any of these individuals for a favor and could locate the perfect resource person or benefactor for a particular project. This was most evident in both his long chairmanship of the Maryland March of Dimes and his twenty-five years as president of the Maryland Historical Society.

Never afraid to ask for a favor, George was, however, basically reserved and without any need for personal recognition. Circumstances had thrust him into both Maryland and Washington spotlights, and he recognized early on that he could market this notoriety for the public good. He always said that he had no remarkable talents, but put him in charge of a project, and his passion, limitless energy, and desire to serve would turn him into a powerful locomotive. He admitted that he often fumbled in a project, but, undaunted, he would charge off on an alternative path. He was never a quitter. As his successes mounted, he was increasingly sought after for projects, and age did not seem to affect his value. He left the Senate at age sixty-nine and accomplished more after that age then most do in a lifetime.

George L. Radcliffe was also the default master of ceremonies for countless events occurring throughout his public life, and these occasions filled up his already overflowing schedule. Once again name recognition may have been the draw, but George's phenomenal recall of local history meant that any event could be put in the proper historical context. Whatever the event, George had the facts and an anecdote to entertain. By his own admission, he was hardly a legendary speaker, and several sources referred to him as a substandard orator. However, on many occasions his brief remarks would turn into an epic oration. Numerous news accounts refer to the audience growing restless as his speech continued, seemingly with no end. This, however, never stopped further groups from tapping this amazing resource.

Part of his success also stemmed from his phenomenal memory. Whether in a committee meeting or speaking extemporaneously, he could quickly retrieve historical facts, budget figures, a relevant anecdote, or a verse of poetry. He also subjected his own views and beliefs to what was needed for a project. Consensus was his goal rather than driving home some point. He was generally progressive in his thinking but combined this with fiscal conservatism.

What was also amazing was how he could hold down several chairmanships while often holding two full-time jobs. He could delegate, and this was especially evident in his years as officer of the Maryland Historical Society, where he attracted many of Baltimore's best, expanding not only its membership but committee membership and adding a full-time director. He always said that the work was mostly done by others, but he sought progress, not attention or recognition.

To just examine one year in this busy life, in 1955 at age seventy, an age when most his age were relaxing and enjoying the fruits of a busy life, George was:

- president of the Maryland Historical Society
- chairman of the Maryland March of Dimes
- president of the Grace Foundation on Taylor's Island
- president of the English-Speaking Union
- honorary chairman of the Baltimore Symphony Drive
- chairman of the Constitution Day Committee
- co-chairman of the Flag House Week observance
- chairman of the USO GI Pal Dinner
- chairman of the Defender's Day program
- member of the WAAM Program Advisory Council (television)
- chairman, of the Baltimore Harbor Tunnel Groundbreaking
- chairman of the Welcoming Committee, Return of the U.S. Constellation to Baltimore
- chairman of Special Gifts, American Shakespeare Festival

- · trustee of St. Mary's College
- · coordinator of a Boy Scout scholarship program

That one year alone would earn him the title of "Mr. Chairman," but this was just a typical year for a man who also managed a farm and went to work each day.

His congenial nature also frequently put him in the role of chairman of a welcoming committee for royalty, dignitaries, and special guests. This would involve considerable planning plus a full day of escorting the individual around Baltimore, Annapolis, or Washington. As he would say, he was often appointed as a committee of one to invite a dignitary to visit and then plan their stay. Their visits would always be followed by a long letter of appreciation, asking them to return, and many did just that. He was even involved in the return of professional baseball to Baltimore in 1954, leading the parade, dressed as Lord Baltimore, to the stadium for opening day.

In 1965, at age eighty-eight, he was called upon in an emergency to plan the dinner for the Maryland chapter of the National Conference of Christians and Jews. Stepping in when another defaulted, he was able to pull the event off in less than two weeks without a major hitch.[3] At age ninety, he was chairman of the Board of the Maryland Historical Society, still coordinating the Maryland March of Dimes, and president of the Grace Foundation, and at the age of ninety-three he founded the Spocott Windmill Foundation, of which he was president. In reality, he never slowed down. He may have been a basically shy individual, but there was no reluctance when it came to civic action. For a child whose parents thought would never make it to the age of twenty-one, he managed to pack several lifetimes into one, and no one was more deserving of the title "Mr. Chairman."

Let us go forward, our hearts always eager, our hands ready to work.
- George Radcliffe, 1955, at a dinner honoring him[4]

His Society

It is the opportunity and privilege of historical soci-
eties to take an active part in seeing that teachings
which history furnish are made readily available. The
man who attempts to make plans, or to carry them
out, without due regard for what experience can teach
is foolish. History is experience.[1]

- George L. Radcliffe, 1930

George L. Radcliffe was an officer of the Maryland Historical Society[2] for sixty-two years. He played a key role in half of the period that the Society had been operating since its founding, and his tenure saw the organization grow from its small office in the Athenaeum to multiple buildings and a large, growing, and active membership, He oversaw the Society's evolution from a small, social group interested in preserving Maryland archives to an organization connected in many ways to the city, providing both a forum for continual historical study and an outreach to area schools and county historical societies. As with so much that he did, ego was never a motivating factor for his efforts. George was focused on documenting history and historical preservation, and the Maryland Historical Society provided the personal vehicle for him to effect significant change.

The Society was founded in 1844 in a period when numerous states were organizing groups to preserve the historical documents and artifacts of the still-young country. The Civil War threatened the existence of the young organization as Maryland, a border state, clearly was split between

Union and Confederacy. The first significant bloodshed of the Civil War occurred on the streets of Baltimore as Union troops attempted to march through the city on April 19, 1861. While Maryland was a slave state, with slaves primarily on the Eastern Shore and in Southern Maryland, one could find both abolitionists and Confederate sympathizers in every section of the state. The Society would grow slowly after the war, but it was in the early to mid-twentieth century that real growth occurred.[3]

With George's legal career with the American Bonding Company well established by 1908. and two years married to Mary McKim Marriott, he had the time to return to his life's passion, history, and to join the Maryland Historical Society. He was initially disappointed as he found the Society to be more a social club for well-to-do white gentleman and quickly made his impact on the organization, becoming its recording secretary in 1912. He was frustrated with his early efforts to advance the organization. George would remark on several occasions that whatever topic was being discussed by the group would ultimately end up with Northern and Southern sympathizers taking sides, as they would then fight the Civil War over again. Early on, George pushed for more diverse programming, and this would become one of his trademarks as his role in the organization grew.[4] He remained recording secretary for the next twenty years. During and after World War I, he played a major role in preserving the war records of Marylanders who had served in the Great War. In 1919, the Society would get a new home on Monument Street—the Enoch Pratt House—a gift from Mrs. H. Irvine Keyser. The previous home had barely survived the Great Baltimore Fire in 1904, and this new home gave the Society both the room it needed to grow and a safer place to store its archives.

George became the Society's vice president in 1933, and although he would be elected to the U.S. Senate late the next year, he stayed active in the group. In 1939, he was elected president of the organization, an office he would hold for the next twenty-five years. His reputation and extensive repertoire of political, civic, and social connections helped make this one of the most productive periods for the organization.

When George became president of the Society, he inherited an organization with almost a century of tradition but one which had suffered through the Depression. With a membership of a little over 1000, an operating budget of about $25,000, and a building with limited storage and meeting space,[5] the Society needed numerous changes if it were to remain relevant in a growing world. Within three years, the country would be at war, and George would have more than his share of challenges. He, however, was well equipped to handle the challenge. First, he had been a member of the organization for over three decades, had been an officer since 1912, and had been vice president for six years. He knew the organization well.

Second, George was a dealmaker and problem solver, and those skills would be needed to move the Society to another level. Being a senator could have been a disadvantage for an officer of the group because of the time requirements needed to be a legislator on the national stage. However, George was still living and working in Baltimore while in the Senate and still used his office in downtown Baltimore almost daily.

Five years in the Senate combined with his extensive connections throughout Maryland made him a Society president with almost unlimited resources. Whatever the problem confronting the Society, George could network with a person qualified to assist. He was also on the Library Committee in the Senate, and his experience on this committee, his passion for books, and extensive knowledge of history made him as knowledgeable as anyone in Maryland in dealing with historical artifacts and collections.

As president, George used a strategy that he was successfully using as U.S. senator: answer every letter. New members were greeted with a welcome letter from George, and those terminating their membership received a kind letter thanking them for their membership and reminding them of the organization's upcoming projects. Never did anyone receive pressure from him. Having full-time secretaries both in his Senate office in Washington and his Fidelity and Deposit office in Baltimore gave him the support he needed, and his letter writing was prolific. Rarely a day went by without considerable Society correspondence emerging from those offices.

In almost three decades as Society president, he was able to oversee many changes:

Membership

On becoming president in 1939, George immediately saw the need to increase membership, which had become somewhat stagnant during the Depression. Following up on the suggestion of Judge Sam Dennis and others, at each monthly meeting, a number of names were introduced for membership, and each of these received a letter, many from George himself.[6] In 1943 alone, they were able to add 700 members.[7] During the period from 1939 to 1945, even with the country completely focused on the war, membership almost tripled, a remarkable feat.[8]

The membership policy may have been the biggest change George and his staff made to the Maryland Historical Society. When George first became an officer in the organization, it was still basically an elitist organization, limited to the wealthy and socially privileged. One had to be nominated and approved by the membership. This didn't set well with George who understood history was for all, not just a limited few. Under his tenure as president, not only would membership be increased significantly, but the Society became open to anyone who could pay the membership fee.[9]

Administrative Structure

One of the most significant changes George made in the Society was recognizing that for the Society to expand, it needed an administrative reorganization. Previously the organization had rested on the shoulders of its volunteers and a handful of part-time employees. Even the office of president was part-time, and daily attention to operation was needed. In 1942 James W. Foster, former head of the Maryland Department of the Enoch Pratt Library and editor of the Society's journal, was appointed full-time director of the Society. This was the initiation of the administrative structure the Society still uses today and paved the way for expansion. George correctly saw that he could not devote full-time to the Society, nor should that be the role of any Society president.[10] As evidence of his commitment to the new director, George paid Foster's salary out of his own pocket for the first two years.[11] As the programs expanded from the 1940s into the 1950s, George and the Society were gradually able to add staff positions: assistant director, secretaries, bookkeeper, hostesses, and registrar. Director James Foster's sudden death in 1962 set back the organization, but Harold Manakee, assistant director, author, and educator, took over as director, continuing until 1972, a period when George was still active with the Society, holding the largely ceremonial position of chairman.[12]

EDUCATION

The teacher in George surfaced in 1944 when he saw that the Maryland Historical Society needed to become a more active organization rather than just a repository of archives. The *Maryland Historical Magazine* had been in publication since 1906, and the Society had offered relevant programs for the public several times a year. However, George and others saw the need to take a more active educational role and to reach out to school children.

This had been an active interest for George for many years, and in 1918, as a key figure in the Eastern Shore Society, he initiated an annual historical essay contest for high school students and chaired that scholarship committee until he became a U.S. senator in 1934. He loved history

Students entering the Maryland Historical Society on April 24, 1950

and felt the essay contest could "stimulate interest in the study of history." He also believed the students could do some legitimate historical research on local topics.[13] It was just logical then that he would want to involve schools more significantly in the Maryland Historical Society.

At a Society meeting on March 24, 1944, George appointed a committee on Maryland history in the schools, and in June a committee of Society members, representatives of historical organizations, and administrators from Baltimore County public schools met to begin discussing possible Society outreach programs in schools.[14] The following year the Society began scheduling tours for school students, hosted teacher workshops, worked with the Enoch Pratt Library to develop materials for schools, and had members run assemblies in the schools themselves. Toward the end of his presidency, George worked to obtain funding for a children's museum on Society grounds.[15]

INCREASED SPACE

Although the move to the current Monument Street location expanded greatly the Society's storage capabilities, the organization quickly outgrew this space. Beginning in 1949, under George's leadership, the Society began buying up buildings on Monument Street and Park Avenue until they owned practically an entire city block. While this was often controversial to the surrounding community, it served three purposes. First, it insulated the Society building from development around it. Second, the buildings generated rent which served as income for the group. However, most important, it provided the land for an additional Society building which was sorely needed. Increased attendance at programs made a large auditorium a priority, and with new acquisitions each year, increasing exhibits, and growing educational programs, all knew an additional building was a must. Planning began in the 1950s, spurred on by an endowment, and when the Society purchased four more houses in 1961, they had the land needed for the major expansion. Amidst a degree of community objection, the buildings were demolished. At a ceremony on November 23, 1964, George L. Radcliffe and Gov. Theodore McKeldin oversaw the groundbreaking for the Thomas and Hugg Memorial Building, completed in 1968.[16]

County Historical Societies

Throughout this period, George saw the need to have each county have its own historical society and was instrumental in assisting many counties in getting these started. Once again, with his extensive repertoire of connections from throughout the State, he was able to find key individuals in many of the counties to initiate the project. Through his prolific letter writing and visits to the counties, he was able to provide the support needed, and his almost encyclopedic knowledge of local history enabled him to relate to each county's history.[17]

Surviving World War II

World War II posed an interesting challenge for the Society. While there were many who felt that it was inappropriate for the Maryland Historical Society to keep up their normal programming during the war, George felt exactly the opposite, since to him history was an active, vibrant process, not just the study of the past. To him the present was a continuum stretching from the past into the future, and he felt that history was more important during wartime than during peace. Rather than cutting back on Society programming, he upgraded it considerably, probably an additional reason that membership increased during this period. In 1943 alone he brought in an amazing array of military dignitaries as speakers to really put the war into both a proper historical and contemporary focus. By providing a forum for actual dialogue on the events and strategies of the war, he felt that the organization could actually further the war effort, and using his connections he had made in the Senate, he was able to tap into the upper echelons of military leadership for speakers: the under secretary of war (Robert Patterson), the undersecretary of the Navy (James Forrestal), War Shipping administrator and Maritime Commission head (Emory Land), chairman of the Senate Foreign Relations Committee (Tom Connolly), assistant secretary of War for Air (Robert Lovell), and assistant secretary of Navy for Air (Artemus Gates). The Society membership in 1943 was literally on the front line of military decision making, and that year alone, Society membership increased by fifty percent.[18]

In 1944, the Society was celebrating its 100th birthday, and George and the officers pulled out all the stops to make this a memorable event. They needed a speaker that would generate a large crowd, and George went back once again to a friend he made in the Senate while serving on the Senate Library Committee. Poet Archibald MacLeish, Library of Congress director, spoke on "The Use of Radio in the Presentation of History."[19]

Once again, despite the war, the membership continued to grow. He was able to top that speaker in 1945, when he chose an individual who had been sworn into the Senate in 1935 on the same day as he. Harry Truman, now vice president, a fellow history buff, and friend of George, spoke to the Society on "Maryland and Tolerance" on March 27.[20] Little did the audience know that he would be sworn in as the thirty-third President of the United States some two weeks later with the death of Franklin Roosevelt. Later that year, George asked Gen. George C. Marshall to speak on "Some Lessons of History."[21] This was actually an easy speaker for George to get as the general's wife was a cousin of George's. This amazing array of speakers did much to put the Maryland Historical Society firmly on both the state and national map.

In 1950, George spearheaded a project for the Society to develop a maritime museum. From his father's shipbuilding days to his work on the Senate Merchant Marine subcommittee, boats and shipping had been a thread which ran through his life. In a 1950 press release from the Society, George said:

> We hope that people all over the state will take an interest in this museum. The Chesapeake Bay has tremendously influenced the history of Maryland. No one can doubt that the history of our state would have been very different without the activities of local shipping and ocean

trade. We are especially interested in the characteristic types that developed on the Bay such as pilot boats, the Baltimore clipper, the clipper ship, the puny, the skip-jack, and the bugeye, as well as boats of today. That collection should have been started many years ago.[22]

Under George's watch, the Society was able to acquire Francis Scott Key's manuscript "Defence of Fort M'Henry," his account of the bombardment of Fort McHenry. This became the lyrics for "The Star-Spangled Banner," our national anthem since 1931. In 1953 Mrs. Thomas C. Jenkins donated the funds to purchase the manuscript from the Walters Art Gallery for $26,400 and also agreed to fund the costs for its preservation and display. On September 14, 1954, George assembled dignitaries to officially dedicate the manuscript's installation.[23] The manuscript remains one of the premier attractions at the Maryland Historical Society.

As president, George L. Radcliffe oversaw many changes, additions, and improvements in the Maryland Historical Society, helping transform the organization from a somewhat elitist group to one with tentacles extending into many parts of the community, from basically a historical repository and research facility to one that brought history out to the common citizen. He surrounded himself with the right people, set up the right administrative structure for the organization, and made the connections needed to facilitate many of the projects. He was always the last person to take credit for any project, and bragging was just not in his make-up. He knew that accomplishments always stemmed from the efforts of a dedicated group. For those three decades of his presidency, he was the poster child for Maryland history and the Maryland Historical Society, and in 1964, at the age of eighty-seven, he finally stepped down as president, becoming the chairman emeritus until his death ten years later.

As a Society officer for over five decades, George was always persistent, and to him roadblocks were just challenges to surmount. Never an inspirational speaker or stereotypical leader, few were more determined and committed, and the Maryland Historical Society was one of the beneficiaries of his boundless energy and unrelenting persistence to achieve a goal. As his close friend and colleague Judge Sam Dennis said in an address at the Centennial Meeting of the Society in 1944: "George Radcliffe, his methods are odd, you think sometimes he will never come through, but give him enough time, let him do it in his own way and he will move the pyramids from Egypt to Druid Hill Park."[24]

THE 200-POUND BIRTHDAY CAKE

On January 30, 1934, at the conclusion of the first Roosevelt Birthday Ball, George L. Radcliffe bought what may be historically one of the largest desserts ever—a 200-pound birthday cake which had been donated to the charity event. He won the cake with the highest bid at the event auction—and he never ate one bite of the massive dessert which cost him $100. In today's dollars, that would be a $2,000 cake. In 1934, George was Maryland chairman for the Birthday Ball Celebration, commemorating President Roosevelt's fifty-second birthday. The Baltimore event was one of over 4,000 events held throughout the country to help raise money for the Georgia Warm Springs Foundation, created by Franklin Roosevelt to support and care for children crippled by infantile paralysis (polio), the disease he had contracted in 1921. The birthday ball tradition continued, evolving several years later into the March of Dimes, and it would become a major part of George L. Radcliffe's life for over forty years. After Roosevelt's death, the Mercury dime was replaced with a dime featuring Roosevelt, both to honor his role in leading the country out of the Depression and World War II, and to recognize his work in ending infantile paralysis.

It was no accident that George L. Radcliffe was Maryland chairman of the 1934 Birthday Ball, and this would evolve into a lifelong relationship between him and the March of Dimes. George never ate a bit of that massive dessert but had the impressive confectionary split in two and delivered the next day to children in two local hospitals: the Children's Hospital School and Kernan's Hospital for Crippled Children.[1]

There were many individuals involved with that first Presidential Birthday Ball in 1934, but none had the motivation that George L. Radcliffe had. Those many days he sat with Roosevelt in 1921 when Franklin first contacted polio made a lasting impression on George,[2] and this experience would fuel a lifetime dedication to the National Foundation for Infantile Paralysis (later known as The National Foundation or the March of Dimes). As George said in 1964 in a letter to Basil O'Connor, long time president of the Foundation:

> My long association with the March of Dimes movement has left me many happy associations. These really began almost immediately after Roosevelt's attack of polio in the summer of 1921. In the first talk I had with him shortly after that attack, he deplored the amount of ignorance regarding polio and stated that he was going to do something about it.
>
> All that time in 1921 he was of course helpless and his opportunities of being active and useful seemed to be entirely negligible. Frequently when I was sitting by his bedside, he would say that he was going to find a way of doing something constructive in such a cause. It was distressing to me to hear a man apparently doomed to complete helplessness, insist he was going again to be active. So really, I can say my association with the fight against polio began in 1921.[3]

George and Franklin stayed close throughout the 1920s, with George often visiting the Roosevelts on his trips to New York. George admired Roosevelt and was acutely aware of and touched by Franklin's condition. After heading up the Maryland campaign to elect Roosevelt in 1932, it was logical that he would welcome the opportunity to head the Maryland Birthday Ball in 1934. Commemorating the President's birthday (January 30), the celebration provided a perfect forum for George to both honor his friend and raise funds to help treat patients with the disease.

The first two balls were successful, bringing in thousands of dollars for local hospitals dealing with crippled children, but the Maryland group decided in 1936 to expand the event to five parties, each offering different entertainment. A one-dollar ticket would get a person into all five events, and quickly over 22,000 tickets were sold.[4]

In 1935, George was instrumental in getting Johns Hopkins to begin research on the dreaded disease. In his characteristic fashion, he would use connections in another area of his life to effect change. He contacted Dean Alan

*Program Brochure from
First Birthday Ball
on January 30, 1934*

Chesney of the Johns Hopkins Medical School and was able to get Hopkins funding to begin research into polio. Chesney was one of George's former students from Baltimore City College. Hopkins would get about $3,000,000 for the National Foundation over the years and would contribute major research leading to the ultimate vaccine.[5]

Many today know little of polio (Poliomyelitis), formerly referred to as infantile paralysis, because of the effectiveness of the vaccine now universally administered. Years ago, it was a disease that spread fear among many, much as cancer does today. Highly contagious, the disease infected the spinal cord and, in some cases, led to paralysis, severe breathing problems, and sometimes death. Its spread was most commonly the result of a person ingesting fecal residue from something handled by a person not appropriately washing their hands. The paralysis often affected the respiratory system musculature; as treatment, the tank respirator, or what became known as the iron lung, was often used to assist breathing, saving many lives.[6] The disease increased in prevalence throughout the first half of the twentieth century, causing people to go to extremes to avoid it. Many stayed away from public swimming pools, and some even stayed inside much of the summer when the warmer temperatures brought people into closer personal contact. The disease reached a high in 1952 with 60,000 children affected and 3,000 dying, and panic was clearly setting in at that point. Polio had become a leading childhood communicable disease, and pictures abounded of children on crutches and in iron lungs.[7] Jonas Salk developed a vaccine early in the 1950s, and toward the end of the decade, Albert Sabin developed a simple and inexpensive vaccine which could be administered orally. This led to a drastic drop in incidence, and the disease is a virtual unknown in this country today.[8]

In 1936, the local birthday ball hit a major obstacle. While previously George had headed up both the Baltimore event and the Maryland effort, that year he was able to get someone to chair the Baltimore activities. Especially busy in the Senate and with the presidential election looming that year, George was thrilled to get the help. However, the individual chairing the Baltimore activity publicly cancelled the event ten days prior to it. George had to scramble, even donating $1,800 of his own money to keep the event alive, knowing that research at Hopkins would cease if the event was cancelled.[9] He kept this incident quiet at the time to avoid any negative publicity, and this demonstrates his marked commitment to both the event and the potential for research.

By 1937 the birthday balls were no longer a novelty, and George needed an incentive to get the people of Maryland to show up at these events. Known as an effective organizer, George set out to make each ball the social and entertainment event of the year in Baltimore. Anyone could purchase admission to the event, but the select tables and those closest to the entertainment carried a good premium. Knowing that local entertainment would not draw the big crowd, and a political speech would hardly be appropriate for a ball, George and his committee turned toward Hollywood, drawing over the years some of the top names in entertainment. In 1937, the group was able to get film star Robert Taylor, still early in his career, but widely popular.[10] In 1938, the group succeeded in lining up tap-dancing and movie star, Eleanor Powell, who would also appear in 1939.[11]

Eleanor's two appearances would fuel a lot of Radcliffe family kidding for years as she and George got along famously, writing each other often over the next several years. Photographs were taken of the two of them, including one with her innocently kissing the senator on the cheek. This was all the family needed for some good old-fashioned teasing, and George would pretend to be embarrassed, always enjoying the kidding. The truth was that Eleanor was a tremendous supporter of the cause and visited Washington in 1941 in support of the fight against infantile paralysis. Writing George after the 1939 event, she said:

> [you] couldn't possibly keep me away from Baltimore next year—if you really want me. I sincerely do hope that I can be with you. Probably it's a little selfish of me, as no doubt I should stand aside and let some other MGM-ite have the honor and thrill of meeting all of you wonderful people. But I know there would be an awful lump in my throat if anyone else were chosen.[12]

By 1939, opponents of President Roosevelt were trying to characterize the birthday balls as political events, prompting an almost angry response from the usually calm George in a press release:

> We have tried to make it clear that the drive for funds for fighting infantile paralysis is non-political and non-partisan. We have emphasized that the movement is of such a nature as to appeal to every citizen whether Demo-

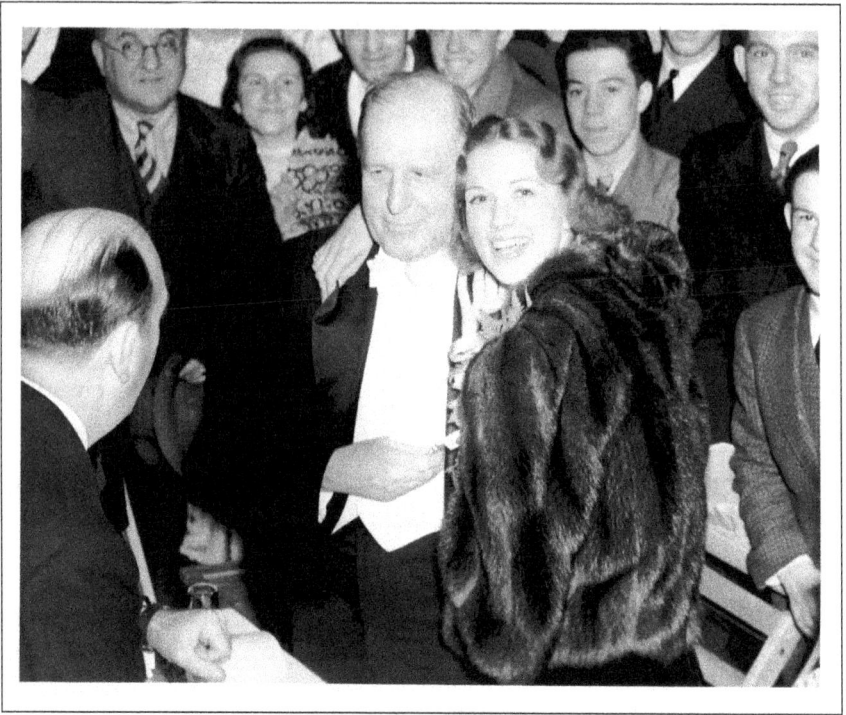

Sen. George L. Radcliffe with Eleanor Powell
Baltimore Birthday Ball on January 30, 1939

crat or Republican, New Deal or Anti-New Deal. At a recent meeting of workers, I explained the nationwide movement was evolutionary, not revolutionary, that out of the Birthday Ball had come the National Foundation for Infantile Paralysis, a permanent organization similar to the Tuberculosis Association and the Red Cross. We all recognize the inspirational value of the president in bringing this great national movement to fight a terrible disease into its present form. Here in Maryland, we are united behind it. We have organized a state-wide survey on what is being done to combat the disease. It is entirely outside of politics. That does not mean, however, that we have shied away from using the name of the president because his opponents might object.[13]

Unfortunately, Eleanor Powell's schedule would prohibit her return in 1940, but Mickey Rooney, former child star and Academy Award nominee, would headline that year. As the event grew, several stars would appear at the Ball in 1941, with singing star and actress Deanna Durbin, actor George Raft, and All-American and Heisman Trophy-winning football star Tom Harmon all appearing. It seemed like half of Hollywood made it to the 1942 event, as the cast included Edward Arnold, Pat O'Brien, Jean Hersholt, Jackie Cooper, and Bonita Granville.[14] The 1942 event occurred not long after the bombing of Pearl Harbor, but the event was still held because of the worthy nature of the cause. However, George and his committee decided in 1943 that a more patriotic program was needed, and most Hollywood stars, if not serving in the military, were either involved in activities supporting the troops and the war or unable to get transportation across the country. George and his able cohorts put together a program recognizing war heroes, the WAACs, WAVES, and even fifty British seamen with a military officer as master of ceremonies. Without the Hollywood stars, the Baltimore ball was still able to attract 7,500 people. George reported:

> Our principle thought this year, as in the past, is to carry on the fight against infantile paralysis. The disease is a fifth columnist—an enemy within our ranks. With men, ships, planes, tanks, and weapons we are engaged in a war against a foe that persecutes and liquidates the weak. At the same time, with our dimes and dollars, we can show the world that America is continuing its fight to aid the weak and afflicted.[15]

The fight to raise funds to combat polio had far surpassed the Birthday Ball format at this point. In 1938, the Warm Springs Foundation had evolved into the National Foundation for Infantile Paralysis, and its fundraising efforts now came to be known as the March of Dimes. Volunteers, in addition to soliciting more generous contributions, used canisters to collect pocket change. George became Maryland chairman of this organization and wore that hat until 1968, when he stepped down at the age of ninety-one.

As an example of George L. Radcliffe's incredible attention to each person is his response to a letter he received from a youth in late December of 1941, just after the Pearl Harbor attack. The boy asked George if he could get either Roy Rogers or Gene Autry (both cowboy movie stars) for the next Ball. With the U.S. now at war after Pearl Harbor and the holiday season fast approaching, one should have expected that this letter would find its way quickly to the waste receptacle, but that was not the way that George operated. The day after Christmas, George penned a full-page response to the youth:

> I know it will be a pleasure for you to meet the movie stars, about whom you wrote me, and doubtless they would be glad to see you. Our plans for the raising of funds for infantile paralysis this year have not definitely been made, but when such is done, and we can do anything to fill in with your wishes, I would be glad to try to do so.
>
> I hope you will have a very Happy Christmas and that the New Year will be very pleasant and helpful for you. These are very serious days when we must all work hard and try to meet the privileges of citizenship which are pressing unusually heavy on us at this time.

This attention to detail is what George was so well known for. Each person felt they were getting his undivided attention. While Roy and Gene did not make it to the 1942 Birthday Ball, this youth was able to get his due notice.

George and the National Foundation for Infantile Paralysis (NFIP) ran into two obstacles in the early 1960s. First, many thought the NFIP was no longer needed because of the universal Sabin vaccination. And second, there was a move to combine charities into single entities, but the charter of the Foundation prohibited this. The two problems were beginning to thwart the Maryland March of Dimes in its efforts, and George resorted to his tried-and-true tactic: a massive letter-writing campaign. George, well into his eighties, was undaunted, and he wrote countless letters to fuel continued support. The local March of Dimes drive was still able to succeed, and by 1965, the March of Dimes stopped the downward fundraising trend.[16]

The NFIP has evolved into The National Foundation, and it funds other crippling diseases such as arthritis, viral diseases, and birth defects. Today the organization is referred to as the March of Dimes, and it continues the fight against birth defects. George remained active, and in 1962, at age eighty-five, he was appointed to the board of the Salk Institute.

As with so many of George's ventures and causes, he gave credit to the many others who did so much work. The amazing thing about the March of Dimes and the drive to find a vaccine was that it was neither a government-funded venture, nor a project that rode on the shoulders of major corporate donations. It was literally funded by nickels and dimes, collected even by school children in the 1950s; I remember carrying my little white cardboard container to school and to neighbors on Halloween to collect change for the cause. George was able to use his extensive repertoire of connections and his boundless energy to help drive the local component of the Foundation.

From sitting beside the bedside of his friend in 1921, his life would be connected for over five decades to the treatment and cure of a dreaded disease. George was neither a medical doctor nor research scientist, but he watched his friend, crippled by polio, rise and go on to heights no one would have imagined after 1921. He and Franklin Roosevelt would see their relationship strained at times by the politics of the day, but George remained devoted to him throughout his life. While most remember George L. Radcliffe for his 12 years in the Senate and his historical preservation ventures, George may have been most proud of his work with the March of Dimes. And to think that for him this would begin with a 200-pound cake.

Essays

———◆———

Family

THE PROMISE

... consider for a moment the early settlers in our tidewater sections. Countless rivers and inlets divided these communities one from the other, and since the most practical means of transportation among these communities was by water, each community was inclined to develop a distinctive form of living. Consequently, we find the growth of numerous communities which, in many respects, are almost like little separate countries.[1]

G eorge, the youngest of many siblings, was the apple of his mother's eye and was devoted to her. While George lived across the Chesapeake Bay in Baltimore throughout his adult life, he always wrote his mother and visited whenever his busy schedule would permit. In 1925, he had rescued his mother's ancestral home just before shoreline erosion on the western side of Taylor's Island turned the house into one large piece of driftwood; he moved the house across the island and up the Little Choptank River to Spocott, where his mother now lived. His mother had been bedridden for several years now, and the end of her long and productive life was drawing near. George's work at the Fidelity and Deposit Company was sending him from coast to coast and occasionally abroad, but he still made it home whenever he could. He and his mother talked frequently about Taylor's Island, where her Travers ancestors had lived since settling there in the seventeenth century, and George had developed the same fascination with family history. In 1926, she insisted that George preserve the history of the island and its many historical entities, including the church which her father had built. George promised he would always stay connected to the island and that he would work to preserve its history and heritage. Work, politics, and twelve years in the Senate would sideline him, but he never forgot. Retiring from the Senate in 1947, he returned to the promise he had made two decades earlier, and his efforts to preserve Taylor's Island history would now be the centerpiece of the remaining quarter century of his life.

Sophie Delila Travers (1837–1927), the oldest of three daughters, was descended from Thomas Broome Travers (1802–1875) and Mary Elizabeth Travers (1820–1843). The two were cousins, but then it was virtually impossible living on that small island to marry someone who was not a cousin. Thus, George was descended from the earliest Travers (or Traverse) settler to Taylor's Island from at least four different lines. William Aip Travers (1640–1701) settled Taylor's Island in 1665, three years after its earliest settlers, John and Thomas Taylor, for whom the island is named. The western part of Dorchester County, on the Chesapeake Bay, was the earliest part of the county settled, and Taylor's, James, and Hooper's Islands, once all connected by land bridges, were important in early county history. Connected to the mainland by ferry until 1856, when a bridge was finally built, the islands were home to many prominent Dorchester families and were the site of an early timber industry, farming, extensive shipbuilding, and more recently of a seafood industry center.[2] Sophie's father, Thomas Broome Travers, continued this shipbuilding legacy and was as successful in the mid-nineteenth century as anyone on the island.

Sophie's great-grandparents through one line were John Critchett Travers (1768–1831) and his wife Mary Dove (1777–1857). John played a prominent role on the island, owning ships and managing the local store, and Mary, who all called Grandmother Polly, was a Taylor's Island legend. When the British were moving up the Bay toward Baltimore in 1814, they came ashore on the island looking for gold, silver, and provisions. Raiding and burning many of the farms, they soon moved to John and Polly's property on the Bay, since John was a well-known leader in the community. John and one of his schooners were captured, but the British were unable to find the valuables which John and Polly surely had. While many island residents hid their valuables in their outhouses, the British had long ago figured out that this was the first place to check. The shrewd Polly came up with a foolproof hiding place. There was a setting goose on the farm, and Polly somehow moved the nest and hid the family silver and gold underneath. Moving the nest back, she correctly assumed that the British would go nowhere near the setting goose.

With her husband and schooner now in the possession of the British, Polly once again took control of the situation. Donning her finest dress, she enlisted the help of friend Mary Gadd and a servant. With the servant rowing, Polly, toting a parasol, set out for the *Marlborough*, the flagship of the British fleet, asking to see its captain, Admiral Cockburn. Treated like royalty, she was led to the captain's cabin, where the two had tea. She had the British take cake out to the servant while she pleaded with Cockburn to free her husband and his ship. Known to be quite persuasive, she succeeded in getting both John and his schooner released. In addition, the Admiral presented her with a silver tea service. The British also forgot to get back the silver platter that the cake had been served on; thus, Polly came out way ahead on that negotiation and soon became a Taylor's Island legend.[3]

Polly and John's granddaughter, Mary Elizabeth, had married another Travers, Thomas Broome Travers, and these were George's grandparents. Mary Elizabeth tragically died at age twenty-two, and Thomas was left with raising his three young daughters as well as the responsibilities of farming and shipbuilding. Rather than remarry, he decided to devote his life to his daughters, taking on the roles of both mother and father. His attention to them was remarkable for the times, and he could afford to send each of them away in their later childhood to get the best education possible at private schools in the Baltimore area. He did this despite being one of the busiest businessmen anywhere. He farmed, managed considerable forest areas for timber, and with the timber, built ships which traveled the Bay and Atlantic Ocean. Inheriting a considerable sum from his ancestors, his wise business practices increased this sum considerably. The end of his life saw the beginning of the decline of life on Taylor's Island as erosion, the decline of the shipbuilding industry, and the loss of enslaved labor worked together to negatively impact life on the island. However, Thomas remained completely devoted to his three girls, going to unusual lengths to provide for them. When his oldest Sophie was to marry, he sent one of his schooners to Baltimore, its only mission to bring the wedding cake to Taylor's Island from Baltimore. As his biography states:

> Possibly the most distinguishing characteristics of Thomas Broome Travers were the personal attention and interest which he gave to the daily life of his daughters, and his constant efforts to give them the best training and education. This was carefully done despite engrossing business cares.[4]

Sophie married Andrew Jackson Robinson in 1861, and the two had six children over the next eight years. However, Sophie, like her father, would lose her spouse, with Andrew dying only months after the birth of their youngest. Two years later Sophie would marry a widower, John Anthony LeCompte Radcliffe, and from this second union would come George L. Radcliffe. While she now lived twelve miles inland from the Island, she never forgot her roots, and trips "home" were frequent.

While only a tiny island barely six miles long and a mile or so wide, Taylor's Island figured significantly in the early history of Dorchester County and of George's heritage. Speaking of the Grace Church, the Island Episcopal Church, and its graveyard, George said:

> My grandfather is buried in that graveyard. So are his wife, his father and mother, his uncle and other of my an-

cestors and my relatives, including Traverses, Spilmans, Keenes, Bosleys, Griffiths, Edmondsons, and Cators, etc. In fact, with very few exceptions, everyone buried in that graveyard is a relative of mine.[5]

At the same time, he saw the Island dying in many ways, and George was one to always yearn for the glory of bygone days:

> They [Taylor's Islanders] were often resourceful and good businessmen and displayed a remarkable amount of self-sufficiency. They lived well and never forecast that loss of slaves, exhaustion of timber, practical drying up deep sea shipping and other factors [which] would bring on economic stagnation and induce active young men to seek their fortunes elsewhere. Practically every home has passed out of the family.[6]

This was all part of the legacy that Thomas' daughter Sophie wanted her son George to preserve and that George saw eroding away just as the disappearing shoreline. By the mid-twentieth century, the islands had eroded considerably from the wave action of the Bay, and the original location of the Travers home George had moved in 1925 was now well out in the Bay. The land bridges were gone, and the once large James Island was now uninhabited, with only a few trees remaining. Cambridge on the Choptank River was now the heart of the county, and the islands were quickly reduced to history. With such a family legacy, it was no surprise that George's mother wanted her son, the historian, to preserve its legacy.

On occasions George attended the church on Taylor's Island which his grandfather had played a part in constructing. Grace Church became a focus for his interest in preserving Taylor's Island history. Prior to Grace Episcopal Church, the nearest church had been Old Trinity on the mainland, some ten miles away. Since that distance was prohibitive for churchgoers, a "chapel of ease" had been constructed on the island. Literally a "bare-bones" wooden structure, the chapel served as the church for the locals until 1873 when Thomas Broome Travers, Samuel M. Travers, and Jeremiah L. Pattison each contributed an equal sum to finally get a church for the island. Thomas donated the land and supervised the construction. In 1936, on the sixty-third anniversary of Grace Church, George L. Radcliffe, then a U.S. Senator, gave a talk in which he recounted the history of his grandfather's church.[7] More than a decade later, he rolled up his sleeves and got to work.

Grace Church was deteriorating like so many colonial structures, and Ella Spilman, one of George's many "Island" cousins had enlisted George's help in getting money for a new roof. This project was the impetus for much discussion on how to preserve the church. In June of 1950, George attended a service at Grace Church and was distressed to find it in deteriorating condition and rather poorly attended. In a letter to Marguerite Ewell, wife of his nephew Emmett Robinson Ewell, he wrote:

> I was disappointed that you and other members of the family were not at church last Sunday. In view of Grandfather Thomas Broome Travers' intimate contact with the church, his splendid qualifications as a man, his devotion as a husband, father, and grandfather, I was sorry that of his many descendants, only three were at the church on Sunday, Sewell [George's brother], Mabel Neild, and I.[8]

What followed was what George did best. Within a short period, he had written over 100 letters to family and Travers descendants. He had been affiliated with the association supporting Old Trinity Church, and he saw that Grace Church needed such a group. Using his position as president of the Maryland Historical Society, he convened a meeting at the Society in Baltimore on December 8, 1950, to discuss the matter. Marguerite Ewell was at that meeting, as were thirteen others. All agreed that an organization was needed and that Grace Church was to be the focal point. The name Grace Foundation of Taylor's Island was hatched at this meeting. George, not surprisingly, agreed to act as temporary chairman of the group. Cousins Ella Spilman and Arnold Travers, and island resident Reynolds Carpenter played key roles right from the beginning.

On March 19, 1951, an informal meeting was held, attended by George, his son George M., and Arnold Travers. Reynolds Carpenter of Taylor's Island and William M. Travers of Baltimore were suggested as vice presidents of the group. An official first meeting date for the organization was set for Sunday, May 13, and George wrote letters to everyone he could.[9] The church was filled that May afternoon with over 200 people, and soon after, Articles of Incorporation were filed. The following year the organization received tax-exempt status, and George finally had his organization, a quarter century after he made that promise to his mother.

However, this organization was never meant to be just a church preservation entity. George and the many Travers descendants and relatives were looking to preserve much of the history of the Island that still existed. While land acquisition for additional grounds and parking, building restoration, and cemetery maintenance were key issues, the group set its sight on acquiring the Chapel of Ease, the original Taylor's Island chapel, built about 1762 to accommodate church goers on the Island, since water and distance prohibited a Sunday round trip to Old Trinity Church on the mainland. Concurrent with the first year of the Grace Foundation, George was also involved with the Eastern Shore Survey, the brainchild of Arthur Houghton; this sought to identify and evaluate historic structures on the Eastern Shore, and the Chapel of Ease was one of the historic buildings identified.

In early 1952, the Grace Foundation purchased the Chapel of Ease for $800 from J. Stapleforte Neild whose wife, Mabel Spicer, was a great-granddaughter of Thomas Broome Travers. The chapel was located near the bridge, where the ferry docked at one time. The Foundation raised the additional funds in 1952 to move the old chapel, and that year it was moved the three quarters of a mile to rest near Grace Church.[10]

George began digging deep into the history of Taylor's Island, and the Grace Foundation was becoming a vehicle for commemorating the role of the island in Maryland history. In 1956, George began to focus on a dispute between William Penn of Pennsylvania and Lord Baltimore over the exact border between the two states, and Taylor's Island had figured significantly in that argument. With Delaware still a part of Pennsylvania at the time, the starting point for the Mason-Dixon Line was being argued, a point which would mark the southwest corner of what was to become Delaware. They determined that the line would begin at the midpoint between the Atlantic Ocean and the Chesapeake Bay at a particular latitude, and in determining where to place this middle point, Penn insisted that Taylor's Island be included as a part of the mainland, thus placing the midpoint two miles farther west, while Lord Baltimore claimed that the western part of the mainland should not include the island. Penn won this argument, thus increasing the size of his holdings.

First Meeting of Grace Foundation Grace Church on May 13, 1951 Taylor's Island, Maryland

Delaware now has 150 square miles which would have been a part of Maryland if Lord Baltimore's argument had prevailed. With talk of commemorating the "Middle Stone" marking this controversial point, George used the attention Taylor's Island was getting in the historical discussion to focus interest on the Chapel of Ease, the only "church" on the Island at the time and probably where much of the original debate over the line would have occurred. This was vintage "George L. Radcliffe," connecting bits of history to accomplish a goal.

In the mid-1950s, renovation was begun on the Chapel of Ease; the roof was replaced, and a new chimney and fireplace were built using bricks retrieved from many of the historic properties on Taylor's Island and nearby areas on the mainland. This clever move directly connected many of the Taylor's Island families to the project. George was clearly making the chapel the focal point of Island history. As he stated:

> The old chapel is rich in history and for most of us, it has long-continued close family associations. It has architectural and historic values. It fully deserves preservation. It can have community uses for all of us, irrespective of religious differences. It can be utilized in part for library and museum purposes. It will be the outstanding physical connecting link for persons living out of Maryland who have close family associations with Taylor's Island. It can be in a sense their local headquarters. It is a unique and very historic survival, fully deserving cherishing preservation and utilization.[11]

At the end of that first decade, the Foundation acquired from the Spicer family the only remaining of four original schoolhouses on the island and had it moved beside Grace Church and the Chapel of Ease. With both an original chapel and schoolhouse on location, Grace Church was becoming the historical venue that the group had wanted. George brought the

Chapel of Ease, 1959
Taylor's Island

commemoration of the Middle Stone to a head with a resolution in the Maryland legislature and a ceremony in 1959 at Grace Church where a plaque was erected commemorating the Chapel of Ease and Taylor's Island's role in the Middle Stone controversy. He was thus able to focus considerable public attention on the Island, the boost needed to continue the work of the Grace Foundation.

While George was clearly the driving force behind all these projects, with his characteristic modesty he downplayed his role. The fact that the Grace Foundation is not only thriving but expanding almost seventy years later is a testament to its being a community organization and not just a

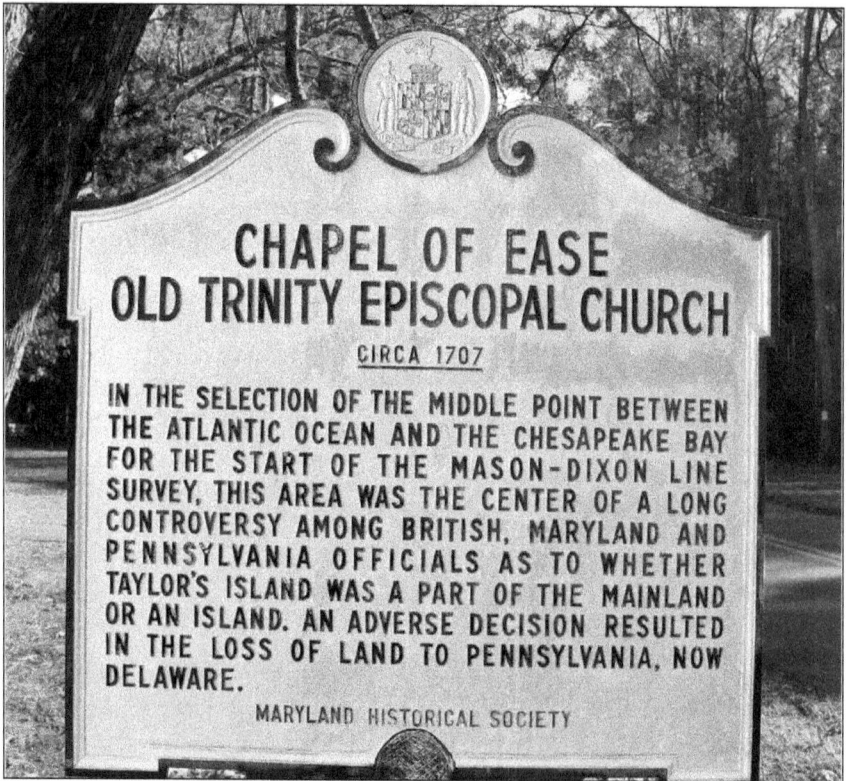

Maryland State Road Marker Commemoriating Both the Historic Chapel of Ease and Taylor's Island's Role in the Maryland-Pennsylvania Controversy Over the Location of the Mason-Dixon Line

pet project of George L. Radcliffe. His extensive network of contacts and his prolific letter writing certainly played a key role, and his seemingly limitless energy clearly helped power the projects in those early days. It was obvious that nowhere in George's efforts was he seeking any personal recognition, but this clearly was personal. All traced back to a promise he had made years earlier to a dying mother. Quite likely he would have done this all anyway as family history and historical preservation were his forte—but then that was all rooted in Sophie Delila Travers, the remarkable mother of a remarkable man.

THE DREAMS OF A TEN-YEAR-OLD CHILD

Winters were more severe when George L. Radcliffe was a child. His brother Tom would don a pair of skates once each winter, skate out the Little Choptank River to the Bay, and then up the Bay to Annapolis. Granted, shipping today would keep the main channel of the Chesapeake Bay open, but the Chesapeake Bay rarely freezes over. The winter of 1888 was likely a cold one, but by early March, faint signs of spring were appearing. On March 11 of that year, it began to rain, but by night it grew markedly colder, and the rain turned to snow. And it snowed and snowed. When the storm finally passed, the Northeast was devastated with some areas getting up to sixty inches of snow. This major winter storm would topple trees, take down numerous telegraph wires, damage barns, and basically halt transportation on the East Coast. On March 13, the New York Tribune described the storm in this way:

> The forcible if not elegant vocabulary of pugilism supplied the phrases which will, perhaps, best reveal to the popular imagination the effect of the storm that visited New York yesterday. New York was simply 'knocked out,' 'paralyzed,' and reduced to a condition of suspended animation. Traffic was practically stopped, and business abandoned. [...] Chaos reigned, and the proud, boastful metropolis was reduced to the condition of a primitive settlement.[1]

Things were not much better in Maryland:

> The visitation was one of the most remarkable storms ever known in this latitude. When the storm was at its

worst ..., the air was so thick with the finest snow that it was impossible to see houses on the opposite side of the street, and the icy blasts chilled warmly-clad pedestrians to the bone. The wind was so strong that it was exceedingly difficult to make headway against it.[2]

When ten-year-old George L. Radcliffe and his father were able to get out and survey the aftermath of the storm, they found considerable damage, but most noticeable was the condition of his father's windmill at the head of Gary's Creek; it was now a pile of rubble. John Anthony LeCompte Radcliffe built the mill in 1852, and for close to four decades, the mill had allowed the family and others in the community to turn grain into the meal needed for cooking. The mill had completely collapsed, and a seventy-year-old John decided not to rebuild it. Quite the shipbuilder, John had built several of these mills in the area, but the farm would now have to operate without one.

Some children dream of accomplishing great things or being a star. Some want to amass a great wealth or travel the world, but young George in 1888 had a novel dream: he would one day rebuild this father's windmill. In the next year, with help, he was able to salvage the two heavy millstones, and the steps leading up from the first to the second story. The remainder of the mill was completely demolished. He moved the stones and steps to a Spocott barn, and told all that someday he would resurrect the mill.

Over eighty years would pass, and all memories of the mill were long erased—but not from George's mind. In 1970, he returned to his never forgotten childhood dream. It was time to rebuild his father's windmill. However, in 1970 windmills were part of the memory of a distant past.

In the nineteenth century in this area of Dorchester County, Maryland, farming, shipbuilding, and mills made a logical trifecta. Because this area was isolated by the Bay and the Choptank River, farmers needed ships to get their crops to a market. Mills were needed to turn the grain they grew into usable flour. While Dorchester County had once been the home of at least twenty windmills (1877), the remains of the last had gone down in a hurricane in the 1950s. Water mills were more practical in areas where there was running water. Western and southern Dorchester County were flat, much of it not much higher than the level of a high tide, and only a wind-powered mill could be built in these areas. Using many of his shipbuilding skills, John Anthony LeCompte Radcliffe built several mills in this area of the county. However, by 1970, these skills were long gone, and George somehow had to find a windmill builder.

While boat building was a dying art, across the road from Spocott there was still a boatyard run by a remarkable gentleman. James Richardson, or "Captain Jim" as so many called him, was a boat builder from the old school and owner of Richardson Boat Yard. His family had built ships since the seventeenth century, and he was nationally known for boat restoration, having restored boats for the Smithsonian Institution, and had just built a colonial-style sailing vessel for the South Carolina Tricentennial. He would later be the one selected to build a replica of the Dove, one of the two ships that landed in St. Mary's City in 1634, the founding of Maryland. George would approach Jim with the task of rebuilding the windmill. We can only imagine what Jim's initial reaction was, but George, in his legendary, low-keyed method of persuasion, did get Jim to agree to the project. However, there was no manual for how to build a windmill, with one not having been built for almost a century.

Quite likely, Jim was the only one who could have built the mill, but even he had no idea where to start. George, of course, had to locate the funding for the project, but this was a skill he excelled in. As he had done many times before, he turned to family. A cousin living in Atlanta, Georgia, Walter Clay Hill, Jr. immediately embraced the project. His mother, Rebecca Beckwith Travers (1886–1967) was the granddaughter of John Anthony LeCompte Radcliffe and had spent considerable time at Spocott as a child. She and George had remained close throughout her life, and her son Walter was more than happy to fund the mill as both a memorial to his mother and his great-grandfather.

Meanwhile, Jim Richardson was beginning his search for how to build a windmill. The original Spocott windmill had been an English post mill, in which the entire two-story mill housing rests on one post, allowing it to be turned into the wind. A tailpole extended out from the building to a wheel, and by turning the wheel, one could rotate the entire building to whatever direction the wind was coming from on a particular day. The blades of the mill were attached to a main shaft, and its rotation was transferred by gears to the top millstone, where the corn, barley, rye, or wheat was turned into meal. All of this occurred in the upper story with the meal falling by chute into the lower bagging room where it first went through a screen sieve. Jim had photos of old mills to examine and found several books from England and Holland, and he knew that historic Williamsburg had a supposedly operational windmill. He headed down there to get ideas but was disappointed to find the officials there remarkably disinterested. However, he was able to get time with the actual miller at the attraction. The older gentleman was enthusiastic but told him the Williamsburg mill did not operate properly on its own and had to have supplemental power. However, he did give Captain Jim some useful tidbits of information, and Jim returned home.

George was not going to let the project die, and Jim Richardson was certainly not a quitter. At his boatyard, Jim started building and continually modified a model of a potential mill. As he would say:

> We couldn't go by the book because there wasn't any book that showed the construction details we needed. We couldn't copy a model, because there aren't any. We couldn't ask anybody because there's nobody left who knows how corn-grinding windmills were put together. What we had to do was construct our mill by trial and error, using our own ideas. When we ran into a problem,

we simply had to figure it out ourselves. Sometimes we guessed right and sometimes we didn't.[3]

This was going to be a process of trial and error, and he eventually had a model which seemed to work. Using this boatyard crew and some additional volunteers, construction began. Jim's son-in-law, Tom Howell, took charge of the construction with Jim supervising every step and doing much of the work. This became a labor of love. The work crew even included Bill Radcliffe, the grandson of George L. Radcliffe, and Walter Clay Hill III, son of Walter Hill. Jim Richardson was the mastermind of the operation and was a perfectionist. Jim may have even lost money on the whole project, but the resulting mill stands as a memorial to a remarkable craftsman and person.

All the timbers for the mill came from the nearby Spocott woodland, exactly where George's father would have gotten the timber for the original mill, and considerable time was invested in finding just the right trees for the construction, which took more than a year. The critical piece of timber was the central post around which the three-ton base was constructed. Jim, George, and others finally located the perfect four-foot diameter oak, and this was dressed down to the central post, two-foot wide at the base. Oak was used for the rest of the framework, and pine was used for the building housing.

The original stones were used, each weighing in at 700 pounds. The mill was assembled in pieces at the Richardson Boat Yard and gradually moved into place. Every step of the operation needed the approval of George L. Radcliffe, but he had complete faith in Captain Jim. George watched with the enthusiasm of that child, who had seen his father's amazing mill years earlier. The four blades were each twenty-eight feet long and had to, along with the building, be perfectly balanced. As Tom Howell would explain, if the mill building were even slightly off or the blades and weight not perfectly distributed, the vibration from the awesome power generated would have ripped the entire structure apart. And they were successful. Almost fifty years after its construction, the mill operates with virtually no vibration as the blades spin and that massive top stone rotates over the stationary bed stone.

George and his son George M. set up a foundation, the Spocott Windmill Foundation, Inc., and the basic construction was completed in 1972. The dedication was set for August 22, 1972, the senator's ninety-fifth birthday. Citizens, family, politicians, and friends showed up for the combination dedication and birthday party at the nearby firehouse. George spoke, of course; even at that age, he was not going to pass up the opportunity to say a few words and to thank the many individuals who had helped him realize his dream. He had waited eighty-five years for that moment, and he relished every moment of that wonderful summer day. He lived just two more years, and he visited that mill many times. One can only imagine how satisfying this must have been to an aged gentleman who had been able to fulfill the dream of an exceedingly long life.

Spocott Windmill - The "George L"
Constructed 1972 by Jim Richardson

The mill was actually not completed when it was dedicated, but then ninety-fifth birthdays only happen once. The following year saw the construction of the gears. The seven-foot oak gear wheel was fitted with fifty-one beechwood teeth which turned the spindle attached to the upper stone. The stones also had to be dressed, one of the many tasks new to Jim Richardson, but by the summer of 1973, the mill was ready to operate. With the sails raised on the four long blades, the blades, main shaft, and gear wheel could rotate up to twenty times a minute, generating up to fifty horsepower. Too old to climb the steep steps up into the mill, the ninety-six-year-old warrior stood silently watching those sail-covered blades whipping around. Never at a loss for words, he was uncharacteristically silent; he must have been remembering back to the last time he had seen that mill turn, almost nine decades earlier. How satisfying it must have been to see a lifelong dream fulfilled. He would die less than a year later.

George L. Radcliffe Beside the Reconstruction
of His Father's Spocott Windmill, 1972

The mill was named the "George L" in honor of him, but then, windmills, unlike boats, always are given a male name. George never wanted a mill named after him, but he was outvoted by all others involved. It had to be named after him. The mill continues to operate two times a year. The sails are raised by halyards on each blade, one at a time, and the lower stone can be lowered slightly to the proper distance to get the coarseness needed for the meal to be produced. The basic framework of the mill is still intact, a testament to Jim Richardson's craftsmanship, and the mill stands today as a monument to two remarkable gentlemen: a boatbuilder and the son of a boatbuilder. Through the efforts of so many, a ten-year-old boy's unusual and remarkable dream came true.

> I don't remember it being built, but I remember it blowing down in the blizzard of 1888, when I was 11 years old. Since then, I've always hoped that some day the old windmill would come home again. Now that we have it, we're going to keep it, and all the angels in heaven and demons down under the sea can't take it away from us. (George L. Radcliffe, Aug. 22, 1972)[4]

The Power of Concentration

It was a cold winter morning, and a young George L. Radcliffe jumped out of bed to get ready for work. He was head of the legal department of the American Bonding Company and, at this point in his life, one of the more respected members of the community. He lived in a boarding house in downtown Baltimore, close enough to work that he could walk to and from his office. This particular day was nothing new, just his typical routine as he was getting himself ready for work and fixing his breakfast.

After putting on the charcoal grey suit he always wore to work, he consumed his usual gargantuan breakfast of bacon, toast, and eggs. He always read while eating, and there was a pile of books and magazines littering every spot in the house. After tying his tie, donning his hat and overcoat, and grabbing his briefcase, he headed out of the row house and started walking south on Calvert Street toward his office. Always deep in thought, he was undoubtedly contemplating some business transaction or the book or magazine he had just been reading. He was always busy processing information, often completely oblivious to what was happening around him.

He had gotten about a block when an acquaintance ran up to him. "Uh, Mr. Radcliffe ... are you alright?"

"Fine, fine, fine" would have been his likely response as it so often was.

"But haven't you forgotten something?" He undoubtedly glanced at his briefcase but obviously did not look down.

"Mr. Radcliffe, you have NO pants on!" One can only imagine that the man who had won the Penn Relay a few years earlier must have made it back to his boarding house in record time.

George L. Radcliffe told this story on himself on countless occasions, always chuckling as much as those hearing the tale, and while we never encountered an actual eyewitness, those who knew him never doubted the story for a moment. George not only had a doctoral degree in history, but he also had one in absentmindedness. It certainly was not for lack of working brain cells. In fact, it undoubtedly was a testament to his amazing powers of concentration. When George was reading or deep in thought, nothing would grab his attention. If his house had ever caught on fire while he was reading, there is no doubt he would have perished without ever knowing what was transpiring. His absentmindedness was legendary, and no one enjoyed poking fun at this trait of his more than he. He never showed embarrassment, seeming to enjoy the comic situation as much as the ones around him. He would finally realize what he was doing, respond with a "my, my, my" and then laugh along with the rest of us. If absentmindedness is a sign of intelligence, then George L. Radcliffe was Mensa material. His delight in poking fun at himself spoke volumes of his self-confidence and ability to accept and enjoy the kind of person he was.

His powers of concentration were evident to all, even when he was a child. His brother Sewell, in later years, would tell story after story of his brother not coming to dinner after being called repeatedly, reading a book from cover to cover without break, or reading by candlelight well into the night. Sewell was the practical one, his other brother Tom was the comic, and George was the absentminded bookworm. George grew up on a working farm where all worked from dawn to dusk, but he obviously found time to read. He came by his passion for reading honestly as his father, John Anthony LeCompte Radcliffe, got up every morning without fail at 4 a.m. and read and reflected until daylight when he would then head out to work on the farm.

George's capacity for concentration and learning enabled him to complete high school early and earn three degrees in a short period of time, taking only one year to complete three years of law school. He was certainly not the typical country youth, although he always considered country to be at his core. His amazing powers of concentration were applied to achieving academic heights rather than to the work on his beloved farm. John remained intensely proud of his youngest son, who was able to pursue a path not available to his father many years earlier.

My grandfather was seventy-two years old when I was born, and most of my memories were of him in his 80s and 90s. I had heard the "no pants" story on several occasions and never doubted it as I was witness to many less significant episodes. On several occasions he showed up on a cold day without a coat or removed his coat to reveal 2 neckties around his neck. I assumed that this is what happened to individuals in the twilight of their life. To me, he was just a loving grandfather who reminisced, told amazing and quite lengthy stories, and had fascinating mental lapses. Only in later years did I realize what a remarkable mind lay beneath this lovable and simple exterior. In high school I soon found that there was no topic of which he was not the master. I could be discussing a poet or author, and he would launch into a long-memorized passage, or I would mention a historical figure only to have him recite a short biography complete with numerous quotes. He could launch into a long recitation of Latin poems he had learned seventy years earlier. He was a walking encyclopedia, easily the most knowledgeable person I have ever met. And he read every day of his life, living in a veritable library.

I remember vividly one period when he was staying with us while we vacationed at Spocott. We had just returned from shopping in town to find him deep into a historical novel. He was sipping on a drink while he read and did stop to look up briefly when we entered the room. We asked what he was drinking, and he informed us that he had fixed a pitcher of lemonade. My mother looked puzzled and seemed surprised since lemonade was one of the items we had just gone into town to purchase. She went into the kitchen to see the lemonade he had made and soon let out a scream. "He's drinking bacon grease!" Yes, the learned scholar had seen a lemonade can on the stove we used for bacon grease drippings, added three cans of water as the directions of the can dictated, and had now half consumed the drink. I naively assumed that my grandfather had finally gone around the bend and only later realized that he was so deep into what he was reading that he was totally unaware of what he was drinking. But bacon grease?

One other occasion also demonstrated that George's ability to concentrate was extraordinary. My grandfather had joined us for a family crab feast on the porch of Spocott, something we often did while visiting the house each summer. He had regaled us with his many stories of family life years ago, and after consuming his share of crustaceans, retired into the living room to read while many continued to work their way through the mountain of crabs. Finally, the table was cleared, and a watermelon appeared to the delight of all. I cut off a slice and took it in to my grandfather to eat. When I told him I had his dessert, without missing a beat in his reading, he simply motioned to the table so that I could put it down. I knew better than to interrupt this sacred activity. I cleared a space on the cluttered table for the plate and then returned to the porch to join the rest of the family. I don't remember how much time went by, but finally the door to the porch opened. We were laughing about something, so no one was looking when he walked on to the porch. "My, my, my, this watermelon tastes a bit sandy." Puzzled, we all looked up. There he was standing on the porch holding his "dessert." Everyone's jaw dropped immediately to the floor. Was this a joke? Although he had a fabulous sense of humor, it was not like him to pull a practical joke. There was no watermelon in his hand, but instead a piece of sandpaper with one bite-sized piece removed. Finally looking at what was in his hand, he muttered, "Oh my, my, my. I've been silly." To this day, everyone who hears the story from a family member either does not believe it or feels it is heavily exaggerated. With George L. Radcliffe, no aspect of this remarkable individual ever had to be exaggerated.

He never made excuses or tried to cover up these silly moments. The family debated for years whether he was pulling a practical joke or had truly "gone over the hill." Only in reflecting on these moments years later have I realized neither was the case. He had an ability to concentrate and block out virtually all stimuli. I could see his father and mother almost a century earlier shaking their heads as their son clearly was blocking out all they said as he was transported back to ancient Greece or Rome while reading another of Plutarch's histories.

Our family has delighted in sharing these stories in the many years since he passed from us, but never are they shared out of disrespect. All understand how remarkable this gentleman was with his extraordinarily powers of concentration. We have long since stopped referring to him as absentminded. He had the ability to completely immerse himself in an issue, transport himself back in time to a particular period of history, and actually relive the events of his life. If he were reading a book, he literally became a part of the book. It is no wonder that history was his passion. He was never in the military, but he marched with Alexander of Macedon on his Egyptian campaign, fought with William of Normandy at Hastings in 1066, spent the winter of 1777–78 at Valley Forge with Washington, and suffered through the human carnage at Antietam in 1862. While many of us find history fascinating, George L. Radcliffe could live it in the most real of ways. With a combination of intelligence and remarkable concentration, he was unique in his capacity to immerse himself in a task. What a contrast to so many today who quickly jump from one task to another. Young children have the ability and imagination to be transported by a book to both imaginary and real places; George never lost that ability in all of his ninety-seven years.

Just a Grandfather

In 1964, President Lyndon Johnson was speaking in Baltimore, and my grandfather asked me to go with him to hear the speech at the Fifth Regiment Armory. Happily sacrificing my homework for an evening, I welcomed the opportunity. I often did things with my grandparents, and getting to hear the president sounded like considerably more fun than solving quadratic equations. It was a standard political speech, but what happened afterwards is what made an impression. Instead of exiting the main door, we used a door at the front of the Armory. I was gazing around at the room we were in when my grandfather started speaking to someone. Turning back toward him, I realized he was conversing with President Johnson. I was introduced and shook the president's hand. However, I remember nothing of what they said as I could only wonder, "My grandfather knows the president?" I was in shock. Yes, I knew he had been a senator, but I had only known him as a grandfather. I never did ask him how he knew Johnson since Johnson did not enter the Senate until two years after my grandfather departed. That is one of many questions I should have asked him and didn't, but then fifteen minutes after leaving the speech, he was back to wearing his grandfather shoes, the role which he most enjoyed at that time.

In 1958, as a fourth grader, I was assigned to do a project on my hometown, Baltimore. The project needed to cover local history and its landmarks, and include as many photos as possible. My grandfather was one of my assistants on this. He could not drive, but he was interested in the project and aided by identifying landmarks and providing historical highlights. I photographed the Shot Tower, but never once did he mention that he had helped save it in 1924. I included the Maryland Historical Society, but he never mentioned he had been president of it for twenty years. Bragging was completely foreign to him, but most important, he just wanted to be a grandfather. And for the first sixteen years of my life, George L. Radcliffe was just a lovable grandfather. I knew that he had been a U.S. Senator, but he had never once talked of his tenure in the Senate. He had received numerous awards throughout his life, but I only found out about these in later years. He was the most modest man I ever knew, never once boasting or drawing attention to himself. For my entire childhood and even into my adulthood, I sat mesmerized as he recounted tales of life in the nineteenth century. He saw the good in all, and each story would highlight the gift that everyone had left us with. His stories cut through the complexities of life to show what was most important: family, relationships, hard work, empathy, and modesty.

This was a time when families all sat down to dine together with no TV or cell phones to distract, and a child did not get up and leave the table after a meal until all were done eating. My grandfather had many meals with us, especially after my grandmother passed in 1963. His stories were of remarkable individuals he encountered in his daily life: the one-armed carpenter who did a lot of construction for him, the relative who pulled a mule out of a well, gathering firewood on a windy sub-freezing night, the spontaneous dances which would occur at Spocott, his efforts to save the 400-year-old Council Oak, and taking the ferry from Annapolis to nearby Travers Wharf, sometimes arriving in the middle of the night. There was no end to the stories, and a family dinner would often run well into the evening. As a young boy, I wanted to go outside and play ball in the last bit of waning daylight, but there was no leaving the table as my grandfather weaved his tapestry of life long ago. I wouldn't be truthful if I said I enjoyed forgoing baseball to hear the clever way that Columbus Wheatley repaired that barn, but years later I am so thankful I was forced to sit through them all. Children do not always know what is best for them, and I was no exception. I may not remember all the details, but the picture he painted for me of life long ago is as clear as if I had lived through it myself. With our family getting its first television set at about this time, I wondered how my grandfather could have enjoyed himself without it. "Books" would always be the answer. They were his treasure and ticket to the world of places and ideas. He traveled the world as a child without ever leaving Spocott, and books provided him the ultimate time machine.

His stories made one almost want to forgo the trappings of modern life and go back to what seemed a better time, especially when put against the fears engendered by the Cold War in which I was growing up. He could even make struggling out to the outhouse on a snowy winter night sound like an adventure, although his description of the barrel of corn cobs just outside the outhouse door certainly killed my desire to build a time machine back to the nineteenth century. Family was paramount, and life was about building strong relationships. The characters he de-

George L. Radcliffe with Grandson William Boggs Radcliffe, 1954

scribed would rival any Dickensian characters: Adaline Wheatley, the cook without equal and weaver of endless tales; Kemp Wilson who could master any farm animal; Columbus Wheatley, former enslaved worker, who lived out his life at Spocott as a master carpenter; Arthur Jones, the first Maryland State Trooper, who hunted with Annie Oakley; Grandmother Polly who single-handedly took on a British frigate in the War of 1812; his uncle Nehemiah Beckwith who was killed fighting for the Confederacy; and his father, the abolitionist slave owner and shipbuilder. He brought all these and many more to life for his grandchildren.

A visit to either his Baltimore home or his home on the Spocott property was an adventure easily topping any museum visit. Books were piled everywhere, relics of the past littered every table, and the odor of holly, pine, and bayberry filled every room. Most of the rooms were vacant but filled with memories of the past. One room was piled high with old shoes and hats he had never thrown away. One contained seemingly every magazine he had ever purchased. The entire downstairs and the giant staircase were lined with family portraits, enhancing the feeling that one had stepped back in time.

Walking through those homes was a walk through the past. His Baltimore house was lit only by small electric candles, probably differing little from the oil lanterns he once used. The hours before bedtime in that house were always spent around a giant open fire, where stories abounded, and a good book was always close at hand. The fires were often too hot, but there was still something unworldly comforting about sitting in front of the fireplace, sipping on hot chocolate (made by melting Hershey's Kisses in milk), hearing a story I had heard many times before, and letting my imagination transport me back 100 years; the house was the perfect time machine.

I spent many nights there, and if ghosts existed, they surely would have congregated in that old house, perched fifty feet above the road below. I would lie in the bed with my imagination running in third gear, keeping sleep far away. The crackling of an open fire, the sound of distant conversation, his frequent piano playing in the evening, the incessantly creaking stairs, and the odors all kept my mind active.

Three aspects of my grandfather left a lasting impression on me. My most vivid memories of him are of a man with incredible modesty. Surely, if there were a person who could have excelled in legitimate bragging, it was he, but the picture he painted of himself was of a shy boy years ago, no different than me. His stories would often poke fun at himself, and the person he described when talking of himself years ago was just ordinary, living his life the best he knew how, sometimes succeeding but many times failing. He had risen far above others in his family, but he saw all as equal, each doing their part to make the world a better place. I never once heard him name-drop. He mingled with presidents, heads of state, entertainers, and sports figures and could have wowed us with story after story about some VIP he had interacted with. It was only in my later years that I got him to talk about Roosevelt and Truman.

He also saw the value in every person. He was far more educated than most around him, but he saw that intelligence manifested itself in many ways. Adaline never learned to read or write, but her wisdom and insight were remarkable to him. The watermen he encountered also had little formal education, but their practical knowledge was unequaled. He would describe the amazing work of a mechanic while poking fun at the fact that he had trouble turning on a radio. He marveled at his wife's artistic ability, a trait he said had clearly passed him by. He saw that the strength of a community was not in its leaders but those whose daily, usually unnoticed efforts, make it strong. As a U.S. senator, it was more important to talk to the common citizen than the Washington establishment, as these ordinary people were the heart and soul of the country. He avoided the political bosses of his day, always knowing who he was truly beholding to.

And finally, his focus was always on the positive. I never once heard him speak poorly of another person. Gossip to him was sharing some positive trait he saw in someone, even if it were obvious to the rest of us that the negatives in that person trumped the positives. Even in his diaries, which I assume were written for his eyes only, he cites all in the most positive way possible. He would mention his frustrations at times, but would remain hopeful for the future. I never saw him get mad or raise his voice at another, and I sometimes wonder if any of his DNA even trickled down to me.

One evening when he was staying with us, I was writing a speech which I was to deliver in school the next day. I was procrastinating, hoping the assignment would somehow evaporate. As a stutterer, I was terrified of public speaking. When he realized what I was working on, he asked me about it, and knowing that he had delivered more speeches than anyone else I knew, I asked him for advice. Rather than offer advice, he asked me why I was having trouble preparing. I rambled on but basically said I was afraid of making a fool out of myself. I then asked him when he stopped being nervous when making a speech. His answer shocked me as he told me that he still got nervous speaking in front of a group but that being scared made him do a better job. Oddly, that comforted me, and the next day I thought about him speaking in front of the Senate as I waited in class for my turn to speak. I had seen him speak numerous times, and he always seemed relaxed while speaking. I have made quite a few speeches myself over the years, and often think of him, taking comfort in whatever pre-speech nervousness I might feel.

Forty-seven years have passed since his death, but rarely a day goes by without one of his stories forcing its way into my head. He was not the grandparent I was closest to when I was very young, as he was hardly the cuddly type that a young child would seek comfort in. Kind, always gentle, never without a smile, he was always accessible. As the years pass, however, he is the grandparent who looms large in my life, and more and more I use him as the yardstick for measuring my own worth as a senior now myself. No one could have a better role model for how to make the maximum impact in our brief existence. Never making excuses for failure, always finding the best in everyone, never quitting, finding humor on even the darkest of days, he continues to inspire me as he did so many others. But it is those stories that are so much a part of me. Because of him, I know that I'm not just a temporary inhabitant of this orbiting rock. I am a link in a long chain. I owe my existence to those who came before as others will look back on me in years to come. Those stories are more than tales of time gone by, but a reminder of the responsibility that the gift of life bestows. I know what so many had to endure for me to live the blessed life that I do, and what I must live up to. I live at Spocott now, and the property is so much more than the buildings and trees found there. I see John Anthony LeCompte building one of his massive schooners, I smell Adaline's biscuits emanating from that marvelous kitchen, I hear one of Columbus Wheatley's highly exaggerated stories of the Civil War, and I see Grandmother Polly rowing out to the British warship to free her husband. I never met any of those individuals, but I know them well. Everyone should be so lucky as to have such a grandparent.

COUSIN GEORGE

F ew today remember George L. Radcliffe for his twelve years in the United States Senate. There were more noteworthy senators at that time, and George was happy to be in the background, just doing the job he was elected to do. In many ways he won't be remembered for his role in the Maryland Historical Society, of which he was an officer for over sixty years, overseeing the Society's rise from a small organization to the significant complex it is today. Some of the young employees of the Society today don't even recognize his name. Most that heard his many speeches have passed on, and his speeches were generally considered more college lectures than oratorical rhetoric. While the history he preserved still stands, his role in its preservation is to a large extent forgotten. This would not bother George L. Radcliffe in the least as he never sought publicity, but he would be proud to see that much of the work of his lifetime has had a lasting effect. The Baltimore Shot Tower still stands, his childhood home remains intact, although its demise at the hands of rising sea level may seal its ultimate fate, and the history and genealogical material which he helped unearth is well recorded.

What George wanted to be remembered for and what he was most proud of was his family. His immediate family was limited, as he had only one child, and only one of his 4 grandchildren lived to have children. I am the only immediate family alive that knew him. George, however, defined his family in a different way than many. He often claimed to be related to everyone in Dorchester County, Maryland, and he may not be far off the mark with that comment. He was, after all, descended from a number of Dorchester County's earliest settlers. With his knowledge of his family history, he probably knew every third and fourth cousin, and with eighteen siblings, his extended family was massive. He had many titles: Senator, Doctor, Professor, and Chairman; however, what he wanted people to call him was "Cousin George." Many referred to him this way who weren't related, or at least didn't know if they were. Many "cousins" couldn't even tell you how they were exactly related. George could.

I experienced this first-hand as a child, as the name of every person to whom he introduced me was prefaced by "cousin". My grandfather might even try to explain the relationship although he usually lost me about halfway through the "this is Cousin Cornelia's daughter's first husband's third child's son." He would often just say that they were a Robinson, Cator, Ewell, Travers, Keene, or one of a dozen other names I could not remember. I soon gave up even trying to figure out who was who and learned quickly to just call everyone "cousin." In hindsight, I wish I had carried a chart around as I have spent the last ten years trying to sort out all the cousins. George L. Radcliffe was the Ancestry.com of the twentieth century.

In 1963, George decided to celebrate the 300th birthday of his beloved Spocott property, and he set out to invite his family and a few friends. At this point, he had outlived most of his contemporaries, but invitations went out all over the country. In typical George L. Radcliffe fashion, his invitation was unique, reading:

September 12, 1963

Three hundred years ago enterprising and colorful Stephen Gary from Looe, Cornwall, England secured in 1663 a grant of land from Lord Baltimore which he called in his will Specott his "Home Plantation," in distinction from his other numerous land holdings.

The gigantic historic oak tree which sheltered Gary died a few years ago. The bears disappeared. So did the deer, but have returned. Corn, turkeys, oysters, and manninoes [clams] will be in close contact with us on October 12th -gastronomically pleasant we hope. Deer, terrapin, rabbits, partridges, and muskrats will be close around us but plead temporary legal immunity from capture and consumption. Tobacco left Specott many years ago and never returned. Since 1663, descendants of Stephen Gary, always relatives and usually ancestors of present owner, have owned Specott and lived there.

You are cordially invited to join a very informal out-of-doors party at Specott of descendants of Stephen Gary and other friends at 2 p.m., October 12th as guests of –

- Some Radcliffe Descendants of Stephen Gary

Sewell was the only of George's eighteen siblings still alive, and many of his first cousins had also passed. Many could not make the long trip to Spocott, but the word was out that Cousin George was having a party. Five hundred people showed up! Or at least that was the number I had reached before giving up as I tried to control the massive overflow of parking on the family property. Spocott was overrun with guests, but the eighty-five-year-old host greeted and talked to every person who showed up, staying on his feet a good twelve hours. Each person, even if not literally a cousin, got the red-carpet treatment befitting the closest of relatives. I attended that party as a fourteen-year-old, and I met all my cousins, probably not one of which I could remember at the end of the day. I could not believe that any person could have that many close friends. That was vintage George L. Radcliffe.

We have all the letters which George received and copies of all that he sent throughout most of his lifetime. He made a point of keeping in close contact with all of his family, regardless of how distant a cousin, even a cousin or two he tracked down in England. None received a cursory reply. His often two- to three-page typed letters would keep them abreast

George L. Radcliffe on October 12, 1963
At the 300th Year Spocott Birthday Celebration

of family news, progress in maintaining and restoring Spocott, and inquiries about the health and welfare of their family. One must believe that each of them felt special and loved, and they truly were. Even while in the Senate, carrying out Fidelity and Deposit Company business, and working on his many causes, a steady stream of letters flowed out of his office. Granted, his secretary typed all those letters, but he dictated each one, often staying in his office well into the evening. While the letters often overlapped in content, they were tailored to each individual person. We need to remember that this was before the advent of word processing; he dictated, and his secretary typed, every letter.

Whenever he was home, either in Baltimore or Cambridge, dropping in on a cousin was standard operating procedure. Traveling on either Senate or Fidelity and Deposit business provided an opportunity to visit a relative in another city. George was the goodwill ambassador for the family. He made sure that all knew their relationship to him, and if it were a distant relationship, George would have sent them enough genealogical information for them to know their exact place in the family. The fact that the two of them shared a seventeenth century ancestor made them family.

George was never wealthy, although he hardly qualified as needy, but he was always the one whom family turned to for assistance. Looking through his extensive archived family correspondence, one can quickly see that he was constantly issuing loans as family members struggled through the difficult times of the 1920s through 1940s. He, the younger brother, constantly looked out for his two brothers, Tom and Sewell. In the late 1920s, he bought their share of Spocott since neither of them was to have children. He then set them up at Spocott, taking on all the house and property expenses for the remainder of their lives. He let them live at the family home while he moved into the tenant home, Windemere. Sewell had serious alcohol problems at one point in his life, even having to be hospitalized. Even with George's insanely busy schedule, he made time for constant visits and frequent letters, and Sewell later attributed much of his recovery to his brother's support. Cousins always knew they could come to him for a loan, and often he was not paid back. He hardly would have operated this way in his Fidelity and Deposit business, but this was family after all.

Cousin George also continued his father's "open house" policy, and all knew they were welcome, even if they just showed up uninvited. They would sit in rockers out on one of the spacious porches at Spocott and talk the day or night away. Stories would drift out over the property as George regaled his guests with talk of his early days on the farm, Christmas feasts, the Spocott Shipyard, and the many colorful characters who populated the Spocott community. There was no Adaline there to prepare an impromptu feast, but he might take them out to dinner at one of the local restaurants where he would, after studiously examining the menu, predictably pronounce, "I think I'll have duck for a change." Before his death he would spend several days sitting on that porch with James Michener, who undoubtedly was beginning work on his novel *Chesapeake*, and Michener got a serious dose of that Cousin George hospitality as George literally rambled on for several days.

Almost more important was the emotional support he provided his "cousins" with his letters and visits. He was hardly a "touchy-feely" person, always remaining somewhat business-like, much like his father, but his presence, the length of his letters, and his continuing interest in them transmitted his unquestionable caring. As an example of the way he wore his "cousin hat" he took quite an interest in the granddaughter of one of his many first cousins. The woman was forty years his junior and had been raised by her grandparents, although both parents were still alive. He became a grandfather-like figure in her life, and when her life became complicated in the 1940s, he was there to support her. She confided in him throughout the whole period, and her letters show George's importance to her. After her grandmother passed, her grandfather seemed to have turned against her. The desperation in her writing is evident:

> Really, Cousin George, I don't know what will come next, and after all I have gone through, life has little for which I can live for. I have tried to live right and do the right thing by everyone. I'm sure I failed at times, but I was sincere and my intentions were good. The next time you are in Cambridge, please come to see me, you are so just and fair, and in you I have a real friend and relative.

And visit her he did. They wrote each other constantly, with George continually offering grandfatherly advice. Several years later when she was planning to get married, sadly still estranged from her family, she reached out to Cousin George again, "Since I seem to be a lone soul, I need a 'father' to give me away, and I have always felt very close to you. I'd be oh so very happy for you to be my dad that day and give me away."

Scenarios like this played out throughout his life. George L. Radcliffe may have achieved national prominence, but his role as patriarch of a large family was most important to him. Marylanders remember George L. Radcliffe as a lawyer, businessman, historian, teacher, civic leader, politician, and office holder, but that is not how he would want to be remembered. He never sought fame, and chance circumstances, not ambition, would allow him to rise to statewide prominence. Governor Emerson Harrington, Judge Sam Dennis, Woodrow Wilson, and Franklin Roosevelt all played a role in pushing that small, shy boy from the Eastern Shore into positions of prominence. If George had met none of them and just played out his life with the engines of hard work, patience, reflection, and wisdom, it is likely so many would still remember him. It is doubtful that he would have entered the political world, but he would have had a significant impact on many.

I saw him frequently in his last few years as he lived in our house for several of those years, especially when his health began to fail. We talked often but rarely of his public life. He had to be proud of that, but those were not the memories which gave him comfort in those final days. His joy was his family, both past and present. He saw his most important role in a genealogical context. While he attended church frequently, he rarely talked of his beliefs. We do not know whether he believed in an afterlife, but I must believe that the afterlife he cherished was the one here on Earth, the one which encompassed his massive extended family. He had affected countless individuals and instilled his passion for family and history in so many that he remains a part of us. His obituaries touted his political, historical, and civic roles, but they are now long forgotten. Cousin George, however, still lives on. His family has grown with the arrival of succeeding generations, who, if they don't know of him, value the things he believed in. And all those stories still live on.

One of our last personal memories of him was of him holding his first great-grandchild in his lap. George was never the cuddly type, but

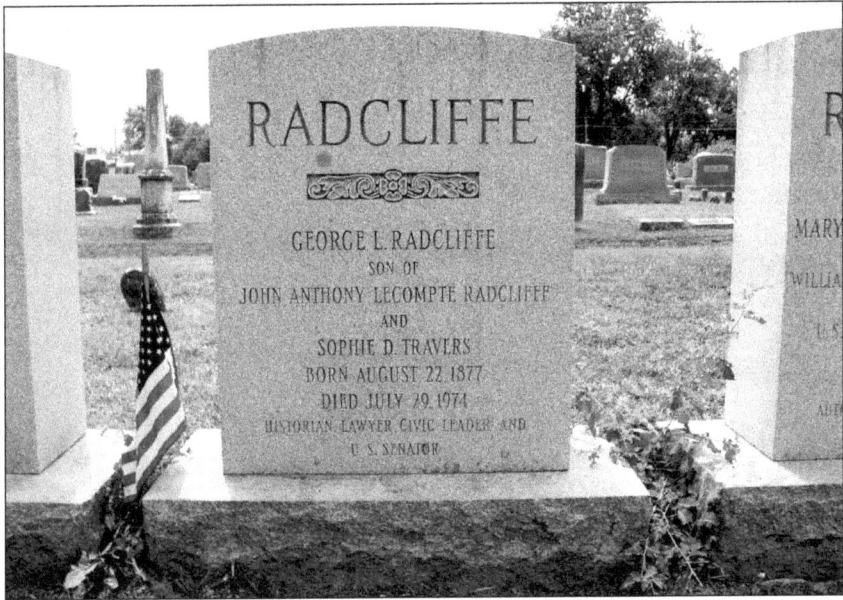

Grave of George L. Radcliffe
Location: Cambridge Cemetery in Cambridge, Maryland

so warm and interested in everyone. As he gently bounced six-month-old Scott Radcliffe on his knee, he grinned, saying "Well young man, what are your plans for this life of yours." He then proceeded to launch into stories about the Spocott worker who could lift a heifer by himself and how much young Scott would have enjoyed Adaline's sweet potato pie. It is doubtful that young Scott would have understood any of what was said, but he seemed to be listening attentively. This was the real George L. Radcliffe—no talk of politics, business, or even history. Family and his beloved Spocott were all that was on his mind.

George L. Radcliffe is buried in Cambridge Cemetery along with his wife, parents, and brothers. His tombstone lists his parents, which it should, as they were so critically important to him. His epitaph reads "Historian, Lawyer, Civic Leader, and U.S. Senator." He would smile to see that senator comes last of those four roles as that was probably the least important to him. However, if he could have written the epitaph himself, there is no doubt that it would read, simply "Cousin George."

Appendices

APPENDIX I

GEORGE L. RADCLIFFE'S
CIVIC INVOLVEMENT BY YEAR

Year	Age	Occupation	Committees/Organizations
1904	27	Head of Legal Dept., American Bonding Company	
1905	28	Head of Legal Dept., American Bonding Company	
1906	29	Head of Legal Dept., American Bonding Company	
1907	30	Head of Legal Dept., American Bonding Company	
1908	31	Vice President, American Bonding Company	*Chair*, 1st Johns Hopkins University Alumni Reunion; *Member*, Maryland Historical Society
1909	32	VP, American Bonding Company	*Member*, Maryland Historical Society; Helped form Johns Hopkins University Alumni Council
1910	33	VP, American Bonding Company	*Vice President*, Johns Hopkins Alumni Association; *Secretary*, Johns Hopkins University Alumni Council; *Member*, Maryland Historical Society
1911	34	VP, American Bonding Company	*Vice President*, Johns Hopkins Alumni Association; *Secretary*, Johns Hopkins University Alumni Council; *Member*, Maryland Historical Society
1912	35	VP, American Bonding Company	*Vice President*, Johns Hopkins Alumni Association; *Secretary*, Johns Hopkins University Alumni Council; *Secretary*, Maryland Historical Society

1913	36	Vice President, Fidelity & Deposit Co.; President, American Bonding Company	*Vice President*, Johns Hopkins Alumni Association; *Secretary*, Maryland Historical Society; *Secretary*, Johns Hopkins University Alumni Council; Johns Hopkins University, *Event Sports Inspector*
1914	37	VP, Fidelity & Deposit Co.; President, American Bonding Company	*Vice President*, Johns Hopkins Alumni Association; *Secretary*, Johns Hopkins University Alumni Council; *Secretary*, Maryland Historical Society; *Alumni Delegate*, Johns Hopkins Athletic Association
1915	38	VP, Fidelity & Deposit Co.; President, American Bonding Company	*President*, Johns Hopkins Alumni Association; *Secretary*, Johns Hopkins University Alumni Council; *Secretary*, Maryland Historical Society; *Vice President*, Maryland League for National Defense; *Secretary*, Hopkins Club
1916	39	VP, Fidelity & Deposit Co.; President, American Bonding Company	*President*, Johns Hopkins Alumni Association; *Secretary*, Johns Hopkins University Alumni Council; *Secretary*, Maryland Historical Society; *Member*, Baltimore City Liquor Board
1917	40	VP, Fidelity & Deposit Co.; President, American Bonding Company	*President*, Johns Hopkins Alumni Association; *Assoc. Dir.*, Bureau of Personnel, American Red Cross; *Secretary*, Johns Hopkins University Alumni Council; *Secretary*, Maryland Historical Society; *Member*, Baltimore City Liquor Board; *Member*, Liberty Loan Committee; *Member*, Maryland Council of Defense
1918	41	VP, Fidelity & Deposit Co.; President, American Bonding Company	*President*, Johns Hopkins Alumni Association; *Assoc. Dir.*, Bureau of Personnel, American Red Cross; *Secretary*, Johns Hopkins University Alumni Council; *Secretary*, Maryland Historical Society; *Member*, Baltimore City Liquor Board; *Member*, Liberty Loan Committee; *Member*, Maryland Council of Defense; *Chairman*, War Records Committee; *Member*, "Over There" Committee; *Member*, Maryland Branch, League to Enforce Peace

1919	42	**MD Secretary of State** VP, Fidelity & Deposit Co.; President, American Bonding Company	*President*, Johns Hopkins Alumni Association; *Chair*, Johns Hopkins University Dormitory Committee; *Secretary*, Maryland Historical Society; *Member*, Baltimore City Liquor Board; *Treasurer*, Maryland League of Nations; *Member*, Maryland Council of Defense; *Chairman*, War Records Committee
1920	43	**MD Secretary of State** VP, Fidelity & Deposit Co.; President, American Bonding Company	*Secretary*, Maryland Historical Society; *Member*, Maryland Council of Defense; *Chairman*, Johns Hopkins University Alumni Committee; *Chairman*, War Records Committee
1921	44	VP, Fidelity & Deposit Co.; President, American Bonding Company	*Secretary*, Maryland Historical Society
1922	45	VP, Fidelity & Deposit Co.; President, American Bonding Company	*Secretary*, Maryland Historical Society; *Member*, Woodrow Wilson Foundation Committee
1923	46	VP, Fidelity & Deposit Co.; President, American Bonding Company	*Secretary*, Maryland Historical Society
1924	47	VP, Fidelity & Deposit Co.; President, American Bonding Company	*Secretary*, Maryland Historical Society; *Chairman*, Inauguration Committee for Governor Ritchie; *Chairman*, Shot Tower Campaign; *Treasurer/Trustee*, Johns Hopkins University Walter Hines Page School of International Relations Planning/Funding
1925	48	VP, Fidelity & Deposit Co.; President, American Bonding Company	*Secretary*, Maryland Historical Society; *Treasurer/Trustee*, Johns Hopkins University Walter Hines Page School of International Relations Planning/Funding; *Chairman*, Shot Tower Campaign; *Chairman*, Eastern Shore Society Historical Essay Contest

1926	49	VP, Fidelity & Deposit Co.; President, American Bonding Company	*Secretary*, Maryland Historical Society; *Chairman*, Eastern Shore Society Historical Essay Contest
1927	50	VP, Fidelity & Deposit Co.; President, American Bonding Company	*Secretary*, Maryland Historical Society; *Chairman*, Inauguration Committee, Governor Ritchie Maryland Historical Soc. Committee to Purchase Flag House; *Member*, National Crime Commission Committee; *Member*, Maryland Tercentenary Commission; *Member*, Motor Vehicle Accidents Commission; *Chairman*, Eastern Shore Society Historical Essay Contest
1928	51	VP, Fidelity & Deposit Co.; President, American Bonding Company	*Secretary*, Maryland Historical Society; *Chairman*, Eastern Shore Society Historical Essay Contest; *Member*, St. Johns College Commission
1929	52	VP, Fidelity & Deposit Co.; President, American Bonding Company	*Secretary*, Maryland Historical Society; *Member*, National Crime Commission Committee to study payroll robberies; *Member*, MD Motor Vehicle Admin. Accident Commission; *Chairman*, Eastern Shore Society Historical Essay Contest
1930	53	VP, Fidelity & Deposit Co.; President, American Bonding Company	*Secretary*, Maryland Historical Society; *Chairman*, Eastern Shore Society Historical Essay Contest
1931	54	VP, Fidelity & Deposit Co.	*Secretary*, Maryland Historical Society; *Chairman*, Inauguration Committee, Governor Ritchie; *Chairman*, Eastern Shore Society Historical Essay Contest
1932	55	VP, Fidelity & Deposit Co.	*Vice President*, Maryland Historical Society; *Chairman*, Maryland Democratic Campaign Committee; *Chairman*, Eastern Shore Society Historical Essay Contest
1933	56	**Public Works Administrator, Region 10** VP, Fidelity & Deposit Co	*Vice President*, Maryland Historical Society; *Maryland Organizer*, 1st Presidential Birthday Ball

1934	57	**Public Works Administrator, Region 10** VP, Fidelity & Deposit Co	*Vice President*, Maryland Historical Society; *Maryland Chairman*, Presidential Birthday Ball; *Secretary*, Maryland Tercentenary Commission
1935	58	**U.S. Senator** VP, Fidelity & Deposit Co.	*Vice President*, Maryland Historical Society; *Maryland Chairman*, Presidential Birthday Ball
1936	59	**U.S. Senator** VP, Fidelity & Deposit Co.	*Vice President*, Maryland Historical Society; *Maryland Chairman*, Presidential Birthday Ball; *Member*, Charles Carroll of Carrollton Bicentenary Comm.; *Chairman of Democratic State Central Committee Chairman*, Maryland Democratic Campaign Committee
1937	60	**U.S. Senator** VP, Fidelity & Deposit Co.	*Vice President*, Maryland Historical Society; *Maryland Chairman*, Presidential Birthday Ball
1938	61	**U.S. Senator** VP, Fidelity & Deposit Co.	*Vice President*, Maryland Historical Society; *Maryland Chairman*, Presidential Birthday Ball; *Manager*, Sen. Tydings Re-election Campaign
1939	62	**U.S. Senator** VP, Fidelity & Deposit Co.	*President*, Maryland Historical Society; *Chairman*, Maryland March of Dimes/Birthday Ball; *Chairman*, Star-Spangled Banner Committee
1940	63	**U.S. Senator** VP, Fidelity & Deposit Co.	*President*, Maryland Historical Society; *Chairman*, Maryland March of Dimes/Birthday Ball
1941	64	**U.S. Senator** VP, Fidelity & Deposit Co.	*President*, Maryland Historical Society; *Chairman*, Maryland March of Dimes/Birthday Ball
1942	65	**U.S. Senator** VP, Fidelity & Deposit Co.	*President*, Maryland Historical Society; *Chairman*, Maryland March of Dimes/Birthday Ball; *Chairman*, War Records Commission, World War II
1943	66	**U.S. Senator** VP, Fidelity & Deposit Co.	*President*, Maryland Historical Society; *Chairman*, Maryland March of Dimes/Birthday Ball; *Chairman*, War Records Commission, World War II

1944	67	**U.S. Senator** VP, Fidelity & Deposit Co.	*President*, Maryland Historical Society; *Chairman*, Maryland March of Dimes/Birthday Ball; *Delegate*, Democratic National Convention, Platform and Resolutions Committee; *Chairman*, War Records Commission, World War II
1945	68	**U.S. Senator** VP, Fidelity & Deposit Co.	*President*, Maryland Historical Society; *Chairman*, Maryland March of Dimes/Birthday Ball; *Member*, Baltimore City College Scholarship Committee; *Chairman*, War Records Commission, World War II
1946	69	**U.S. Senator** VP, Fidelity & Deposit Co.	*President*, Maryland Historical Society; *Chairman*, Maryland March of Dimes
1947	70	VP, Fidelity & Deposit Co.	*President*, Maryland Historical Society; *Chairman*, Maryland March of Dimes; *Chairman*, Baltimore Sesquicentennial Committee; *Chairman*, Baltimore Symphony Campaign; *Chairman*, Inauguration Committee, Governor Lane; *Chairman*, Inauguration Committee, Mayor D'Alesandro; *Chairman*, United Nations Association's – UN Week; *Member*, Greek War Relief Fund Committee
1948	71	VP, Fidelity & Deposit Co.	*President*, Maryland Historical Society; *Chairman*, Maryland March of Dimes; *Manager*, Maryland Truman Re-election Committee; *Chairman*, Lee-Jackson Statue Dedication; *Chairman*, Maryland Religious Toleration Celebration; *Chairman*, Maryland Committee to Support Marshall Plan; *Chairman*, Baltimore Symphony Campaign
1949	72	VP, Fidelity & Deposit Co.	*President*, Maryland Historical Society; *Chairman*, Maryland March of Dimes; *Chairman*, Maryland Religious Toleration Celebration; *Member*, Hall of Records Commission; *Chairman*, Baltimore Symphony Campaign

1950	73	VP, Fidelity & Deposit Co.	*President*, Maryland Historical Society; *Chairman*, Maryland March of Dimes; *Business Chairman*, Gov. Preston Lane Election Campaign; *Treasurer*, Maryland Citizen's Committee for the Hoover Report (government reorganization); *Trustee*, St. Mary's College
1951	74	VP, Fidelity & Deposit Co.	*President*, Maryland Historical Society; *Chairman*, Maryland March of Dimes; *President*, Grace Foundation; *Chairman*, Flag Day Ceremony in Baltimore; *Chairman*, Inaugural Ceremony for Mayor D'Alesandro; *Director*, Baltimore Contractors, Inc.; *Trustee*, St. Mary's College
1952	75	VP, Fidelity & Deposit Co.	*President*, Maryland Historical Society; *Chairman*, Maryland March of Dimes; *President*, Grace Foundation; *President*, English-Speaking Union; *Trustee*, The Truman Library; *Maryland Chairman*, Crusade for Freedom; *Chairman*, Chesapeake Bay Bridge Dedication Committee; *Maryland Delegate*, Democratic National Convention; *Director*, Baltimore Contractors, Inc.; *Chairman*, Baltimore's United Nations Week activities; *Co-chairman*, I am an American Day, Defender's Day, and Constitution Day Activities; *Trustee*, St. Mary's College
1953	76	VP, Fidelity & Deposit Co.	*President*, Maryland Historical Society; *Chairman*, Maryland March of Dimes; *President*, Grace Foundation; *President*, English-Speaking Union; *President*, University Club; *Maryland Chairman*, Crusade for Freedom; *Chairman of Dinner Committee*, Silver Jubilee, Baltimore Chapter of National Conference of Christians and Jews; *Chairman*, Constitution Day Committee; *Committee Member*, King George VI Memorial Fund; *Chairman*, Joint Fund-raising Appeal for Old Trinity Church and Grace Foundation; *Trustee*, St. Mary's College

1954	77	VP, Fidelity & Deposit Co.	*President*, Maryland Historical Society; *Chairman*, Maryland March of Dimes; *President*, Grace Foundation; *President*, English-Speaking Union; *President*, University Club; *Chairman*, Constitution Day Committee; *Chairman*, USO GI Pal Dinner; *Chairman*, Committee on Historical Markers in Maryland Planning Committee; Baltimore Oriole's Baseball Opening Day Parade, led parade dressed as Lord Baltimore; *Trustee*, St. Mary's College; *Committee Member*, Clair Bee's Youth Sports Program; *Co-chairman*, Baltimore Chapter of National Conference of Christians and Jews; *Co-chairman*, Sponsoring group to bring Shakespearean theater to Stratford, Connecticut
1955	78	VP, Fidelity & Deposit Co.	*President*, Maryland Historical Society; *Chairman*, Maryland March of Dimes; *President*, Grace Foundation; *President*, English-Speaking Union; *Honorary Chairman*, Baltimore Symphony Drive; *Chairman*, Constitution Day Committee; *Co-chairman*, Flag House Week observance; *Chairman* of USO GI Pal Dinner; *Chairman*, Defender's Day program; *Member*, WAAM Program Advisory Council; *Chairman*, Baltimore Harbor Tunnel Groundbreaking; *Chairman*, Welcoming Committee, Return of the *USS Constellation* to Baltimore; *Chairman*, Special Gifts., American Shakespeare Festival; *Trustee*, St. Mary's College; *Coordinator*, Boy Scout Scholarship Program
1956	79	VP, Fidelity & Deposit Co.	*President*, Maryland Historical Society; *Chairman*, Maryland March of Dimes; *Chairman*, Constitution Day; *President*, English-Speaking Union; *President*, Grace Foundation; *Chairman*, Nominating Committee, Baltimore Symphony Orchestra Association; *Trustee*, St. Mary's College; *Coordinator*, Boy Scout Scholarship Program

1957	80	Fidelity & Deposit Co	*President*, Maryland Historical Society; *Chairman*, Maryland March of Dimes; *President*, Grace Foundation; *Chairman*, Constitution Day; *President*, English-Speaking Union; *Trustee*, St. Mary's College; *Advisory Board*, United Nations Association of MD; *Coordinator*, Boy Scout Scholarship Program
1958	81	Fidelity & Deposit Co	*President*, Maryland Historical Society; *Chairman*, Maryland March of Dimes; *President*, Grace Foundation; *Chairman*, Civil War Centennial Commission; *Chairman*, Constitution Day; *President*, English-Speaking Union; *Trustee*, St. Mary's College; *Advisory Board*, United Nations Association of MD; *Coordinator*, Boy Scout Scholarship Program
1959	82	Fidelity & Deposit Co	*President*, Maryland Historical Society; *Chairman*, Maryland March of Dimes; *Chairman*, Civil War Centennial Commission; *Chairman*, Constitution Day; *Trustee*, St. Mary's College; *Advisory Board*, United Nations Association of MD; *Coordinator*, Boy Scout Scholarship Program
1960	83	Fidelity & Deposit Co	*President*, Maryland Historical Society; *Chairman*, Maryland March of Dimes; *Chairman*, Civil War Centennial Commission; *President*, Grace Foundation; *Advisory Board*, United Nations Association of Maryland; *Trustee*, St. Mary's College
1961	84	Fidelity & Deposit Co	*President*, Maryland Historical Society; *Chairman*, Maryland March of Dimes; *Chairman*, Civil War Centennial Commission; *President*, Grace Foundation; *Trustee*, St. Mary's College
1962	85	Fidelity & Deposit Co	*President*, Maryland Historical Society; *Chairman*, Maryland March of Dimes; *Chairman*, Civil War Centennial Commission; *President*, Grace Foundation; *Board Member*, Salk Institute for Biological Studies; *Trustee*, St. Mary's College

1963	86	Fidelity & Deposit Co	*President*, Maryland Historical Society; *Chairman*, Maryland March of Dimes; *Chairman*, Civil War Centennial Commission; *President*, Grace Foundation; *Trustee*, St. Mary's College
1964	87	Fidelity & Deposit Co	*Honorary Chairman of the Board*, Maryland Historical Society; *Chairman*, Maryland March of Dimes; *Chairman*, Civil War Centennial Commission; *Chairman*, Samuel Friedel's Congressional Campaign; *President*, Grace Foundation; *Trustee*, St. Mary's College
1965	88	Fidelity & Deposit Co	*Honorary Chairman of the Board*, Maryland Historical Society; *Chairman*, Maryland March of Dimes; *Chairman*, Civil War Centennial Commission; *Planned*, Dinner for Maryland Chapter of National Conference of Christians and Jews; *President*, Grace Foundation; *Trustee*, St. Mary's College
1966	89	Fidelity & Deposit Co	*Honorary Chairman of the Board*, Maryland Historical Society; *Chairman*, Maryland March of Dimes; *President*, Grace Foundation
1967	90	Fidelity & Deposit Co	*Honorary Chairman of the Board*, Maryland Historical Society; *Chairman*, Maryland March of Dimes; *President*, Grace Foundation
1968	91		*Honorary Chairman of the Board*, Maryland Historical Society; *Chairman*, Maryland March of Dimes; *President*, Grace Foundation
1969	92		*Honorary Chairman of the Board*, Maryland Historical Society; *President*, Grace Foundation
1970	93		*Honorary Chairman of the Board*, Maryland Historical Society; *President*, Grace Foundation
1971	94		*Honorary Chairman of the Board*, Maryland Historical Society; *President*, Grace Foundation; *President*, Spocott Windmill Foundation

1972	95		*Honorary Chairman of the Board*, Maryland Historical Society; *President*, Grace Foundation; *President*, Spocott Windmill Foundation
1973	96		*Honorary Chairman of the Board*, Maryland Historical Society; *President*, Grace Foundation; *President*, Spocott Windmill Foundation
1974	97		*Honorary Chairman of the Board*, Maryland Historical Society; *President*, Grace Foundation; *President*, Spocott Windmill Foundation

Appendix 2

Heigh-ho. Sing Heigh-ho
Unto the Green Holly

A Wood Fire, Books, Memories ... and Castle Building

The following was written by George L. Radcliffe for a Christmas card he and Mary sent out. It was also included in a magazine article.

Someone has said a wood fire on the hearth is a window looking out on many scenes. That is certainly true at Christmastime.

Infinite variety of form and expression is one of the delightful aspects of Christmas. This I began to realize when I was a boy living on a farm on the Eastern Shore of Maryland. Later on, access to books not available on the farm, especially when I was doing research work as a graduate student in history at Johns Hopkins University, taught me that Christmas is boundless in scope.

Usually, when I was a boy, I made my plans for Christmas in front of a blazing wood fire. The dancing flames of the gleaming brass andirons seemed to present fleeting glimpses of Christmas. What a fascinating succession of them! None more beautiful than the Christmas story in the Bible, quaint Christmas carols, hymns, and Milton's immortal poem on the Nativity written probably when he was a student.

As a very small boy I accepted readily the story of Santa Claus, not knowing that it was a variation in name and theme of the deeds of Nicholas, Bishop of Myra. It was probably natural that for a while I shared the ambition of many children who have wanted to live at the North Pole as voluntary unpaid assistants to Santa Claus.

When the wind was cold and howling, it was instinctive for me, when basking in the glow of a genial wood fire, to browse over tales of old Scandinavian, Germanic, and English customs, especially alluring when concerned with Christmas. It was easy to visualize Christmastide celebrations around roaring fires after long voyages over bitter wintry seas. Maybe we glamorize the charm of the Viking Yuletide's tumultuous celebrations and of those held within "castle walls ... old in story." Certainly, they were spontaneous and colorful. Sir Walter Scott's picturesque poem on Christmas was a never-ending source of delight to me. It gives a vivid description of an old time Christmas in England and Scotland, beginning:

> *Heap on more wood – the wind is chill;*
> *But let it whistle as it will*
> *We'll keep our Christmas merry still*
>
> *   *   *   *   *   *
>
> *The fire with well dried logs supplied*
> *Went roaring up the chimney wide.*

Modern ways of living have made impractical many features of old time Christmas celebrations. I can see many changes even in my day, or as a writer of about three hundred years ago once referred to the change, "Since this old cap was new." Transition from old-fashioned country to city life doesn't permit the opportunity our parents or grandparents had of making, not buying, much of what Christmas calls for. City folks usually can't select and cut in the woods their Christmas trees, holly, pine, bayberry, and mistletoe. In my boyhood, for months before Christmas I was inspecting critically hundreds of small cedar trees on my father's home farm before I made my final choice. Selecting, cutting and bringing home one's own Christmas tree was to my mind a necessary part of Christmas celebration. Even today the pungent odor of the cedar tree suggests Christmas to me.

The tree was trimmed almost entirely with what I found in the woods or made during many wintry evenings. Long strings of white popcorn came from grains of corn planted by me in the Spring, cultivated in the Summer, and harvested in the Fall. Ears of corn were hung for a month close to a woodstove in the kitchen so that the grains would pop more readily. Part of the popcorn was shipped to commission merchants in Baltimore for sale. It was traditional that money spent for Christmas should be *earned*. Doubtless the toys and other articles made by me for my Christmas tree were not artistic, but they were quite satisfying to me. Of course, a few things were bought for my Christmas tree. These always included figures of three candy lions inspired in the last sentence in Dickens' account of the Battle of Hastings in "A Child's History of England" –

And the three Norman lions kept watch o'er the field.

How thrilling it was to gather bayberries from bushes growing on the farm near the salt water and then to utilize these berries in the making of bayberry candles in candle molds once used by my great-grandfather! I hope my bayberry candles displayed more magic powers than evidence of skill and workmanship.

The housewife of today would be appalled if she were called upon to make the enormous variety and number of cakes, pies, and plum puddings which her grandmothers took naturally in their stride. Of course, her ancestors often had servants or other kinds of help not available to the housewife today. Fortunately, I was raised in a family which adhered closely to many old English family traditions, and our preparations for Christmas were always much bigger than our finances would seem to warrant. During the many weeks of preparation everyone at my home was busy, and it was true, as Wither says of the days preceding Christmas,

Now every lad is wondrous trim
And no man minds his labor.

No workers at our home, just before Christmas, were more enthusiastic and indefatigable in their efforts than the colored folks who had "always belonged on the place." Families of their descendants are still there with us, continuing with festive cheer to carry on many of the same old Christmas customs.

Once, when I was a young man, I was one of several guests at the Christmas dinner of a very hard-working prosperous tenant farmer of ours. He was a man having little education, but much regard for tradition. For dinner he had beef, lamb, pork, ham, sausage, poultry, wildfowl, seafood, vegetables, pies, puddings, custards, nuts, and so on in seemingly endless procession. When I commented on the amazing variety and abundance, he replied, "You know the old folks say that's what you ought to do at Christmas." He also gave us frumenty, an old English Christmas dish that I had never before seen served. And he carried out several simple Yuletide ceremonies brought to Maryland in the days of the Stuart Kings and today almost forgotten.

Never will I forget my happy surprise when first I saw a copy of Washington Irving's "Old Christmas", illustrated by Caldecott, certainly the most painstaking and colorful account ever written of an old-fashioned English Christmas. Be sure to read it, if possible in front of a blazing wood fire, when you also enjoy Dickens' "A Christmas Carol" or read the glamorous Christmas issues of English magazines.

Among the many writers on Christmas, none delighted me more than those 17th Century contemporaries Robert Herrick, a clergyman, and George Wither. Herrick's poems on the Nativity are charming, but he is best known for his numerous short poems on oldtime Christmas customs. You may recall the one beginning:

> *Come bring with a noise, my merry, merry boys,*
> *The Christmas log to its firing.*

George Wither, often a grim, contentious man, yet could write his rollicking "Christmas Carroll" – not a Christmas carol as we ordinarily use the term.

At times when I was young, I pleased myself by weaving a fantastic and wholly groundless tale about an imaginary visit by Herrick and Wither, when old men, to Maryland about the year 1670. I had them landing by accident at the shore of the plantation where I was born and which I now own. In 1670, it belonged to an ancestor of mine who had patented it from Lord Baltimore.

Herrick and Wither gave expression to sentiments which unfortunately have largely slipped away during intervening centuries. Today we hasten to stress the religious and humanitarian aspects of Christmas. We have made the holiday, as it should be, more and more a children's day. We have satisfying family reunions. But haven't we lost some of that exuberance of spirits – not alcoholic – which Herrick and Wither reflect so charmingly? No other writer has given us a more vivid picture of sheer joyousness of Christmas spirit, as illustrated by some of Wither's verses. Consider:

"So now is come our joyfullest feast,
Let every man be jolly;
Each room with ivy leaves is dressed,
And every post with holly.
Now all our neighbor's chimneys smoke,
And Christmas blocks are burning;
Their ovens they with baked meats choke,
And all their spits are turning.
Without the door let sorrow lie;
And if for cold it hap to die,
We'll bury it in a Christmas pie,
And evermore be merry."

That joyousness of spirit found expression in another custom now almost incomprehensible. It was indeed topsy-turvy. Maybe the Scandinavian word Yule does not mean a wheel, but surely there was, as Christmas approached, an amazing turning of the wheel of human relations. When you consider the cruel harshness of rank and living conditions of those days, it is amazing that such sharp distinctions were often suspended at Yuletide. Rich and poor, master and servants dined together on a basis of outright equality. Often masters waited at dinner upon the servants, or serfs, as they really were. For the time being, sitting "above the salt" or "below the salt" had no significance. Boy kings held sway. After Twelfth Night, back to work and to static distinctions of rank. – But did they entirely return? Didn't something of the friendly and formal relations persist?

Let me also refer to a story about King Henry V of England. He was besieging Rouen. Food had almost disappeared in that city. The inhabitants were facing either surrender or starvation, when the season of Christmas came 'round. Henry V, eager as he was to capture the city at the earliest moment possible, nevertheless was possessed with the thought that on Christmas Day everyone should eat a Christmas dinner. Therefore, he sent into the city food sufficient for one meal for the entire population. What an extraordinary evidence of Christmas spirit! After the end of that day, King Henry pressed the siege vigorously to victory.

When I was a boy, I was told that cattle go on their knees to pray on Christmas Eve. Naturally I hear much about hordes of spirits, persistently prone to harass good citizens but quite powerless to bedevil anyone at the hallowed Christmastime. Can you imagine living in a world beset by such noisesome pests? You will recall what Shakespeare writes so delightfully in Hamlet:

> Some say as ever 'gainst that season comes,
> Wherein our Saviour's birth is celebrated,
> The bird of dawning singeth all night long;
> And then, they say, no spirit dares stir abroad;
> The nights are wholesome; then no planet strikes,
> No fairy takes nor witch hath power to charm
> So hallowed and so gracious is the time.

I have a real grievance against Shakespeare because he wrote so seldom about Christmas!

No longer do we "bring in the boar's head" with elaborate ceremony. In these days of refrigerators and dependable lock-up facilities no one guards, during the long night watches, the Christmas pie. This wonderful pie was enclosed, often, in the old days, in the skin and plumage of peacock. Herrick describes it –

> *"Come, guard this night the Christmas pie*
> *That the thief though ne'er so sly*
> *With his flesh hooks, don't come nigh to catch it;*
> *From him, who alone sits there*
> *Having his eyes within his ear*
> *And a deal of nightly fear, to watch it."*

Nothing written in this country about Christmas has deservedly been more frequently quoted than Dr. Clement C. Moore's, "A Visit from St. Nicholas". During his lifetime the author was a bit embarrassed by the thought that his poem was too frivolous to have been composed by a scientist.

Many of the quaint old Christmas customs have faded away, many remain with us in happy blend with new forms of observances reflecting remembrance, affection, good will, and good cheer. Today more people are eager and able to celebrate Christmas than ever before. My wife, family, and I are among the joyous multitudes who are finding such a combination of the old and the new a source of unfailing happiness. In Christmas today there is much of the religious, much of the secular, much to enlighten, much to amuse. Yet is the real spirit of Christmas with us unless "we feel it in our bones"? If circumstances force you to be alone during Christmas, in adverse surroundings, would memory and fancy envelop you in the happy mystic atmosphere of Christmas? If so, you have abundantly the true Christmas spirit "—so hallowed and so gracious is the time."

— *George L. Radcliffe*

Appendix 3

The Man for U.S. Senator: George L. Radcliffe

Campaign Brochure, 1934

The man who seeks the office of U.S. Senator should be able to prove beyond question that he possesses certain fundamental qualities necessary to discharge the duties of the exacting office.

He should have character, high standards of conduct and the backbone to maintain those standards unyieldingly. He should have mental capacity of a high order. He should have experience in large affairs. He should be able to see another man's point of view. He should have the power to make friends. He should know and feel the peculiar quality of life in Maryland.

The sketch of George L. Radcliffe which follows is a mere outline of the man's life. It is presented so that readers may judge what order of man they are asked to place in the United States Senate.

George L. Radcliffe has given more than 25 years of service to the people of the State in which he was born, and in which he has lived for 57 busy, useful years.

It is one of the chief characteristics that he does not seek the limelight – that he prefers the knowledge of a service well rendered to the sight of his name in the headlines. And that is why the story of the things he has done for Maryland and Marylanders will come as an impressive surprise even to many who know him well and who know the State well.

At the age of 28, George L. Radcliffe was the ranking vice-president of a bonding company which became one of the most important in the country.

He did not get the position because of his financial or family backing. His father was a farmer and shipbuilder in Dorchester County and was unable to send his son to college. But the son met the situation in characteristic fashion. In the main, he worked his way through college. He enjoyed working, and he enjoyed playing. He was a star athlete and even today carries a watch he won as a member of the Johns Hopkins University relay team.

But he was also a good student. For a while, he taught school after getting out of law school. But he preferred the active life of business. He entered the law department of the American Bonding Company and only a few years elapsed before he was first vice-president.

But private business—the quest of private gain—has never been sufficient to fill the man's life. Always he had a sense of public duty; of public obligation.

Consider, just briefly, some of the things he has done for his State and his neighbors.

In the last two years he has served, unofficially but incessantly, getting help from Washington for Maryland interests which needed help badly.

When a Maryland banker found himself helpless while trying to release money to his depositors, and turned to George L. Radcliffe, he secured his aid. And this aid helped put millions of dollars back into the pockets of their rightful owners.

Did a Maryland official get entangled in red tape or differences of opinion with Federal officials? Usually, it has been George L. Radcliffe who, quietly, without fanfare or publicity, helped to disentangle him.

As Public Works Advisor for this region, his work has been invaluable not only to Maryland but to six other States. He did not ask for this appointment. It is reported that he took it only at the urgent request of President Roosevelt. That itself indicates the quality of the man. For Roosevelt knows Radcliffe well. He worked with him for many years. He knows what the Marylander can do.

The work which Radcliffe is doing as Public Works Advisor will have a permanent effect upon the United States. For it involves planning huge projects, to furnish present work and future use. It involves, in the first place, the coordination of Public Works projects in all the States of the region, so that the activities of one section may not nullify or decrease the benefits of work done in another.

Millions of dollars, giving many thousands of jobs, have been expended on projects evolved with his help. In this work, he has acted as advisor and, when necessary, umpire, and the extent and rate of the work has been, generally speaking, in accordance with the cooperation received from authorities of the several localities involved.

So well did he work that he was sent to other parts of the country to give advice and guidance.

He visualized national planning, taking stock of economic conditions in given areas, and considering whether industries which had been expected to support populations in the past were still capable of such support in the future. He considered it a part of his job to probe into such problems and to try to discover what economic planning for the future could accomplish.

A board was organized, various parts of the work assigned to various members. The Chesapeake Bay authority was created to conserve commercial and recreational possibilities of the Bay and its rivers, to reduce sewage pollution and to halt land erosion. The Board is still functioning actively.

Colonel J. M. S. Waring, a New York engineer who associated himself with Mr. Radcliffe early in the latter's work as regional advisor, developed in Mr. Radcliffe's board, with the encouragement of Mr. Radcliffe, a plan for a study of economic and industrial conditions in the manner just described. He was invited to Washington and is now there studying the application of his plan to the Nation. The idea represents the abandonment of the old hit and miss economic development of the past and an effort to adapt industry to a given area, or to make the area support its population by deliberately planning means by which the support may be furnished.

The fact is that no citizen of Maryland has worked harder in the public interest and with less thought about whether he did or did not get credit for his work than has George L. Radcliffe.

His capacity for friendship is probably a large element in his ability to do those things. Quiet of bearing, with a sense of humor, his mind open to the other man's point of view, with no touch of arrogance about him, he binds other men to him.

He has been Executive Vice-President of the Fidelity and Deposit Company since 1913 (Incidentally he has had his own work to do in connection with that office all the time he has been doing the work described here). Franklin Roosevelt became Vice-President of the Company in New York in 1920 at a time when no one thought of associating Mr. Roosevelt's name with the Presidency. He remained in that Position until he became Governor of New York. Between him and Mr. Radcliffe a warm attachment was formed.

When the campaign in which Mr. Roosevelt was elected opened, Mr. Radcliffe was made chairman of the Maryland campaign committee. Public knowledge of the relations between the Marylander and the President undoubtedly led men of responsibility in the State to seek Mr. Radcliffe's aid in discharging those responsibilities.

Mr. Radcliffe has supported Governor Ritchie each time the latter has been a candidate for Governor and arranged the ceremonies incident to the inauguration of the Governor at three of the inaugurations. He supported Mayor Jackson in his two campaigns for the Mayoralty as well as his earlier campaign for the office of Register of Wills. He has been a consistent Democrat all his life, although he had not run for public office until he entered this campaign.

He was a member of the Board of Liquor License Commissioners for Baltimore City in the administration of Governor Harrington and later as Secretary of State under Governor Harrington.

During the War he was active in the Liberty Loan Drives and was associate director of the Bureau of Personnel of the American Red Cross in Washington when the organization was engaged in its vast war program.

As a member of the Maryland Council of National Defense he was asked to take charge of the work of preparing suitable records of Maryland's participation in the War and of the service performed by each of the 60,000 Maryland men who were in the fighting forces. That work has been done with an efficiency which every veteran approves.

An alumnus of The Johns Hopkins University, from which he has the degree of Doctor of Philosophy, Mr. Radcliffe has been extremely active in the affairs of the alumni association and has served as its president. He is an LL.D. of Washington College.

Born in Lloyds in Dorchester County, near Cambridge, August 22, 1877, he received instruction in his home for several years and then went to public schools. He was graduated from the Cambridge High School, entered Johns Hopkins, received his degree of B.A. in 1897, returned to Hopkins for graduate work and took his Ph.D. there in 1900. His thesis for his Doctor's degree was "Governor Hicks of Maryland and the Civil War." He returned to Cambridge and was principal of the High School there for the year 1900 – 1901. In 1903 he was graduated from the Law School of the University of Maryland and was admitted to the Bar.

Mr. Radcliffe was married on June 6, 1906, to Miss Mary McKim Marriott, of Baltimore. Her family, like her husband's, have been Marylanders for generations. They live at 12 Edgevale Road, Roland Park, and have one son, now fifteen years old.

No man illustrates in his character and bearing the qualities which Marylanders like to associate with themselves – tolerance, open-mindedness, capacity for lasting friendships, hospitality – more completely than does Mr. Radcliffe. His fellow Marylanders have frequently proved their faith in his capacity for large affairs in the most practical manner in which men can prove that faith – by asking that it be used in their behalf and in behalf of those whom they have served.

Appendix 4

The Merchant Marine

Radio Address of Sen. George L. Radcliffe of Maryland
Delivered April 7, 1941
Printed in Congressional Record on April 25, 1941

For a few minutes I want to discuss several aspects of our Merchant Marine. What do we mean by our Merchant Marine? There are probably more opinions as to what it is than were colors in Joseph's coat. Possibly no definition of the term would be quite satisfactory, but I will refer to a few aspects of it. For instance, we know, naturally, that our Merchant Marine concerns primarily methods of transportation by water – not by land. We know it embraces really more than ships – the small ones as well as big ones. In its largest sense it includes men, organizations, policies, activities, and the many other elements which make the industry function.

The word "merchant" in the term "merchant marine" is somewhat misleading. The operations of the Merchant Marine are not, as we know, necessarily restricted to merchants and merchandising. Naturally nearly every kind of industry might at times function with it.

Ordinarily ships of a merchant marine are engaged in private commerce, but they may be used to help battleships or other forms of armed agencies, whether on land, on water, or in the air. The Merchant Marine has duties, very important, in connection with our defense program. It is an invaluable adjunct in time of war. A navy, and often an army or air force, would be practically impotent if it did not have as handmaidens auxiliary vessels to carry troops, fuel, ammunition, and various other materials, and to assist in many other ways.

The United States approaches our present problem in ship construction and operation with historical precedents and helpful traditions in spite of serious mistakes at times. The history of our shipping is an interesting one.

The first immigrants to this country came by water. They were, to a very considerable extent, especially in colonial days, a seafaring people. The water in many parts of the country in colonial United States was the chief means of transportation. This fact helped greatly in the development of our country in colonial days and in the conduct of the Revolutionary War. In the War of 1812, our Navy played a role much more effective than our Army. The people of Maryland furnished at least half of the American ships which fought in the war and as large a percentage of their crews. While Napoleon, like Hitler, was planning to invade England, his brother, Jerome Bonaparte, once Secretary of our Navy, married Betsy, daughter of William Patterson, a big shipowner of Baltimore, whose operations carried him to the four corners of the earth.

Following the War of 1812 there was a dramatic and glorious development of our shipping. This was so in New England and along the Atlantic coast. The Baltimore clipper sailing vessels became known all over the world. *Anne McKim*, most famous of Baltimore clippers, had a world-wide reputation for speed, beauty, and efficiency which was richly deserved.

In those days there seemed to be no limit to the opportunities offered to American shipping industry, inland and on the seas. Canals were being built and soon in time began the industry of the great railroads.

This is not the place to dwell upon the glories of American shipping or the decline which came to it. Our shipping became relatively unimportant. Our exports and imports were more and more in foreign bottoms.

The World War brought us sharply to the realization of our grave lack of necessary ships. The necessity of building ships as quickly as possible was acutely obvious. The result was a tremendous stimulation in the building of ships in America, mainly by the Federal Government, but from this program with all its energy, not a single new ship of ours reached the other side before the armistice. Vessels built in this country for the Allies did, but the vessels undertaken in the huge expansion program of the Emergency Fleet Corporation, did not.

After the World War our American shipping again began to fall into relative insignificance but later events demanded we again build ships. We did not ignore that need until the present war in Europe began. Before that we had taken steps to increase the number of American built and owned ships. For instance, in 1936 we passed legislation which launched us again upon a shipbuilding program.

In doing so we realized difficulties arising from the fact that other nations could construct and operate ships cheaper than we could. We tried then to solve the problem by providing for grants of money from the Federal Government to equalize the differences in cost of production and operation. This act of 1936 stated that this Merchant Marine, while providing shipping service on trade routes essential to our foreign commerce, should be "capable of serving as a naval and military auxiliary in time of war or national emergency."

The Maritime Commission, created by that act, has reestablished our merchant fleet on a solid basis. There had been no new dry cargo ships built for foreign trade since 1922 until the Donald McKay, the Commission's first freighter, was launched at Chester, Pa., in April 1939.

Shipbuilding in the United States had reached a low ebb and there were only six building yards capable of constructing merchant ships. By 1941 the Maritime Commission had increased the merchant shipbuilding yards from 6 to 16. Instead of being located within a small area on the northeast Atlantic coast, these yards were spread over three coasts, the Atlantic, the Gulf, and the Pacific. In the Commission's long-range building program for the twin purposes of commerce and defense, 196 vessels have been started. Of those, 102 have been launched and all but 29 of those 102 completed, delivered, and now in operation.

These vessels were considered by naval architects and marine experts the finest of their type ever built. They have become well known everywhere, as the C types: the C-1, a small but efficient freighter; the C-2, a medium-sized fast freighter with extraordinarily economical engines; and the C-3, the large, fast freight ship which also has been designed for carrying passengers.

Twenty-seven of these new vessels built by the Commission have already become naval auxiliaries. They have been acquired by the Navy for such diverse purposes as ammunition carriers, seaplane tenders, submarine tenders, and supply and repair vessels. Among the finest of the group are twelve 19-knot tankers, the fastest of their kind in the world today. These ships were undertaken by the Commission at a time when normal commercial tanker speeds were 10 to 11 knots. With the cooperation of the Standard Oil Co. of New Jersey, these 12 ships were built, and everyone is now serving our naval forces.

To a battle fleet, tankers are a symbol of freedom of action. They mean that the fighting vessels will not be towed to their land bases. These 12 tankers will carry more than 72,000,000 gallons of oil at a speed which will enable them to keep up with the battle fleet. On the basis of the rate of fuel consumption of the battleship, they will enable vessels of our fighting fleet to steam a total of more than 800,000 nautical miles without putting in at a naval base.

The quickness with which these vessels were built and converted into naval auxiliaries testifies to the careful planning of the Maritime Commission's program. A complete understanding was had with the Navy Department from the inception of the original building-plan basis of cooperation. Fortunately, President Roosevelt appointed Rear Admiral Emory S. Land, former Chief Constructor of the Navy, as chairman of the Maritime Commission in 1938. That appointment has been a most fortunate one. Admiral Land and his associates on the Commission are justifying fully the confidence placed in them.

Designs for vessels were made with Navy needs in mind and were approved by the Navy. Gun locations, accessibility of cargo space and compartmentation were all planned for Navy use. The care which went into this designing and building is proving itself entirely warranted.

Also, the value and the necessity of freighters and tankers to maintain foreign commerce of the United States is beyond question. This fact has been demonstrated over and over again in normal peaceful times. It is being doubly proven at present when our American ships are bringing in load after load of rubber, tin, manganese, and other raw materials, which are being converted into instrumentalities of defense.

As chairman of the Merchant Marine committee of the Senate Commerce Committee, I am in close touch with developments in the Commission's building program. Recently the Commerce Committee of the Senate reported favorably on legislation which will further facilitate the building of first-class naval auxiliaries. That committee and the Maritime Commission believe in competitive building. However, the Army and Navy now want the negotiated-bid system for quick deliveries. The Maritime Commission has asked for similar authority and will doubtless get it, which will be used only when competitive bidding is apparently not feasible or sufficiently expeditious.

The United States is in a position to make effective use of sea power. Our battleships are supported by one of the largest merchant fleets in the world. The fleet aggregates more than 7,000,000 tons. More than 1,200 ships are engaged largely in domestic commerce. The American people more than any other people in the world use ships to transport goods from one portion of their country to another. The fleet of American ships sailing in foreign trade is also substantial. More than 300 vessels of various types are carrying the burdens of foreign commerce of the United States.

The United States in many respects is as well-equipped as any other country to be self-sufficient. Some commodities essential to us must, however, be imported. No nation has ever really thrived which did not engage regularly in foreign trade. No isolationist today is going to claim that we can forego foreign trade without serious danger of stagnation.

In addition to our heavy imports, an important export movement is in our defense program. The Army has advised the Maritime Commission that more than one and one-half million tons of supplies must be moved to Army bases such as the Canal Zone, Puerto Rico, Hawaii, and the Philippines. The Navy lists more than 500,000 tons to be transported to our naval bases. It is the job of our Merchant Marine to see that all of these materials are carried, and carried quickly.

The Maritime Commission, which is operating the preference or priority system for ship cargoes, knows what must be moved for the Army, for the Navy, and for the Office of Production Management, which is coordinating the needs of the defense-production program.

The Office of Production Management has determined the amount of imports which must be made during the calendar year 1941. Its list includes such obvious items as manganese and tungsten, also other items not generally realized as vital in the national emergency, as for instance, teakwood for the decks of naval vessels, tanning materials, pulpwood for newsprint, sugar, and coffee.

The amounts of these and other important defense materials have been totaled, and for the year 1941 reach the astonishing figure of more than 19,000,000 tons. On the basis of the average capacity of a freight ship, this represents 2,500 shiploads of material which must be brought in during the calendar year from overseas.

Although we are not convoying our ships or sending them into war areas, we are exporting many articles of various kinds to certain nations, especially to Great Britain and its allies, but these articles are carried in ships other than those belonging to the United States and its citizens.

The scope of war activities, ever broadening, is stressing the necessity for the use of these materials which were practically unknown to warfare years ago. So, the interpretation as to what is contraband of war has broadened so much that it includes now almost all kinds of fuels, metals, crops, manufactured or mechanized products, and other commodities of countless varieties.

Even before Mahan wrote his immortal book on the subject, it was realized that sea power is a controlling factor in the life of a nation. It is almost indispensable to the existence of a nation which is not an island one, and all inland nations suffer for lack of their own channels for water transportation. The inability of Germany and her allies to use the seas freely during the World War was a grave and never-ending menace to them. Today, Germany, although having conquered much of continental Europe, is seriously restricted because of her very limited use of the Atlantic Ocean and the Mediterranean Sea. Although possessing the western coastline of continental Europe, Germany is encountering trouble in efforts to secure certain metals or other commodities which she could easily get if the oceans were open to her. She suffers from a lack of prevailing sea power.

Sea power has a dual nature; it consists of war vessels which seize and hold the power; and merchant vessels which use the power. Yet the sea power of the battleship and airplane would be useless if not accompanied by the sea power of the merchant fleet. The effectiveness of British resistance in the war has lain largely in its ability to use successfully the seas as a source of strength.

We have, as you know, transferred ships to Great Britain and her allies. More than 200 American ships with a gross tonnage of more than 750,000 have gone to them. The ships have been of priceless value to the British in her effort to keep sea lanes open. Five million tons of shipping through hostile sinkings have occurred, it is said.

The additional number which may be transferred is a matter for the President to determine under the terms of the so-called lend-lease bill.

The 3,000 or more miles of water which separate us from the continents of Europe and Asia have been and will remain invaluable in helping to protect us from aggression. However, everyone knows that certain modern methods of warfare, as exemplified by the airplane and the submarine, have lessened materially the security which these oceans afford us. We have recently acquired naval and aviation bases, in some cases hundreds of miles from the boundaries of the United States. Modern methods of defense require such stations. To safeguard our own shores, we must go many miles beyond them to secure and use naval and aviation bases. Do not forget, however, that these naval and aviation bases would be of little use to us if the oceans of the world were dominated by a combination of naval powers hostile to us. It is needless to add also that the Monroe Doctrine in its friendly developments of cooperation among the republics of North and South America would be outmoded.

The vessels now in the American Merchant Marine are being used steadily. Likewise, there are reservoirs of ships such as those in use in coastwise and intercoastal trade which could be tapped in case of need.

The 212 ships announced by the President are in addition to the 200 emergency ships already under construction, the 60 ships now building in American yards for the British, and the 124 vessels of the Maritime Commission's regular long-range program.

Our government has undertaken the building of 300 simple, slow, but efficient freighters. They have been called ugly ducklings. The name certainly is not flattering but these ducklings will doubtless do their job well. These ships will cost considerably less than the ships of the government's regular long-range building program. They will be capable of mass production on a prefabrication basis.

Engines, machinery, navigation equipment, and supplies will be acquired from plants all over the country. These will be shipped to the building yards at tidewater and there assembled. Seven new shipyards are now being built to assemble these parts into finished ships. The Maritime Commission is handling this program which is going ahead steadily.

As far as possible new facilities will be created and materials for the ships acquired without interference with defense production for the Army and Navy. Ships will be built in Baltimore and in a new shipyard on Curtis Bay. They will also be constructed in Wilmington, N.C., in Mobile, New Orleans, and Houston; likewise on the Pacific coast in Portland and Los Angeles. In every case these new shipyards will be sponsored by existing well-established shipbuilding organizations. This arrangement justifies confidence as to rapid construction and workmanlike product.

One hundred and twelve of these newly authorized ships are to be of the "ugly duckling" type and the remainder of standard designs of the Maritime Commission, including C-type cargo ships and tankers. This will be done by expanding existing yards on all three coasts. This means a shipbuilding program of great magnitude. But it is a program which our experts in the Commission are confident can be accomplished.

What about the operations of the vessels which this country owns? Are they being used in the interest of the United States as a whole rather than that of a few shipowners? The answer undoubtedly is "yes". Shipowners of the United States have voluntarily coordinated the operations of their vessels through the Maritime Commission which has created a Division of Emergency Shipping headed by experienced ship operators, to see that American vessels are used with the highest efficiency obtainable.

In normal times American ship lines operate as individual business enterprises. They carry cargo available on their trade route only. As a result, ships are not always used to capacity in normal times. Nowadays ships are being rerouted and reassigned to carry strategic materials to this country and supplies to our defense bases.

As an example, ships bring copper ore from the west coast of South America to the port of Baltimore. Then they use to discharge and return in ballast to Chile. In normal times this would be a shipping operation sufficient to meet cargo conditions. Recently the Maritime Commission arranged for certain ore carriers, instead of returning in ballast after discharging their cargo, to proceed from Baltimore to New York and there take on a load of supplies and equipment for our enlarged Army posts in the Canal Zone. After delivering these materials in the Canal Zone, the vessels go again to the west coast of South America to pick up copper ore.

By this means the carrying value of those ships to the country has almost doubled. It is believed that this voluntary cooperation between shipowners and the government will be sufficient to insure suitable and adequate movement of these materials which are essential to our defense program.

Strikes by labor have not seriously interfered with construction of our ships. It is imperative in our defense program that such delays should not occur. Occasionally sabotage is suggested as a danger to our shipbuilding and ship-operating activities. We know that such crimes would anger the American people as few other offenses could do and would meet with summary and severe punishment.

You will recall that the President of the United States, in a recent speech, quoted certain well-known lines from Longfellow, which begin:

> Thou, too, sail on, O Ship of State!
> Sail on, O Union, strong and great!

He was using the word "Ship", of course, in a figurative sense as referring to the government of ours and these United States. Especially in these days it is pertinent to emphasize the vital importance of "Ship" in its material or normal sense. We have the need to strive for peace – to take such steps by way of preparedness as seem possible to protect this country from the horrors of war on this continent. We are creating a big army and providing military training for civilians. We are building ships of war. We are developing an airplane industry immeasurably greater than was contemplated even a year or so ago. We are trying to do effectively the things in industry which are needed to meet dislocations in our agricultural, industrial, and general economic life caused by war conditions.

We have the will and the purpose to try to reckon with the harrowing conditions existing in the world by taking such steps as seem necessary for our welfare. Our efforts will be grossly inadequate if we do not have suitable and adequate facilities for transportation and defense upon the water. Our "Ship of State" cannot "sail on" unless we have, in addition to many other things, necessary vessels and other craft of wood and steel.

APPENDIX 5

PRESERVATION OF FREEDOM AND LIBERTY UNDER THE AMERICAN FLAG

Speech of the Hon. George L. Radcliffe of Maryland in the Senate of the United States

June 15, 1942

Mr. President, yesterday in celebrating Flag Day, we realized that our flag has recently taken on a new significance and has acquired luster. A few years ago, in accordance with a resolution passed by the Congress of the United States, a committee, of which I was chairman, was appointed to arrange for the national celebration of the one hundred and twenty-fifth anniversary of the writing of the Star-Spangled Banner. That celebration, as Senators may remember, was held in September 1939, most appropriately, in Baltimore at Fort McHenry, where the Star-Spangled Banner was written, and it was largely attended. As we joined in homage to our flag, none of us foresaw the events, momentous and tragic to this country and to the world, which have since happened. On that day in 1939, our flag was recognized as an outstanding symbol of liberty and democracy. Today most assuredly it is still so regarded, and with ever increasing brilliance, glory, and promise.

Never before have the eyes of the world looked more intently and eagerly upon the flag as an outstanding symbol of justice and humanity. Our flag bears witness today that the cause of liberty, though fiercely and cruelly flouted and assailed, is more firmly entrenched than at any time since the bloody war of aggression against Europe was begun by the Nazis, and since the slimy treachery of Pearl Harbor.

It may be said that Germany and Japan, after making enormous conquests of territory, have not been required to surrender their loot; that they have not been stopped in their tracks; that they are still carrying on their nefarious schemes of conquest. True it is, but the world for them is changing fast. We hear of the capture by the Germans of a city in Africa and of most violent assaults by them on Sevastopol. We realize the gravity of a pincer movement by which the African and European armies of Germany seek to form a coalition in Asia Minor and Suez, with the hope that they may join the Japanese forces in forming a continuous line of conquest from the Atlantic to the Pacific. We face the still but partially controlled fury of the submarine and the resulting menace to our shipping, and, thereby, to the cause of ourselves and our Allies. These events and dangers do not frighten us; they do not dishearten us. We now know that the Nazi might is not invincible, and must soon reckon upon a second front, being obliged to do what Bismarck had dreaded, that is, to fight at one and the same time upon both eastern and western fronts.

We know that in a short time the Japanese will be faced with a force which they cannot withstand. The battle of Midway Island a few days ago may not have turned the tide of the war, but it shows that the sinister schemes of the Japanese to dominate the Pacific will come to naught; that the day of reckoning for them and their fellow conspirators, Germany and Italy, is inevitable. The Axis Powers can see no end of signs of eventual defeat. The convincing demonstration of the effectiveness of our fighting forces; the indomitable patriotism and persistence of Russia; of Great Britain and her Dominions; of China; the epoch-making treaty between England and Russia and the understanding between the United States and Russia, both of which were recently announced; the rapid growth of the war resources of the Allies, especially in the air – all these are gloomy portents of disaster to the Nazis and their fellow conspirators against the peace and security of the world.

The world was shocked a day or so ago by the hideous destruction of a town in Czechoslovakia, by the murder of all the male citizens in the town, and by the carrying away of all its women and children. It was a cruel illustration of the savage butchery which has made Tamerlane and Attila, the Hun, infamous in the pages of history.

Certainly, the bloody act was prompted by a premonition of defeat. It betrayed the foreboding and the desperation which is beginning to possess the minds of the Nazis, especially as the haunting thought seizes them that their bloodthirsty efforts to superimpose their will upon conquered Europe will eventually fail completely, and that the nations which are now under their heel will, at the first possible moment, arise and drive out the bloody invaders. All these are signs of the times and they bring ever-mounting despair to the Axis.

For long dreary months those who resisted the Nazis could reckon upon little except hope. Now they see, actually or potentially, within their hands the means of stopping full in their tracks the Axis marauders and of driving them back to their own countries, thereby relieving the world from the incubus and misery of subjugation. The way to that end may be long, arduous, and fraught with much suffering, but quite definitely that gleaming goal is visible. It can be reached provided the members of the Allied Nations will make that effort of which they are capable. No one, whether in the ranks of the Allied Powers or in the hosts of the Axis, now doubts for a moment that such effort will be made, and made successfully. But we, the people of the United States, those of Great Britain and her dominions, of Russia, China, heroic Greece, and all the other peoples of the world who have not been tortured by the brute might of the Axis, must put forth the greatest possible effort. This they must realize and this they are ready to do.

It is necessary that we win a just peace. It is even more essential that we preserve it, after it shall be won. Peace will not be durable unless it is just. We must not make the mistake of 20 years ago, thinking that a lasting peace could be secured in one stroke, and that then the job was done. We believed at the time the Versailles Treaty, whatever its merits, was made that the task was really completed. We should have known that the work of keeping peace had only begun. Had we really understood the problem, many mistakes in policy could have been avoided, and probably the Nazis would not have attempted to clutch at world domination.

Almost invariably a patient underestimates the time necessary for a full recovery from a serious operation, or from any form of grave illness. Nature requires a long time before there can be a complete physical re-adjustment. Meanwhile, a sensitiveness of mood persists, and an erratic instability of opinion is often quite noticeable.

The result is also true of nations, especially those which have been subjected to severe strains, as from a long war. The recovery period really is protracted far beyond what apparently is necessary. Public opinion is fitful. Internal unrest and disorders frequently arise. Often there is logical discontent with what has been and is, and continued attempts at experimentation, often ill-advised, are characteristic of a nation in process of recuperation. Under the most favorable circumstances this war-racked world cannot heal readily, Sufferings have been too acute to permit an easy and quick recovery. So, at the best, the next 20 or more years will be a period of continued convalescence. For years we must reckon with acute cases of the irritation of convalescence, as an inevitable problem in the life of nations, as it is in that of individuals. During those years, those of us who are young today will have much of the responsibility for international health. Never in history has such an opportunity been given to work for the healing of nations and the welfare of humanity. But do not be surprised nor disheartened if we meet again and again with the often-seen irritation of a convalescent.

We hear much in these days of stockpiles and inventories, of the vast number of aeroplanes which we are constructing. In fact, the suggestion a year ago that we might build as many as 50,000 airplanes a year seemed merely a fantastic iridescent, and Utopian dream. Now it is, in essence, a reality. Already our rate of airplane production is greater than that of any nation in the world. The submarine remains a serious menace, but we are building ships faster and faster. We are launching two a day, and soon three a day, and even more will be our record.

Our armed forces are increasing rapidly. They are being outfitted with all the necessary equipment. Many of our mistakes are being rectified, and solutions have been found for many of our harassing problems.

In spite of setbacks, some of which should have been avoided, we have made tremendous progress in carrying out our war program under the farsighted, resourceful, and vigorous leadership of President Roosevelt, assisted by his many competent aides, and in cooperation with the Congress of the United States—cooperation which has been very effective.

The Bible says, in substance, that a people without vision will perish. We know that we need vision, sound and constructive vision. We know also that it is essential that we now do many concrete things, more in both variety and number than ever before. We must spend money freely whenever necessary for our war purposes. But we must economize, saving every dollar and every penny the spending of which is not essential. We must be ready to make any changes in our policies that our war program demands. But let us continue to cherish the basic principles of our government, and to hold fast to those economic, industrial, financial, and political policies which have been so helpful in the building up of our Nation. Let us preserve them except insofar as the temporary demands of our war program require otherwise, or whenever our judgment, after very mature consideration, approves permanent changes.

As I said a moment ago, we hear much of stockpiles and inventories of war materials that are essential to our war program. One of the stockpiles which we are accumulating is very real, indeed, although it is intangible and invisible. It is the spirit of our people and of the people of our allies. It is the conviction that we will find a solution to our problems as will bring an end to the insolent attempt of the Axis to subjugate and control the world. That is not overconfidence. That opinion rests upon a clear knowledge of many dominant facts. One is that we are not going to be disheartened by further conquests of the Axis should they occur. Another is that in this war we can finish successfully what we have begun.

So, when we consider our ever-mounting stockpiles and inventories of war materials, we realize that one of our most valuable possessions is our firm and unshakable purpose to help preserve for ourselves and the remainder of the world freedom and liberty. We shall rest from our labors only when that essential and indispensable result shall have been accomplished.

APPENDIX 6

PROPOSED CONSTITUTIONAL AMENDMENT PROVIDING EQUAL RIGHTS FOR WOMEN AND MEN

Speech of Hon. George L. Radcliffe of Maryland in the Senate of the United States

Thursday, May 3, 1945

Mr. President, I ask unanimous consent to introduce, on behalf of various Senators and myself, a joint resolution calling for a constitutional amendment providing that the rights of women and men shall be coequal.

I feel strongly that the adoption of this amendment would be a step forward and a wise one. Its adoption would certainly be one of the most important stages in the development of opportunities for women. Of course, I realize that for many years in countless indispensable ways women have had many varied fields of usefulness which they have utilized for the benefit of humanity. However, ever-changing economic factors and processes have made constantly more urgent the demand that women be given the right to exercise certain other privileges which have so far in a measure been denied them. It may be that economic conditions of other days did not make imperative that such rights and privileges exist in a full sense. Nevertheless, for many years, women have given unmistakable and entirely convincing evidence that they are entitled to equality of opportunity with men, and that society in the broad sense of the term would be greatly benefited by the exercise of women of such rights.

The wholesome trend toward such a realization has received a tremendous impetus because of and during the progress of the present

World War. The tragic intensity and all-comprehensiveness of our war program have found women not only willing but also ready and competent to do a large part in the fight for freedom and democracy. Their contribution on the home front and on the battlefield during the present war has been outstanding and indispensable.

We are reminded that the equality of opportunity will call also for equality of responsibility. Certainly so, but both terms in application are relative as to persons concerned, whether men or women. As individuals, whichever our sex, we can avail ourselves of our opportunities and also meet our responsibilities only as our physical fitness, special talents, other facilities, and circumstances will permit.

Some people fear that by the adoption of this amendment, women may be deprived of certain necessary protective legislation now existing which was enacted for their special benefit and was so designated. Certainly, we should be sufficiently resourceful to guard against injurious results occurring, bearing in mind the fact that opportunity and responsibility should be considered really from the standpoint of each individual and not from the standpoint of sex. I feel confident that with the adoption of an equal rights amendment, the availability of individuals, whether they are men or women, to exercise specific duties, or to sustain successfully demands of responsibility, can be regulated with increasing success. We will continue to seek that goal at which no one, man or woman, will be forced to attempt to do that for which there is neither mental qualification nor physical fitness.

It is obvious that the adoption of an equal-rights amendment may require changes in certain existing remedial legislation. Surely adequate legislation designed to suit individual needs and limitations can be framed and passed. A period of moratorium is provided in this proposed amendment during which the most obvious requirements for enactment of legislation can be satisfied. Further legislation can and doubtless will be passed from time to time as conditions seem to warrant and to require.

I hope and believe that an amendment creating equal rights for men and women will become the law of the land.

There being no objection, the joint resolution (S. J. Res. 61) proposing an amendment to the Constitution of the United States relative to equal rights for men and women, introduced by Mr. Radcliffe (for himself, Mr. Capehart, Mr. Capper, Mr. Chandler, Mr. Chaves, Mr. Ferguson, Mr. Fulbright, Mr. Guffey, Mr. Hawkes, Mr. Johnson of California, Mr. Kilgore, Mr. Langer, Mr. McClellan, Mr. Magnuson, Mr. Myers, Mr. Pepper, Mr. Robertson, Mr. Stewart, Mr. Thomas of Oklahoma, Mr. Thomas of Idaho, Mr. Tunnell, Mr. Tydings, Mr. Willis, and Mr. Young) was received, read twice by its title, and referred to the Committee on the Judiciary.

Appendix 7

My Message to My People

Campaign Speech, Delivered May 25, 1946
Pocomoke City, Maryland

I have served my people in the Senate for nearly 12 years. However able and perfect one may be (and surely, I am neither) criticism at least from a rival candidate might be anticipated. Nor should my worthy opponent expect your votes unless he can show I have failed in my duty, or he and his programs are better than I offer. Has he done either?

No Criticism of Me or My Record, The Governor's Case

We must take it that in his platform announced May 1st, the Governor intended to state his whole case, and all his claims to the nomination.

1. He criticizes not one act of mine. It was his duty to speak if he believed I am in any way unfit, derelict, or mistaken. From his silence, we may infer that he approves of my record; and would have done what I have done.
2. He offers a platform both conventional and vague. It suggests no reference applicable to any one of the burning stupendous questions, and controversial measures before Congress affecting the welfare not alone of the United States, but of the world. It is hard to extract a single practical definite issue from his platform planks, or to forecast how he would have voted or might vote.

By contrast to the Governor's generally approved abstractions I have voted or spoken or both on hundreds of measures. My parliamentary record is an open book for all to read; and from that you have estimated my worth. He has no parliamentary record. His course can be charted in reference to legislation only by his utterances. Since he has said nothing regarding myself, and nothing specific or practical touching the questions which affect this globe, the Senatorial campaign boasts no public issue whatever, exhibits no attempt on my rival's part to meet the burden of proof as to why he, a gentleman, inexperienced in Senatorial duties, should be put in, and I, a veteran, should be put out.

Naturally, I am gratified that neither my temporary rival, nor any responsible, respectable party charges me with lack of diligence, lack of intelligence, lack of integrity, poor judgment, or failure in the performance of my Senatorial duties. They do not even charge me with honest mistakes. That is generous, for I know I have made my share.

Too Busy on Official Duties to Campaign

I like people. It is an inspiration to talk to my constituents. In season and out, whenever possible I seek contacts with them. Hence, it was my earnest desire to afford myself the gratification of visiting every section of the State and report face to face, to my employers, the people, as their representative and agent, simply, sincerely, and generally what in the main I have done and some of the things I hope to do. Due to the continued sessions of Congress that pleasure must be denied me. I am too busy attending sessions of the Senate and helping constituents in Washington to spend much, if any, time out of the Capitol campaigning for myself.

A wag has said the State should have 3 junior senators; one to attend to parliamentary duties, pilot bills through the Senate, study bills, sit in committee hearings, write reports, - a full time job; one "to service" the people, get them hearings, information, press their claims for consideration this way and that, rescue constituents from misunderstandings with the O.P.A., etc.—a myriad of things—and a full-time job; one to make a canvass for re-election.

Senatorial duties are exacting. Visits to departments, the "cases" to be handled (some string out for years) the incessant telephoning, study, conferences, hearings eat up time.

Letters come by hundreds; sometimes by thousands when inspired by propagandists who urge people to write to senators. The mail is a task. Answers to many letters require study and investigations. Senators might have their secretaries open, read, and answer mail; all done promptly. But the respondent gets the secretary's thought when he thinks he gets his Senator's. Thought it often means delay, I prefer to give my corresponding constituents my own thought, and to myself just as many letters as possible; or at least to direct what others write for me. That means long hours. I seldom get through under 12 to 14 hours' work any day. Not infrequently I am at work on bills, reports and mail until 2 to 3 a.m., occasionally all night. The above is neither to brag nor to complain; only to explain why it is impossible for me to be off the Senatorial task to seek my re-election. I like to work; my health is excellent, and work does not hurt me. Constituents are entitled to all and the best in my shop. I have no need, no desire to take Florida vacations in winter or even summer vacations. Foolishly, perhaps, I have had no vacation for fifteen years. My duty, my pleasure, and my ambition is to turn out a good, sincere, unostentatious, successful record of service to my constituents, whether they earn their living with a pen, a hoe, or a pinmall. They all look alike to me. I often find it necessary, with growing duties, to employ two extra clerks at my own expense to help me serve my people well.

I Am No Denouncer

People advise me "to stand up and denounce" this and that. I am not by nature cruel, I shrink from causing people pain or mortification. I have no commission, no duty to denounce; and I doubt the sportsmanship of denouncing when protected by Senatorial immunity from suit for statements made in the Senate. Besides denouncing in lieu of consultation, consideration, patience has the world enough hurt already. Vituperation is neither as legitimate or as convincing as my votes, which express my views impressively and often.

I Believe Maryland is Richer, Better for My Efforts

I may with modesty and truth claim credit for many things through Government aid which make Maryland and her people richer and better. For example, the Savage River Dam, the Ocean City jetty, the Choptank River Bridge, the Susquehanna River Bridge, the Potomac River Bridge, improvement of the C & D Canal. The Government was of inestimable aid to banks, building and loan associations, many industries, and surety companies at a critical time. It helped save loss and ruin to their owners and creditors when hard times were our lot. In fact, I can scarcely remember the great numbers of indispensable business, educational and financial concerns which would have gone under, never to rise again in the depression, but for the aid and influence, their managers are gracious enough to say, I was able to exert in the 1930's. And it was a glory and a pleasure to have had that great opportunity. And every dollar was repaid by the borrowers. Now there is some disposition to criticize that governmental aid, eagerly, desperately sought and welcomed then. Government money in aid of projects within this state is eagerly welcomed now.

The Housing Situation

It was my opportunity in the Senate to play a part in the F.H.A. and the H.O.L.C., to assist our people to get shelters over their heads. Those governmental projects worked out, paid out remarkably well. Looking back, we know the pity is they were not extensive enough. The housing situation is pitiful now, would be desperate beyond measure save for governmental enterprise and help.

Seafood and Farming

I was born within a hundred feet of salt water. My early experiences were in my father's shipyard, on his farms, working in our canning factory, mingling with the farmers, fisherman and oysterman who were our neighbors and good friends. The lives of those who toil on farms, on the oyster bars are open pages to me. They struggle against harsh odds, adverse labor and marketing conditions. I was of some help in getting laborers from a distance in recent years. I lose no fair opportunity to aid them.

As a health and revenue measure, I was helpful in retarding the import of Japanese crab meat as our competitor; helped secure the Bay from contamination, and loss of seafood markets, through peril of typhoid infected oysters; and the destruction of fish and wild fowl. I sought and got governmental studies made of sources of disease in marine life, and warded off danger of disaster to seafoods in Sinepuxent and Chesapeake Bays. I believe many men in Crisfield, Oxford and elsewhere in Tidewater Maryland, many farmers, canners, poultry raisers, will bear witness to my always available ear, my always available effort, regardless of the time and trouble involved to get them good, square, decent treatment in every phase of the seafood and farming industries.

Rationing and Price Control

Rationing and price control and the administration of the law are nightmares. The complications, the paperwork and instances of maladministration in a novel field which affects every individual, old or young, are exceedingly irritating. The only excuse for the inauguration or continuation of rationing and price control is summed up in one word, "necessity." Wiser men than I assert that without price control people in moderate circumstances simply would starve, the Well-to-do-left in want. Prices would rise to the sky, and up, up. Canners, butchers, grocers, food producers, retailers, farmers, poultry men have sought and had my help numberless times in clearing up problems ranging from the trivial to the most serious with the administrative officers of O.P.A. My function was to secure hearings, to clear up misunderstandings of fact, misconceptions of industrial conditions and problems, and where possible help to get kinks out of the law. The administrative heads as a rule are receptive of truth and welcome detached, sincere, accurate factual statements. We must remember that they stand between two irreconcilable rival forces, and can't please both. All should rejoice when production is so nearly normal as to justify the complete repeal of the O.P.A. It is a war created affliction as are enormous taxes. I get work and worry from the law in my home, on my farms and in my official position. O.P.A troubles furnish me more departmental missions than any law, possibly all the laws, on the books.

The Constructive Side of the Work

I rejoice in the constructive side of my work. There is a zest in helping to develop transportation facilities, aviation, shipping, especially for overseas. As a member of committees and sub-committees, it was my privilege to help pass a bill to provide for the development of airports in cooperation with states and cities; to aid in the modernization of the Baltimore airport without cost to the city; generally to develop that fast-expanding industry – commercial aviation; and:

Shipping

For five busy years it was my special and exacting responsibility as chairman of a sub-committee to frame and pass bills in the Senate to aid in that gigantic enterprise, the creation of a merchant marine sufficient to meet the unprecedented demand of the war; then after the war to find a way to dispose of the ships the government had built. For days as Committee chairman, I had to explain, defend, and urge necessary legislation on the floor of the Senate. Those were perhaps the greatest responsibilities I ever faced in view of the billions involved and the imperative tragic need for transportation, and called for every atom of business experience I had. Out of that vast experience grew in me an unqualified admiration for Admiral Land and the other executives who built and operated the ships, and a feeling of even more intense admiration for the seamen who manned the ships, many to meet the death of heroes from submarines, bombs, starvation; admiration for those who shipwrecked once or twice, cheerfully sailed again. What fortitude, what courage!

Reorganization of Weak Corporations

For many years the reorganization proceedings of weak or insolvent corporations involved great expense; the payment of unjust taxes I framed and pushed through the "Radcliffe Amendment" permitting reorganization of such companies without oppressive and intolerable income tax burdens based on the entirely fictitious theory of profits if they bought in their own outstanding bonds below par.

Financial Legislation

Maryland, since Senator Gorman's days, has had no Senator on the Finance Committee until I made that assignment.

As a member of the Finance Committee for years I have helped to frame tax bills. I have been chairman of sub and special committees; for instance, the Pensions Committee, which constantly studies improved legislation for the creation of pensions, and retirement plans among corporations; one way by giving them suitable reductions in taxation as to such reserved funds.

I supported the Ruml plan on the theory that an income taxpayer should have an opportunity of knowing what he owes and paying the Government income taxes the year he earns the money, and not start a new year in debt for the past year's tax.

Very recently I supported a substantial reduction in taxes. I will continue to advocate similar reductions as often as the state of our federal budget will permit. I am working for drastic reductions in expenditures. Not many months ago, I introduced and secured passage by the Senate of legislation calling for, and providing for reduction of expenditures, and for balancing the national budget.

As a member of the Finance Committee, I have aided in framing and enacting measures touching Social Security benefits; various benefits to veterans; have helped to develop and improve such legislation from time to time.

Just to mention those measures in a dry paper is not dramatic. But it makes my heart glow with pride and gratification that it was given to me to cooperate in acts, some pioneer efforts, which means so much for the happiness and welfare of our country.

Interest in History – Health

No one ought to grow narrow and allow official duties in the Senate, however necessary, to crowd out all recreational capacity. I turn for rest through a change of work to historical research, and get real relaxation out of the fascinating office of head of the Maryland Historical Society. It grows. As an officer of the Society for 30 years, I have seen it increase in size and importance with delight.

Again, for fourteen years I have been stimulated and diverted from petty and selfish things by participating in that gloriously humane work for the treatment, care and study of infantile paralysis. I am head of the organization in Maryland. Amazingly enough, about 20,000 zealous men and women in Maryland lend their time and give their money to organize and sustain that great task. It is my pride, my diversion. But back to my report to my employers.

Attitude Toward Labor, Labors Attitude Toward Me

My good friend, and temporary opponent, the Governor, if the papers are correct, seems to be embarrassed by the hearty endorsement of his candidacy by the C.I.O., Political Action Committee. He doubtless welcomes their secret votes, and his diffidence is in welcoming the C.I.O.

voters openly. If he regards the C.I.O., and as to that I do not know, as stigmatic supporters, I am sorry. I never experienced his sensation for I was never endorsed by the P.A.C. Personally, I am not dismayed that the political managers of the C.I.O. now, as always, oppose me. The result of that opposition is told by the election figures in my ever-increasing majorities.

C.I.O. opposition now is no surprise. For, I opposed the so-called "Fair Employment Bill", a misguided measure. Its name "Fair" was a fraud. It violated many of the rights free men have fought for and lived by since Maryland was founded in 1634. A few C.I.O. political leaders told me in unparliamentary language that I had "ruined the labor union cause"; that punishment awaited me.

Again, it is conceded that Senator Taft and I secured a modification of the so-called "Full Employment Bill" which made an otherwise intolerable bill fairly tolerable. As framed, the bill pledged the resources of the United States to a policy of keeping labor employed, regardless of the effect upon government and the people.

I am the last to dispute the importance of labor and labor unions. They are quite necessary. Nor do I oppose the establishment of unions or collective bargaining, or deny labor full and complete justice. I am unalterably in favor of such measures. I am also the last man to pledge the sacrifice of all other callings, occupations, all treasury funds for the supposed advancement of labor and to make about one hundred and twenty odd million people subservient to a single prior preferred interest, let it be labor or any other interest. The act as originally drawn, in my judgment (and many wise labor leaders agree), would have been Labor's sorrow; would set one hundred and twenty million or more citizens against about seventeen million labor unionists; would have destroyed the union's public relations and invited retaliation. Again, I was threatened with punishment for doing my duty as I saw it. Again, I did not yield. I have no idea of bartering my vote in the Senate for favorable votes in the June 24th primary. Again, I was told I had "ruined" Labor (a second time), which seems to have been an overestimate in the light of so many strong and generally successful strikes.

I, in no way resent the opposition of the C.I.O. Its opposition has not and will not alter my views or votes.

In the future, as in the past, I shall support legislation aimed at giving labor fair opportunities to obtain larger incomes commensurate at least with increased cost of living; and sound working conditions. In the conversion from war to peace activities, labor ought to be given an opportunity for readjustments in employment and to receive certain security while in process of doing so.

I have favored unemployment insurance in worthy cases subject to safeguards against mismanagement and other forms of abuses; and believe that unless labor remains on a stable basis, our national economy will be disrupted.

It is unfortunate that present arrangements and policies of adjustment of differences between management and labor are not adequate. They should and can be improved; and the light of truth turned on; decisions made.

Which side is right? Who without study can say? We get in the main only hearsay from violently interested contestants. Public opinion is therefore based upon feeling not facts. Management and Labor bear joint and all-too-often forgotten responsibility to the country to keep production going, and avert suffering to that third interested party, the public, which in the end usually pays the price. An aroused exasperated people will likely read both without discriminating justice. Labor and management had best quit violence (physical, economic, political violence) and resort to reason, the law, to some established judicial process or to arbitration while there is time, or face the whirlwind.

Veterans

Years ago, I voted to pass the bonus for the veterans of the first World

War over the President's veto. I have supported increased salaries for members of the armed forces and measures designed to give them benefits upon returning to civilian life.

I favored the GI Bill of Rights; legislation permitting veterans returning to civilian life the opportunity to regain their old positions and introduce legislation to the same effect giving the merchant seamen like opportunities.

I supported measures for building veteran's hospitals and for increased facilities for hospitalization and medical care; and supported legislation providing for veteran priorities in employment and education facilities; and for veteran priority in the purchase of surplus property; also, for veteran's housing; and for veteran's loans. In fact, I have supported every measure before the Senate reasonably calculated to benefit veterans.

Keep Government Off Schools, Medicine, Business

I am doing my level best to get and keep the government out of competition with private business consistent with the war effort wherever possible; to keep the hand of Federal control off public schools, off the practice of medicine, and off private industry. For instance!

The Insurance Dilemma

The Supreme Court recently overruled a precedent of seventy-five years, held that all insurance business was interstate commerce, was subject to Federal control; that insurance officials who agreed on rates, though compelled in many states to charge the same rates, were liable to prosecution for alleged violations of the Sherman Anti-Trust Law. That revolutionary decision played havoc with a great industry. If the government had insisted and exercised its power to take control, the State Insurance Departments would be superseded, revenues and control by State authorities lost. The proof is absolute that my efforts with President Roosevelt resulted in the suspension of Federal prosecutions and the assumption of Federal control until the States are given a reasonable opportunity to make and enforce satisfactory regulatory laws. If done, it was understood that the Federal Government will let the matter rest. The effect of President Roosevelt's act, which he wrote me was due to my intercession, saves the companies and the States much revenue, insures the peaceful conduct of the business, and incredible relief; saves the public, stockholders and policy holders complications and losses. State insurance commissioners, Federal authorities and the insurance companies approach a settlement satisfactory to all. Frankly, I am proud of that job.

Preparations for War, the War, Peace

In relation to international trade agreements, the elimination of currency and trade barriers, preparations against attack, upbuilding of the Army, Navy, shipping aviation, to perfect lend-lease, the acquisition of bases, the Bretton-Woods inaugurated legislation, etc., the conduct of the war, the steps leading the way to peace, the story is short. I supported each and every measure to the utmost.

Prosperity Here Impossible with a Pauper Europe and Asia

We cannot have permanent prosperity in America if the nations of Europe and Asia continue on the verge of starvation, continue bankrupt and disorganized. They cannot manufacture goods we need and cannot buy merchandise we have to sell. Nor can peace reign in distressed and desperate countries; which brings me toward the end of this long report.

My Absorbing Ambition

Going, striving incessantly, spending twice my salary to keep my work moving, why do I seek six more years in office? Simply because I am interested in the millions and millions of the people of the Earth, the black, the brown, the yellow, and the white. Many domestic and international questions possess me. I am fired with an ambition, if I can, to help correct ills and improve the institutions, nations and governments.

The end of war is the most supreme fruit of statesmanship, if not of prayer. Much must be corrected, rebuilt, to enjoy that prize.

The Means at Our Hands

The Poles, a brave people, war-torn, their land portioned, mangled, our friends in the Revolutionary War, unconquerable, appeal to us. We offer them relief from now imminent starvation, a loan on terms they should meet. We can well afford to furnish them with ships. With Poland's sweeping access to the Baltic Sea, Polish merchant vessels will again grace the ports of the world. We want to see Polish soil free from the presence of foreign troops, and Poland restored to her old independence, to become a prosperous nation. That will make for peace.

The Jews. Who can crave leisure so long as there is need for help in any capacity left for those victims of unutterable grief, who survived the oppression and murder which swept the majority of the race in Europe out of existence during World War II? The remnants of one of Earth's greatest people seek a tiny national home, a bit of land the size of Vermont, surrounded by a vast semi-waste land which have been held by the Arabs undeveloped and deteriorating for thousands of years.

The Jewish people want a national home. Who does not want a home? A home bought and paid for, which beautifies and improves the neighborhood; where they can be independent and at peace. Such a home they propose is as helpful to the Arabs as to them. The Arabs do little to build up their enormous and thinly settled desert. They don't work. They leave the land unsowed, when needed to replenish the food and goods so tragically sought by starving neighbors. They should give up resources they won't use, and make way for others. Why not back the men who will work, who will irrigate, plant and improve, who will buy for a fair price a small part at least of that neglected soil? That will make for peace; for ease of conscience.

Greece. We hope and pray for the quick restoration of Greece because her burdens are so grievous, the Greek spirit so indomitable, the country's means so small, the Grecian example so inspiring. By loans, by supplies of food and necessaries, we must aid the Greeks to set up again; again, to become successful in shipping, farming, the arts, and industry. That will ease the tension in Europe.

Italy. Who can regard Italy as our enemy? Italy and the United States had a common enemy, a treacherous, deadly enemy in Mussolini. Terribly, he made them suffer. In mercy and fellowship, we must help Italy; trade with Italy; foster the great Italian civilization, come to peace terms with her. That will go a long, long way on the right road.

The whole foreign field, particularly China and the European nations, their history, their present, their future intrigue me. China, England, France, Belgium, Holland, Norway, an honest debtor Finland, lie gasping from war fatigue; hungry, disorganized, they saw the works of their hands swept away, The Czechs, the Lithuanians suffered grievously, still suffer, still struggle, and struggle supremely. What their future will be, whether these brave stricken nations fall to the depths, or arise to march towards the goal of a restored civilization and the prize of world security rests primarily in their hands, and in a lesser, but indispensable part in ours. Will we stand by them understandingly, generously, sympathetically? I pray that we do.

Germany, the hard international problem, is its own grief; our grief. Must we say its future, our future, in German affairs is hopeless? Aside from war criminals, the German people supply much we can admire sincerely. It is an ultra-pessimism which says that the bulk of the German people, orderly, common, intelligent, educated, thrifty, prodigiously energetic are blind to the lessons of history, are forever indifferent to international utility, "materialism" if you will; and forever deaf to the call of Christ.

In fundamental essentials German people are just folks as other advanced nationals. Their national aggressiveness and devotion to war are the fruits of tradition, of centuries of training, and environment. It will take much treasure, many years of effort and infinite patience to neutralize their past trends. But it is worthwhile. It is the best possible investment we can make.

An answer to the pessimists, and one proof of my belief, lies in the many thousand men and women of pure German blood who absorb the American point of view, who fought and worked in both world wars with thoughtless patriotism and supreme courage. Nor was the German born population who came to our shores guilty, except in rarest instances, of any sabotage or subversive acts. It is the environment, not the blood. German people expand and develop under the American way. For example, measured by blood lines General Eisenhower is German. The accident of birth, the accident of American environment made General Eisenhower a great patriot, and a general greater under the American way than any brother by German blood who served on the German General Staff ever was.

Russia. Ten years ago, our feeling toward Russia was antagonistic, unreasonable, ill advised. A great, though as yet incomplete change over spreads our thinking now. Men of intelligence and patience in Russia and America can see the objectives of the two countries approach a closer harmony, a lasting understanding.

My soul is on guard against the enemies of peace, the enemies of world security. All aspirations, all hopes, all efforts are dwarfed by that supreme necessity; peace. And that effort, in my small way, to the best of my abilities, I wish devoutly to take part. I dedicate every gift that God gave me and every opportunity given me to use in the Senate to preserve and forestall the Earth from World War III.

APPENDIX 8

Speech by Sen. George L. Radcliffe, Maryland Chairman of the Presidential Birthday Ball for the benefit of the National Foundation for Infantile Paralysis

Baltimore, Maryland

January 30, 1940

This day, the 30th day of January, has a special significance for many reasons. One of these is the anniversary of the birthday of the President of the United States, a matter which, naturally is of particular interest to us Americans. It is instinctive at this time to offer our most hearty congratulations and wish him many happy returns of the day. There is also another reason why this day is significant. It commemorates the beginning of a movement which already has had a wide humanitarian appeal and the results of which are most far-reaching. It records a splendid fight against terrific odds made by a brave and courageous man because out of that fight a human plan has evolved and a great good to mankind has resulted.

I seemed to be in quite close contact with the President of the United States when he was stricken with infantile paralysis, making such a remarkable effort to restore his health. Never have I seen such energy, resourcefulness and courage and patience more freely illustrated. The successful fight to the return of health as made by President Roosevelt is an inspiring record which forms the basis. It is stimulating. It suggests what can be done against terrific odds. That example in itself would be a stimulating one, but that is only part of the story. The example of that fight suggested a practical plan by which other people, who might be victims of that disease, could be benefited. Little was known of infantile paralysis, except that it was a dreadful disease and most distressing in its effects. A suggestion was made that the birthday of President Roosevelt could remain a rallying place for those who desire to combat infantile paralysis. All of this required treatment; it also required research into the causes of the disease and methods of its treatment.

And so, as we know, on Jan 30th, 1934 the first birthday balls were held, and the objective in mind was to raise funds to fight infantile paralysis. These balls were held all over the United States and approximately $1,000,000.00 was raised.

That was the beginning of a series of similar events which have been highly successful. Each year these balls and dinners were held in commemoration of the President's birthday and for the purpose of raising funds for infantile paralysis. These balls have reached almost universal support. People, men and women, in private and public life have freely contributed their time, their services and their money. The members of the theatrical profession have been especially helpful. And so, during the seven years, these balls have been held each year with the result that approximately $1,000,000.00 annually has been raised for this worthy cause.

But that is not all of the story. What began seven years ago is a series of joyous balls which have continued as such, but in addition a permanent association or foundation has evolved which always will be an assistance in helping to fight this dreadful disease. It is similar in constitution to other great medical foundations which have been formed. It will work much along the same lines. It is, of course, non-partisan in constitution, and it is controlled or supervised by outstanding experts in the country. The work of the foundation is manifold. It is a clearinghouse for research and methods of treatment of epidemics and all of the many activities.

So, what started out as merely a celebration of a joyous evening to raise funds for a worthy cause has now developed into a well organized fight which is doing the splendid work for the treatment of the most dreaded disease which inflicts the human race. The splendid example, the courage and resourcefulness which President Roosevelt gave against infantile paralysis has furnished the original incentive and has always been a most stimulating factor.

Out of this fight has been worked out successfully something which is a great benefit to the human race. I have been in an unusually fortunate position in seeing and knowing what is being done. I was practically in daily contact with the President when he was making his heroic and successful fight. Also, I have been Chairman for Maryland for the Birthday Balls each one of the seven years.

APPENDIX 9

MEMORIAL TO GEORGE L. RADCLIFFE
SAM HOPKINS, 1974
MARYLAND HISTORICAL SOCIETY

George L. Radcliffe, 1877-1974

United States Senator for Maryland, 1935-1947
Member of the Maryland Historical Society, 1908-1974
Secretary 1911-1931, Vice President 1931-1939,
President 1939-1964, Chairman 1964-1974

For ninety-seven years from birth at Spocott Farm near Lloyds in Dorchester County on August 22, 1877 until death came in Baltimore on July 29, 1974, Senator George L. Radcliffe enriched the lives of others with warm friendship as he followed a strong urge to use his boundless energy and wide range of interests and abilities. Throughout his life, the Senator's old associations grew richer. As his activities and usefulness widened with each passing year, he increasingly cherished his family, neighbors, and growing new friendships. He particularly enjoyed returning home to the Eastern Shore on every possible weekend. For sixty-nine years, he happily attended each annual meeting of the Baltimore City College Class of 1905. They had named him their favorite teacher and dedicated the 1905 *Green Bag* and its supplement 40 years later to him.

In describing his early years, in a speech at Pocomoke on May 25, 1946, the Senator said, "I was born within a hundred feet of salt water. My early experiences were in my father's shipyard, on his farms, working in our canning factory, mingling with the farmers, fisherman and oysterman who were our neighbors and good friends. The lives of those who toil on farms, on the oyster bars are open pages to me." Referring to his view of his service as United States Senator, he said, "My duty, my pleasure, and my ambition is to turn out a good, sincere, unostentatious, successful record of service to my constituents, whether they earn their living with a pen, a hoe, or a pinmall. They all look alike to me." In the same year, Judge Samuel K. Dennis, the Senator's long-time friend and former Chief Judge of the Supreme Bench of Baltimore said of the Senator, "... nor is he partisan. He has an idea his services belong to anyone, everyone. Hence, men of high and low degree, of all political affiliations, in business and in office alike find him approachable, amiable, infinitely kind and obliging."

Senator Radcliffe thoroughly liked people. He was at ease with others regardless of place, background, or differences. He made them feel comfortable and enjoy being with him. A person full of innate goodness and blessed with ability and good judgment, the Senator was instinctively turned to by people when they wanted a man in whom they could place their trust and from whom they would receive fair and wise help or advice. Individuals and groups, often those with conflicting views, turned to him for help in resolving their differences or accomplishing a task. He was a man of patience, quick to forgive and who just could not harbor a grudge. His very nature rebelled at man's cruelty to man. It was never for him to cause pain or mortification to others.

From early childhood the Senator carried with him and constantly renewed warm memories of Christmas and the happy time his mother made for her family at Christmas. In school Christmas was his favorite subject for compositions. Later he collected over 2,000 books and 500 articles about Christmas. It was the subject of his first address to the United States Senate. The Christmas spirit represented to the Senator the happy bringing together of family and friends, generous impulses, and kindly deeds to others. These things appealed to his deeply ingrained sense of love of people, equality, goodness, and justice in dealing with others.

Beginning early in life, Senator Radcliffe was deeply influenced by his father's emphasis on independence and work, and his mother's love of reading and literature. Following graduation from the Cambridge High School and pursuing his desire for work and education, he received degrees from the Johns Hopkins University, A.B. 1897, in history and political science and Ph.D., 1900, in history. His doctoral thesis, "Governor Hicks of Maryland and the Civil War" was published by the Johns Hopkins Press in 1901. A lifelong source of satisfaction to the Senator was that those who read his work were unable to determine whether his sympathies were with the Union or the Confederacy. While at "Hopkins", the Senator was a member of the one-mile relay team which won that event at the University of Pennsylvania Relay Carnival at Philadelphia in 1898. The gold watch awarded him became his favorite possession and a constant reminder of this happy occasion. An active and appreciative alumnus, Senator Radcliffe served as President of the "Hopkins" Alumni Association (1913–1920) and Chairman of the successful 1919 campaign to raise funds to build the "Alumni Memorial Dormitory".

Among the Senator's happiest memories were those of his service as principal of the Cambridge High School (1900–1901) and Professor of History at the Baltimore City College (1901-1902). During the years 1902–1903, he attended the University of Maryland Law School from which he received an LL.B. degree in 1903. In later years, he received honorary degrees from Washington College (LL.D., 1934) and the University of Maryland (LL.D., 1943).

In 1903 Senator Radcliffe began his seventy-one-year business association with the American Bonding Company of Baltimore and the Fidelity and Deposit Company of Maryland. His responsibilities in various capacities included Head of the Legal Department, Vice President, Chairman of the Executive Committee and member of the Board of Directors. Judge Samuel K. Dennis, a fellow Director, in referring to the Senator as a businessman, said, "He became valuable to his Company, not as a master of routine, but in stronger fields as a "trouble shooter", idea man, pioneer thinker, policy maker, diplomat." J. Harry Schisler, a business colleague for most of the Senator's career, describes him as "the man to handle serious things" and "an accomplished negotiator." Senator Radcliffe's other business interests included membership on the Board of Directors of the Fidelity Trust Company and Baltimore Contractors (1951–1974).

Senator Radcliffe and Miss Mary McKim Marriott of Baltimore were married on June 6, 1906. Among the Senator's greatest joys were his home and family. After his wife's death he derived special joy from knowing that his son George, his daughter-in-law Augusta, and their children shared his love for Spocott Farm.

In 1908 Senator Radcliffe became a member of the Maryland Historical Society, and for sixty-six years contributed immensely to its growth in size and usefulness. For sixty-four years he served as an officer—Secretary (1911–1931, Vice-President (1931–1939), President (1939-1964), and Chairman (1964–1974). The Senator often said that the Society was not work but a place to which he could turn for a restful change of pace and recreation.

The highlights of the Senator's service as President included an address to the Society by his close friend, then Vice-President Harry S. Truman, soon to succeed as President another close friend, President Franklin D. Roosevelt. The subject, "Maryland and Tolerance", was dear to the Senator's heart. Speaking of intolerance that evening, March 16, 1945, Vice President Truman said, "There is no lasting cure except that found in the impartial recording of history." Turning to history again, Vice President Truman spoke words to the Senator. "The pages of history remain open for all to read. They stand as an eternal warning against the tragic disasters of the past ... of course, every generation must meet new problems in light of new developments, but surely they must profit by the experience of the past."

Developments at the Maryland Historical Society which meant much to Senator Radcliffe would include the Keyser Memorial, including the gift of the Enoch Pratt House, the gift of Francis Scott Key's original manuscript of "The Star-Spangled Banner", the Thomas and Hugg Memorial Building and endowment, the Jacob and Annita France Auditorium and the Jacob France Endowment Fund, the Darnall Young People's Museum of Maryland History, and the 1973 decision to rename an expanded maritime museum "The George L. Radcliffe Maritime Museum."

The Senator supplemented his devotion to the Maryland Historical Society by accepting other responsibilities related to Maryland history. These included: Chairman of the 1924 City Commission which saved the "Shot Tower"; Chairman of the Star-Spangled Banner Committee (1939); Maryland War Records (1942); Chairman of the celebration of the 300th anniversary of the Religious Toleration Act in Maryland (1949); Chairman of the Committee on Historical Markers in Maryland (1954). The Senator's long-time encouragement to local historical societies played an important role in their growth to the point where at least one is in every Maryland County.

When interviewed and recorded on tape last summer by his friend Walter Finch as part of the Society's Oral History project, the Senator responded to a question about his first introduction to politics saying. "According to tradition, the first thing that an Eastern Shore baby does is look west to Annapolis." His early public service included appointments by his former Cambridge High School principal, Governor Harrington, to membership on the Baltimore City Liquor License Board (1916–1919) and Secretary of State (Maryland) (1919–1920). Senator Radcliffe served as chairman of four Gubernatorial Inauguration committees – Governor Ritchie, 1923, 1926, 1930; and Governor Lane, 1947. In 1932 his friend Franklin Delano Roosevelt, who had been a Vice President of the Fidelity and Deposit Company before becoming Governor of New York State, named Senator Radcliffe as Maryland Chairman of his successful campaign for election as President of the United States. To help President Roosevelt in that difficult period, Senator Radcliffe accepted an appointment in 1933 as Regional Director of the Public Works Administration. In 1934 Senator Radcliffe was elected to the first of his two terms in the United States Senate. His Senate committee assignments included Finance and Maritime. As Chairman of a Maritime Subcommittee, Senator Radcliffe was the chief architect and author of the Merchant Marine Act of 1936. This basic legislation has been described as "the keystone and foundation upon which our maritime laws and our merchant marine function." Just as had been his way in business, the Senator thrived in the United States Senate on work and problems. Never one to set people against each other, he had no sympathy for legislation and programs which advantaged groups at the expense of others.

The Democratic State Central Committee for Maryland chose Senator Radcliffe as its Chairman for the Presidential Campaign year 1936. He later served as Maryland Chairman of his close friend President Harry S. Truman's successful 1948 re-election campaign. In 1952 Senator Radcliffe served as Chairman of the Chesapeake Bay Bridge dedication.

The Senator's additional interests and contributions to Maryland were many. His ability to enlist people in getting jobs done was reflected in his being called on as just the right man for many responsibilities. One of these responsibilities which meant much to the Senator was leadership for thirty years of the March of Dimes (Infantile Paralysis Programs) in Maryland. A quick project the Senator often recalled was the construction of a horse-drawn coach within forty-eight hours by Victor Frenkil and Baltimore Contractors for the Oriole's 1954 Homecoming Celebration. Other opportunities for service the Senator responded to were the presidencies of the English-Speaking Union, the University Club, and the Eastern Shore Society.

Perhaps closest to Senator Radcliffe's heart were the parts he played in projects related to the Eastern Shore. These would include the Dorchester County Historical Society, Grace Foundation of Taylor's Island, the restoration of historic Old Trinity Church, and the Chapel of Ease.

One of the happiest occasions of the Senator's life took place on his ninety-fifth birthday. On that day he realized a childhood hope for the reconstruction of Spocott Windmill, which was originally built by his father, used for grinding grain into flour, and blew down in the blizzard of 1888. His vigorous address and the appreciation he expressed on the dedication day for the reconstructed mill will always be remembered by those present.

The Senator steadfastly looked to the future with hope. Each of us who know and study his life will find in his example strength for our own futures. At every stage of life, he lived as though he were entering a new career. Those who are fifty-nine will see great possibilities for their futures as they realize they are at the same age as the Senator when he began a twelve-year career in the United States Senate. At any age until ninety-six, they can look forward with success, as the Senator did, to the realization of his childhood dream that "the old mill would come back." Each of us can, as was true of the Senator, continuously re-live the joy of Christmas and share with the Senator the lifelong happiness and inspiration he found in the Christmas spirit of goodness to all men.

It is an inspiration to look back on the life of Senator George L. Radcliffe. He lived a life in which a sense of the past was linked so beautifully with the realities of the present and an optimistic view for the future.

Samuel Hopkins
October 1974

Endnotes

PREFACE:

1. Radcliffe, George L. Letter to Kenneth N. Anglemire, Marquis, *Who's Who,* Inc., 22 Jun 1965.

THE LIFE OF GEORGE LOVIC PIERCE RADCLIFFE (1877-1974)

1. Radcliffe, John A. L. Cash Book, 1846 – 1851, pp. 136-37.

2. Radcliffe, George L. *Governor Thomas H. Hicks of Maryland and the Civil War,* Baltimore: Johns Hopkins Press, 1901.

3. "Wilson Coming in May." *The Baltimore Sun* (Baltimore, MD), 28 Apr 1915, p. 7.

4. "Plan Hopkins Militia." *The Baltimore Sun* (Baltimore, MD), 18 Sep 1915, p. 12.

5. "Memorial Dormitory for Hopkins Heroes." *The Baltimore Sun* (Baltimore, MD), 22 Jun 1919, page 16.

6. "To Work for Dormitory Fund." *The Baltimore Sun* (Baltimore, MD), 7 Mar 1920, page 14.

7. "Plans for Hopkins Dormitories Nearly Completed by Architect." *The Baltimore Sun* (Baltimore, MD), 23 Jul 1920, p. 20.

8. There is no specific documentation of his participation in the "Dollar-a-Year Man" program, but Sen. Radcliffe always talked of meeting Roosevelt in this capacity, and the Senator's son, George, expounded on this in notes he recorded in 2000 and an interview in 2008.

9. The incident was shared by his son, George M. Radcliffe, in a 2008 interview.

10. "George L. Radcliffe Is Appointed Works Adviser for Tenth Region." *The Surety Producer,* Sept. 1933, page 40.

11. Bell, Ulric. "10 Regional Public Works Heads Named." *The Courier-Journal* (Louisville, KY), 26 Jul 1933, p 1.

12. "Builds Model Public Works Advisory Board." *The Evening Sun* (Baltimore, MD), 21 Dec. 1933, p. 44.

13. "Radcliffe Withdraws from Gubernatorial Race to Seek Senate." *The Sun* (Baltimore, MD), 8 Jul 1934, p. 1.

14. Radcliffe, George L. *Notes on His Political Campaigns*, 1946. Maryland Center for History and Culture, *The George L. Radcliffe Papers, ca.1895-1972*, MS. 2280, p.7.

15. Miles, Clarence W. agent. *The Man for U.S. Senator: George L. Radcliffe*, 1934.

16. "Nice's Margin of 6149 in Md. Cost $39,798." *The News Journal* (New Castle, DE), 28 Nov 1934, p. 4.

17. Radcliffe, George L. *History of the United States Merchant Marine.* Maryland Center for History and Culture, *The George L. Radcliffe Papers, ca.1895-1972*, MS. 2280.

18. Schulman, Bruce J. *From Cotton Belt to Sunbelt: Federal Policy, Economic Development, and the Transformation of the South, 1938 – 1980*. Duke University Press: Durham, NC, 1994, p. 45.

19. O'Neill, Thomas, M. "Kicks at Naming of Radcliffe as Campaign Chief." *The Evening Sun* (Baltimore, MD), 29 Aug 1936, p. 16.

20. O'Neill, Thomas, M. "Radcliffe Says 'No, Thanks' to Boss-ship Bid." *The Evening Sun* (Baltimore, MD), 5 Nov 1936, p. 46.

21. Radcliffe, George L. Personal Diary, unpublished, 1937.

22. Radcliffe, George L. *Notes on His Political Campaigns*, 1946. Maryland Center for History and Culture, *The George L. Radcliffe Papers, ca.1895-1972*, MS. 2280, p.14.

23. "Radcliffe Replies to B.A. of C. Letter." *The Baltimore Sun* (Baltimore, MD), 12 Mar. 1939, p. 18.

24. "Radcliffe Pledges Efforts for Peace." *The Baltimore Sun* (Baltimore, MD), 5 Sep 1939, p. 22.

25. "Senator Radcliffe Urges Repeal of Neutrality Act." *The Baltimore Sun* (Baltimore, MD), 27 Oct 1941, p. 7.

26. "Women in Men's Field." *The Baltimore Sun* (Baltimore, MD), 23 Feb 1921, p. 4.

27. Amadeo, Kimberly. "Bretton Woods System and 1944 Agreement." *The Balance*. https://www.thebalance.com/bretton-woods-system-and-1944-agreement-3306133. Accessed 3 Sep 2020.

28. Radcliffe, George L. "The Bretton Woods Agreement." Speech before the U.S. Senate, 18 Jul 1945.

29. Radcliffe, George L. *Notes on His Political Campaigns*, 1946. Maryland Center for History and Culture, *The George L. Radcliffe Papers, ca.1895-1972*, MS. 2280, pp. 24 – 25.

30. Radcliffe, George L. Summary of Battle of Brooklyn, unpublished, 1950.

31. Hopkins, Samuel. "George L. Radcliffe, 1877 – 1974." *Maryland Historical Magazine* 69 (1974), p. ix.

A CONFLUENCE OF GENES AND ENVIRONMENT

1. Tepper, Michael, ed. "The Sailing of the Ship *Submission* in the Year 1682, With a True Copy of the Vessel's Log." *New World Immigrants: A Consolidation of Ship Passenger Lists and Associated Data from Periodical Literature, Volume 1*, Genealogical Publishing Company, 1979, pp. 235 – 241.

2. "First Supply (Fleet), sailed Oct 18, 1607." *WikiTree*. Accessed 13 Jan 2021. https://www.wikitree.com/wiki/Category:First_Supply_%28Fleet%29%2C_sailed_Oct_18%2C_1607.

3. This is based on conversations George L. Radcliffe had with James Michener at Spocott during the spring and summer of 1972. The details were relayed to the family by Bill Radcliffe, grandson of George L. Radcliffe. Bill sat in on most of the conversations.

4. Spencer, Richard Henry, ed. "John Anthony LeCompte Radcliffe", *Genealogical and Memorial Encyclopedia of the State of Maryland, Vol. I*, New York: The American Historical Society, Inc., 1919, pp. 257 – 261.

JUST A FARM BOY

1. Michener, James. *Chesapeake*. New York: Random House, New York, 1978, p. 16.

2. Radcliffe, G. M. *Spocott, It's Owners and Buildings: From 1662 to Date*. Unpublished, 2003, pp. 1 – 3.

3. This information comes from the many hours that George L. Radcliffe shared stories of his childhood and of the stories which had been passed down through the generations. Additional verification comes from a 2008 interview with his son George.

THE MYSTERIOUS MIDDLE NAME

1. Radcliffe, George L. Letter to Talbott Denmead, 30 Aug 1963.

2. Jakes, John. *The Furies, Vol. IV, The American Bicentennial Series.* Open Road Media (New York, NY), 1976.

3. Jakes, John. Letter to George M. Radcliffe, 9 Feb 1976.

4. Northen, William F., ed., Caldwell, A. B. "Lovick Pierce", *Men of Mark in Georgia, Vol. II.* A. B. Caldwell Publisher (Atlanta, Georgia), 1910, pp. 76 – 78.

5. Smith, George G. *The Life and Times of George Foster Pierce, D.D., LL.D.* "Chapter 1" [The Bishop's sketch of his father]. Hancock Publishing Co. (Sparta, GA), 1888, p. 3.

6. Ibid, p. 4.

7. Ibid, p. 31.

8. Ibid, pp. 34 – 35.

9. Stone, Phillip. "How the Methodist Church Split in the 1840s." Wofford College: From the Archives, 30 Jan 2013. http://blogs.wofford.edu/from_the_archives/2013/01/30/how-the-methodist-church-split-in-the-1840s/.

10. "Episcopal Methodist Conference." Baltimore Sun, Baltimore, MD, 7 Mar 1867, p. 1. *Macon Weekly Telegraph* (Macon, GA), 22 Mar 1867, Vol. 2, Issue 17, p. 5.

11. *Macon Telegraph* (Macon, GA), Issue 7910, 18 Jul 1877, p. 2.

12. Radcliffe, George M. "Mysterious Middle Name of Senator Radcliffe." South Dorchester Folk Museum DVD, Presentation #67, 5 Sep 2007.

13. George L. Radcliffe shared this story on numerous occasions.

14. "Death of a Venerable Man." *Augusta Chronicle* (Augusta, GA), 11 Nov 1879, p. 4.

15. Pierce, Dr. Lovick. Letter from the Rev. Dr. Lovick Pierce, "To Men of Calm Reflection I speak", *Augusta Chronicle* (Augusta, GA), 9 Nov 1860, p. 3.

16. Northern, p. 78.

- Source for the image of Reverence Lovick Pierce: Northen, William F., ed., Caldwell, A. B. "Lovick Pierce", *Men of Mark in Georgia, Vol. II.* A. B. Caldwell Publisher (Atlanta, Georgia), 1910.

THE RUNNER

1. Schmidt, John, C. "At 80, George L. Radcliffe is Still Running." *The Baltimore Sun* (Baltimore, MD), 30 Jul 1958, p. 181.

2. "The Relay Team.", *The News-letter.* Johns Hopkins University, Spring 1898, p. 11.

3. "Score Another for Hopkins." *The Baltimore Sun* (Baltimore, MD), 2 May 1898, p. 8.

4. "At 80, George L. Radcliffe is...", p. 181.

5. "G.L. Radcliffe Dies at 96." *The Evening Sun* (Baltimore, MD), 29 Jul 1974, p. 9.

- Source for the image of the Johns Hopkins University Mile Relay Team: *Hullabaloo '99* (the Johns Hopkins Yearbook), Williams and Wilkins Company Press (Baltimore, MD), p. 186.

A TEACHER AT HEART

1. Baker, R.S. and Dodd, W.F., eds. 'The Spirit of Learning', in Woodrow Wilson." *College and State: Educational, Literary and Political Papers (1875 – 1913.* New York and London, 1925, vol. 2, p. 112. Retrieved from The Isaiah Berlin Virtual Library. "Woodrow Wilson on Education", 2004. http://berlin.wolf.ox-.ac.uk/lists/nachlass/woodrow.pdf. Retrieved 4 Feb 2020, George L. Radcliffe took classes from Woodrow Wilson at Johns Hopkins, was mentored by him on his Ph.D. research, and then worked in Wilson's 1912 Presidential campaign.

2. Maynard, W. B. "More Than a Mere Student." *Johns Hopkins Magazine,* Vol. 59, No. 4, Sept. 2007. Retrieved in 2020 from https://pages.jh.edu/jhumag/0907web/wilson.html.

3. Senior Class of Johns Hopkins University. Wilson lectures. *Hullabaloo '97,* Guggenheimer, Weil, & Co. (Baltimore, MD), 1897, pp. 17, 29.

4. Maynard, "More Than a Mere Student."

5. "A Teacher Elected." *Baltimore Sun* (Baltimore, MD), 30 Dec 1900, p. 8.

6. Letter from unknown to George M. Radcliffe, Dec. 1983.

7. "History of Baltimore City College." *Wikipedia*. Accessed 6 Jun 2020. https://en.wikipedia.org/wiki/History_of_Baltimore_City_College.

8. Highton, R. "Only Played 4 Good Butlers." *The Evening Sun* (Baltimore, MD), 20 Jun 1962, p. 36.

9. Radcliffe, George L. "Lares et Penates." *The Green Bag*, Baltimore City College (Baltimore, MD), 1905.

10. "Fortieth Anniversary Reunion of The Class of 1905." Class of 1905, Baltimore City College Reunion Brochure, 4 Jun 1945.

11. Ibid.

12. "To Lecture on Suretyship" *Baltimore Sun* (Baltimore, MD), 20 Oct 1920, p. 7.

13. Arnett, E. "Boys of 1905 Class Meet Again, Recall Their Own Uniqueness." *Baltimore Sun* (Baltimore, MD), 12 Jun 1974, p. 21.

ONE FOOT IN THE PAST, ONE IN THE FUTURE

1. Radcliffe, G. L. Letter to Franklin Roosevelt. Aug. 1939. Maryland Center for History and Culture, *The George L. Radcliffe Papers, ca.1895-1972*, MS. 2280. George L. Radcliffe composed the letter to Roosevelt in reply to a letter Roosevelt sent to him on 31 July 1939. In the letter George summarizes his efforts to support the President over the years and which he denies ever trying to get a favor from the President. George did not indicate why the letter was not sent.

2. Anderson, P.D., ed. "A History of the Maryland Historical Society: 1844 – 2006." *Maryland Historical Magazine*, Maryland Historical Society (Baltimore, MD), Vol. 101, no. 4 (Winter 2006), pp. 452 – 481.

3. Radcliffe, G.L. "Faith of George Washington." Speech delivered at Episcopal Pro-Cathedral, Baltimore, MD, 22 Feb 1948.

4. Radcliffe, George L. Speech on the Maryland involvement in the Battle of Long Island. Delivered at Prospect Park (Brooklyn, NY), 17 Sep 1950.

5. Tawes, Gov. J. M. Remarks at the Dedication of the Middle Marker for the Mason-Dixon Line, Grace Episcopal Church (Taylor's Island, MD), 24 Oct 1959.

6. Radcliffe, George L. *History of the United States Merchant Marine*. Maryland Center for History and Culture, *The George L. Radcliffe Papers, ca.1895-1972*, MS. 2280.

7. George's personal daily diaries document his daily activities. He visited England at least once a year, often on business, and he would often add vacation days to extend the trips. He documented in detail his visits and meetings with officials and potential relatives as he tried to uncover clues as to his family's background in England.

8. Culhane, David. "Former U.S. Senator Radcliffe Espouses the Vigorous Life." *The Evening Sun* (Baltimore, MD), 24 Aug 1961, pp. 45 – 46.

"Born a Red-Hot Rebel"

1. Radcliffe, George L., Interview conducted by Walter Finch and Donna Shanklin, Document OH8075. The Maryland Historical Society (Baltimore, MD), 7 May 1974, Page I-1-5. *The George L. Radcliffe Papers, ca.1895-1972*, MS. 2280.

2. McQuilty, G.W. Letter to John Anthony LeCompte Radcliffe, 11 Jul 1862.

3. Account by William Henry Radcliffe, Jr., great-grandson of William Harris Radcliffe.

4. Radcliffe, George L. Letter to Rebecca Hill, 14 Apr 1965.

5. McQuilty, G.W. Letter

6. Radcliffe, George L. *Governor Thomas H. Hicks of Maryland and the Civil War*, The Johns Hopkins Press (Baltimore, MD), 1901.

7. Radcliffe, George L. Eulogy Given at Service/Burial for Aline Bracco Marriott, Baltimore, MD, 29 Mar 1939.

8. Ibid.

9. U.S. Dept. of the Interior. "First Winchester", *Study of Civil War Sites in the Shenandoah Valley of Virginia*, Sept. 1992. http://www.nps.gov/abpp/shenandoah/svs3-4.html.

10. Reed, Emilie McKim. Her speech to the Daughters of the Confederacy of Maryland on March 19, 1897, from her personal diary.

11. Radcliffe, George L. Speech on Governor Hicks and the Civil War, date unknown.

12. George L. Radcliffe. Speech at the Dedication of the Robert E. Lee – Stonewall Jackson Equestrian Statue in Wyman Park, Baltimore, MD, May 2, 1948.

WOOD FIRES, DICKENS, AND BAYBERRY

1. Obrecht, Victoria B. "Radcliffe's Christmas Carol." *The Sun Magazine* (Baltimore, MD), 22 Dec 1946, p.5.

2. Myres, Karen. "The Windmills of His Mind." *The Dorchester News* (Cambridge, MD), 23 Aug 1972, p. 5A.

3. Radcliffe, George L. "Heigh-ho, Heigh-ho Unto the Green Holly." Essay published in an unknown magazine but also included in a Christmas card he sent in the 1950's.

4. Ibid.

5. Radcliffe, George L. "Christmas and War." Speech before U.S. Senate, Delivered 15 Dec 1942.

6. Personal Remembrances of George M. Radcliffe and George M. Radcliffe, Jr.

7. Radcliffe, George L. "Heigh-ho, Heigh-ho Unto the Green Holly."

- Source for the image of George L. Radcliffe and his Christmas book collection: *The Baltimore Sun*, 22 Dec. 1946, p. 105.

SAVING A LION

1. Beirne, Francis F. *Baltimore: A Picture History, 1858 – 1958.* Hastings House (New York, NY), 1957, pp. 96 – 99.

2. Radcliffe, George L. "A Lion in the Street." *The Sun Magazine* (Baltimore, MD), Feb. 7, 1954.

- Source for the image of George L. Radcliffe and the bronze lion: *The Baltimore Sun*, 7 Feb. 1954, p. 199.

Endnotes

"Fine Old Timbers"

1. Anderson, J. "Shot Tower – How Lead Shot is Made." *Engineering Clicks*, 15 Oct 2018, retrieved from https://www.engineeringclicks.com/shot-tower/.

2. Letter from George L. Radcliffe to potential subscribers

3. "Plans Final Effort to Save Shot Tower." *The Baltimore Sun* (Baltimore, MD), 11 Oct 1924, p. 10.

4. Numerous notes and records of George L. Radcliffe

5. Scarborough, Katharine. "The Shrines of the Shore." *The Baltimore Sun* (Baltimore, MD), 23 Aug 1953, p. 75.

6. Scarborough, Katharine. "The Williamsburg Idea in Maryland." *The Baltimore Sun* (Baltimore, MD), 29 Nov 1953, page 73.

7. "Old Trinity Now Rebuilt." *The Baltimore Sun* (Baltimore, MD), 7 Aug 1960, p. 19.

8. Chappelle, Howard I. "The Story of the *Constellation*." *The Constellation Question, Part 1*. Smithsonian Institution Press (Washington, DC), 1970, pp. 3-4.

9. "Bill Seeks to Bring Frigate Constellation to City Permanently." *The Baltimore Sun* (Baltimore, MD), 21 Mar 1941, p. 36.

10. "Historian Claims Constellation was built in Norfolk, Not Here." *The Baltimore Sun* (Baltimore, MD), 16 Mar 1948, p. 12.

11. Text of speech used by George L. Radcliffe, 1949

12. "Historian Claims *Constellation* ...", p. 12.

13. "Fight Continues to Regain Ship from Navy." *The Evening Sun* (Baltimore, MD), 19 Nov 1953, p. 35.

14. "*Constellation* Due on Tuesday." *The Baltimore Sun* (Baltimore, MD), 5 Aug 1955, p. 34.

15. "Admiral Leahy Opens Drive for Frigate." *The Evening Sun* (Baltimore, MD), 7 Sep 1957, p. 18.

16. "Board the *USS Constellation*." *National Park Service*. https://www.nps.gov/thingstodo/board-the-uss-constellation.htm.

- Source for the image of the shot tower: the Library of Congress.
- Source for the image of the *USS Constellation*: National Archives at College Park.

THE LITTLE WOMAN

1. "Ferry Rescues Dog from Water." *Evening Capital* (Annapolis, MD), April 11 – 16, 1938.

2. "Death Plans Well Laid." *Baltimore Sun* (Baltimore, MD), 18 Mar 1908, p. 14; "Life Worth the Candle." *Baltimore Sun* (Baltimore, MD), 23 Mar 1908, p. 12.

3. Meyer, Adolf. Letter to Mary Marriott Radcliffe, 13 Mar 1917.

4. "History: Over 120 Years Strong." *National PTA*, https://www.pta.org/home/About-National-Parent-Teacher-Association/Mission-Values/National-PTA-History.

5. Roosevelt, Theodore. Letter to Mary Marriott Radcliffe, 26 Sept. 1918.

6. Radcliffe, Mary McKim Marriott. "Over the Carnage – Comes a Voice." Undated published booklet, most likely written 1918 – 1919.

7. Radcliffe, George L. Unpublished Biography of Mary McKim Marriott Radcliffe.

8. Radcliffe, George L. Unpublished speech given to several groups, 1939 – 1949.

9. "Women in Men's Field." *The Baltimore Sun* (Baltimore, MD), 23 Feb 1921, p. 4.

10. "Radcliffe Approves Susan Anthony Plan." *The Evening Sun* (Baltimore, MD), 23 Oct 1939, p. 32.

11. Radcliffe, George L. "Proposed Constitutional Amendment Providing Equal Rights for Women and Men." *Congressional Record* Reprint of Speech, Proceedings and Debates of the 79th Congress, First Session. 3 May 1945.

12. Hamlin, Kimberly A. "Are Women People? The Equal Rights Amendment Then and Now." *Origins*. Ohio State University and Miami University History Departments (Columbus, OH), Vol. 10, Issue 10 (July 2017), https://origins.osu.edu/article/are-women-people-equal-rights-amendment-then-and-now.

13. National Women's Party, "Equal Rights Amendment Reaches Vote in Senate, July 19, 1946." *Equal Rights* (Washington, D.C.), Vol. 32, no. 4, July-August 1946.

ENDNOTES

General Sources:

- Interviews with George M. Radcliffe (her son) in 2008 and personal recollections of George M. Radcliffe, Jr. (grandson).

- Many letters between George L. Radcliffe and Mary McKim Marriott Radcliffe.

THE JUDGE

1. Radcliffe, George M. "Mysterious Middle Name of Senator Radcliffe." *South Dorchester Folk Museum*. DVD, Presentation #67, 5 Sep 2007.

2. Radcliffe, George L. "Memorial Minute." *Chief Judge Dennis Honored by Bench and Bar at Memorial Services Held at Court House.* Published Proceedings, Remarks by George L Radcliffe. (Baltimore, MD), 20 Mar 1953.

3. "Judge Dennis Dies Suddenly at His Home." *The Baltimore Sun* (Baltimore, MD), 12 Jan 1953, p. 26.

4. Radcliffe, George L. Professional Diaries, 1936 – 1963, unpublished.

5. Dennis, Samuel K. Letter to George L. Radcliffe, 7 Sep 1931.

6. Radcliffe, George L. Letter to Sam Dennis, 27 Jun 1952.

7. Radcliffe, George L. "Memorial Minute."

8. Burke, Joseph M. "Maryland Memories: Swing and Sway with Sammy K." *Extra*, 26 Sep 1971.

9. "Judge Dennis Dies...", p. 26.

- Source for the image of Judge Samuel K. Dennis: Maryland State Archives.

CHIMLEYS, ZINKS, AND BULL TURKLES

- Radcliffe, George M. Interview (Cambridge, MD), 20 Dec 2008.

- Personal experience and stories recounted by George M. Radcliffe.

THE PICTURE ON THE DINING ROOM WALL

1. United States Federal Census, 1850, Maryland, Dorchester, District 1, pp. 62 – 63.

2. 1860 U.S. Federal Census – Slave Schedules, District 7, Dorchester County, page 43; *Robert Bell's Book of Slave Statistics, 1864 – 1868: Dorchester County*

3. Spencer, Richard Henry, ed. "John Anthony LeCompte Radcliffe", *Genealogical and Memorial Encyclopedia of the State of Maryland, Vol. I,* New York: The American Historical Society, Inc., 1919, p. 260.

4. Hooper, Edith Robinson, Letters to George M. Radcliffe with remembrances of past Spocott visits, 1995, 1999.

5. Delmarva Eastern Shore Association. "Epicurean Gems: A Rare Collection of Delectable Dishes Handed Down from the Earliest Colonial Days", Nationally Distributed Brochure, 1928.

6. Earle, Swepson. *The Chesapeake Bay Country,* Thomsen-Ellis Company (Baltimore, MD), 1923, p. 398.

7. Conversation with John Creighton shortly before his death in 2015; Maryland State Road Marker, Greenbriar Rd., Dorchester County, MD. https://mht.maryland.gov/historicalmarkers/TourDetails.aspx?tour=African%20American&recNum=12.

An Unusual Friendship

1. Radcliffe, George L., Interview conducted by Walter Finch and Donna Shanklin, Document OH8075. The Maryland Historical Society (Baltimore, MD), 7 May 1974, T*he George L. Radcliffe Papers, ca.1895-1972,* MS. 2280, pp. I-1-38 - 39.

2. "60,000 Should Sign." *The Evening Sun* (Baltimore, MD), 11 Aug 1919, p. 9.

3. "Tablet is Unveiled Honoring First 800." *The Baltimore Sun* (Baltimore, MD), 14 Jan 1920, p. 3.

4. Radcliffe, G. M., Unpublished Notes on the Life of George L. Radcliffe, 2000. George L. Radcliffe always shared with others that he and Franklin Roosevelt met while George was volunteering in the Department of the Nay and that they had become good friends before Roosevelt was hired by the Fidelity and Deposit Company in 1921.

5. Radcliffe, G. M., Unpublished Notes.

6. Schmidt, John, C., "At 80, George L. Radcliffe is Still Running", *The Baltimore Sun* (Baltimore, MD), 20 Jul 1958, p. 181.

7. Radcliffe, G. M., Unpublished Notes.

8. Sutton, Antony C. *Wall Street and F.D.R.* Arlington House (New Rochelle, NY), 1975, Chapter 2.

9. Radcliffe, George M. "Mysterious Middle Name of Senator Radcliffe." South Dorchester Folk Museum DVD, Presentation #67, 5 Sep 2007. Personal recollections of George L. Radcliffe shared with his son.

10. Roosevelt, Franklin. Speech Placing Alfred E. Smith in Nomination. Houston, TX, 27 Jun 1928 p. 7. http://www.fdrlibrary.marist.edu/_resources/images/msf/msf00262.

11. Radcliffe, George L., Interview, p. 1-1-18.

12. Radcliffe, G. M., Unpublished Notes.

13. Dave Leip's Atlas of U.S. Presidential Elections, "1932 Presidential General Election Results – Maryland." https://uselectionatlas.org/RESULTS/state.php?f=0&fips=24&year=1932.

14. "George L. Radcliffe is Appointed Works Adviser for Tenth Region", *The Surety Producer*, Sept. 1933, p. 40.

15. "Roosevelt Attends Bridge Dedication", *The Philadelphia Inquirer* (Philadelphia, PA), 27 Oct 1935, p. 5.

16. George L. Radcliffe shared this story with family and friends on any occasions.

17. "Senator is Roosevelt's Former Boss", *Daily News* (New York, NY), 23 Dec 1934, p. 81.

18. Radcliffe, George L., 1937 Professional Diary

19. Dorsey, John. "Portrait of a Gentleman of the Old School." *Sunday Sun Magazine* (Baltimore, MD), 15 May 1966, p. 16.

20. Roosevelt, Franklin D. Letter to George L. Radcliffe, 7 Apr 1945.

THE GENTLEMAN POLITICIAN

1. The quote incorrectly identifies the election in which George L. Radcliffe opposed Howard Bruce in the Democratic Primary. He opposed Bruce in the 1940 primary, not 1934.

2. Azrael, Louis. "He Loved History and Made It." *The News-American* (Baltimore, MD), 4 Aug 1974, page 11G.

3. Hopkins, Samuel. "George L. Radcliffe, 1877 – 1974." *Maryland Historical Magazine*, Baltimore, MD, Vol. LXIX, no. 4, Winter 1974, p. vi.

4. "Ritchie, Mayor Asked to Get Out of Fight." *The Baltimore Sun* (Baltimore, MD), 27 May 1934, p. 20.

5. O'Neill, Thomas M. "Radcliffe Says 'No Thanks' to Boss-ship Bid." *The Evening Sun* (Baltimore, MD), 5 Nov 1936, p. 46.

6. O'Neill, Thomas M. "Trenton Club's Attacks Fail to Excite Senator." *The Baltimore Sun* (Baltimore, MD), 31 Aug 1936, p. 30.

7. McKeldin, Theodore. Letter to George L. Radcliffe. 16 Aug 1965

8. McKeldin, Theodore. *Washington Bowed*. Maryland Historical Society (Baltimore. MD), 1956, Forward p 3.

9. Radcliffe, George L., Letter to Gov. Theodore McKeldin, 3 Oct 1956.

10. Radcliffe, George L. Letter to Board of Governors of the Maryland Club, 20 Nov 1937

11. Hopkins, Samuel, p. vi.

12. Dorsey, John. "Portrait of a Gentleman of the Old School." *Sunday Sun Magazine* (Baltimore, MD) 15 May 1966, pp. 14, 16.

THE MERCHANT MARINE

1. Rembski, Stanislav. "George L. Radcliffe." *The Baltimore Sun* (Baltimore, MD), 7 Aug 1974, p. 14.

2. Burnham, Robert. "Why Did Napoleon Fail in Russia in 1812?" *The Napoleon Series*, https://www.napoleon-series.org/faq/c_russia.html.

3. Radcliffe, Sen. George L. "Our Merchant Marine Must Be Second to None." *The American Magazine*, Vol. CXXXVI, no. 6, Dec 1943, p. 40.

4. *History, Art & Archives, U.S. House of Representatives*. "BLAND, Schuyler Otis." https://history.house.gov/People/Listing/B/BLAND,-Schuyler-Otis-(B000545)/ (January 29, 2021).

5. "Merchant Marine Act, 1936." *American Merchant Marine at War*, 18 Nov 2004. http://www.usmm.org/mmact1936.html; "Putting the New Merchant Marine Act to Work." Asbury Park Press (Asbury Park, Monmouth, NJ), 8 Jul 1936, p. 8.

ENDNOTES

6. Radcliffe, George L. "The Merchant Marine." Radio Address, 7 Apr 1941. Printed in Congressional Record on April 25, 1941.

7. Radcliffe, George L. "Launching of the Patrick Henry." Radio Address, 27 Sep 1941, Printed in The Congressional Record 6 Oct 1941.

8. Radcliffe, Sen. George L. "Our Merchant Marine ....", p. 91.

9. "Liberty Ships and Victory Ships, America's Lifeline in War." *ParkNet*. National Park Service, U.S. Department of the Interior (Washington, DC), 29 Jan 2021. https://www.nps.gov/articles/liberty-ships-and-victory-ships-america-s-lifeline-in-war-teaching-with-historic-places.htm.

10. Radcliffe, George L. "The Merchant Marine."

11. Ibid.

12. Radcliffe, George L. Letter to Helen Delich, 7 Jun 1955.

13. Hanes, John W. "The American Merchant Marine: A Bridge to the Future." Speech delivered before the Academy of Political Science, New York City, April 5, 1945. http://www.ibiblio.org/pha/policy/1945/1945-04-05b.html.

14. Radcliffe, George L. "Peril in Small Merchant Marine." Letter to the Editor, *The Baltimore Sun* (Baltimore, MD), 15 Feb 1954, p. 12.

General Sources:

Radcliffe, George L. "Maritime Day." Unpublished Speech, 22 May 1942.

Radcliffe, George L. "The Merchant Marine and Admiral Emery S. Land." Speech in the U.S. Senate, 23 Jun 1944.

- Source for the image of *SS Patrick Henry* launching: National Museum of the U. S. Navy.

A FRIEND FROM MISSOURI

1. "Radcliffe to Hunt Deer with Garner." *The Evening Sun* (Baltimore, MD), 30 Nov 1937, p. 16.

2. Osgood, Charles, ed. *Funny Letters from Famous People*. Broadway Books (Random House, Inc., New York, N.), 2003, pp. 35 – 36.

3. Radcliffe, George L. Letter to President Harry Truman, 1 Dec 1948.

4. Truman, Harry S. "Maryland and Tolerance." *Maryland Historical Magazine*, vol. 40, no. 2 (1945), pp. 85-89.

5. Radcliffe, George L. "Our New President." Radio Address, WBAL (Baltimore, MD), 21 Apr 1945, Printed in the Congressional Record on 14 May 1945.

6. Radcliffe, George L. Speech at Democratic State Convention (Maryland), 1948.

7. Radcliffe, George L. Letter to President Harry Truman, 19 Aug 1948.

8. Radcliffe, George L. Letter to James M. Thomson, 24 Dec 1948.

9. Radcliffe, George L. Letter to Harry S. Truman, 18 Aug 1953.

10. Truman, Harry S. Letter to George L. Radcliffe, 3 Jun 1970.

- Source for the image of the hunting party: Harry S. Truman Library and Museum.

THE CONTRADICTION

1. Radcliffe, George L. Speech to the National Negro Business League, 25 Aug 1943. Delivered at their 43rd annual convention in Baltimore.

2. "New Housing Site for Negroes Urged." *The Baltimore Sun* (Baltimore, MD), 22 Jun 1943, p. 30.

3. "Would Hear Black First, Says Radcliffe" *The Evening Sun* (Baltimore, MD), 16 Sep 1937, p. 21.

4, "Editorial: Why the Afro Backs O'Conor." *The Baltimore Afro-American* (The Afro, Baltimore, MD), 25 Jun 1946.

5. Patterson, James T. *Congressional Conservatism and the New Deal.* University of Kentucky Press (Lexington, KY), 1967, pp. 97 – 99.

THE 1946 ELECTION: HIS ONLY DEFEAT

1. Palmer, Brian. "Democracy or Gerontocracy: Is Congress Getting Older?", *Slate*, 2 Jan 2013. https://slate.com/news-and-politics/2013/01/average-age-of-members-of-u-s-congress-are-our-senators-and-representatives-getting-older.html.

2. Radcliffe, George L. *Notes on His Political Campaigns,* 1946. Maryland Center for History and Culture, *The George L. Radcliffe Papers, ca.1895-1972*, MS. 2280.

3. O'Donnell, Louis J. "Radcliffe as Governor. He Says 'No!'", *The Sun* (Baltimore, MD), 19 Oct 1945, p. 26.

4. Radcliffe, Sen. George L. "My Message to My People." Speech delivered at Pocomoke City, MD, 25 May 1946.

5. "O'Conor Takes Radcliffe to Task on Trip." *The Sun* (Baltimore, MD), 27 May 1946, p. 24.

6. "Job Keeps Him from Personal Campaigning, Radcliffe Says." *The Sun* (Baltimore, MD), 22 Jun 1946, pp. 7, 20.

7. "Editorial: Why the Afro Backs O'Conor." *The Baltimore Afro-American* (The Afro, Baltimore, MD), 25 Jun 1946.

8. Pearson, Drew. "How OPA Deadlock Was Broken." *The Times Herald* (Port Huron/St. Clair, MI), 29 Jun 1946, p. 4.

MR. CHAIRMAN

For a complete listing of all that George was involved in over his long life, go to Appendix 1.

1. "Well-wishers Pack Dinner to Pay Radcliffe Tribute." *The Baltimore Sun* (Baltimore, MD), 25 Jan 1955, p. 5.

2. "Miss Joseph Gets Inaugural Commission." *The Baltimore Sun* (Baltimore, MD), 5 Dec 1948, p. 28.

3. Dorsey, John. "Portrait of a Gentleman of the Old School." *Sunday Sun Magazine*, (Baltimore, MD), 15 May 1966, pp. 14 – 17.

4. "Well-wishers Pack Dinner ...." p. 5.

HIS SOCIETY

1. Radcliffe, George L. "Historical Relationship Between Maryland and Virginia." Speech to the Virginia Historical Society, Richmond, Virginia, 19 Jan 1950.

2. In September of 2020, the Maryland Historical Society was renamed the Maryland Center for History and Culture. (https://www.mdhistory.org/)

3. Anderson, Patricia Dockman, ed. "A History of the Maryland Historical Society: 1844 – 2006", *Maryland Historical Magazine* (Baltimore, MD), Vol. 101, no. 4, Winter, 2006, pp. 401-501.

4. His many letters and interviews document his initial frustrations with the Maryland Historical Society.

5. "Proceedings of the Society: 1939." *Maryland Historical Magazine* (Baltimore, MD), Vol. XXXV, 1940, pp. 93 – 98.

6. Dennis, Samuel K. Letter to George L. Radcliffe, 26 Jan 1943.

7. Radcliffe, George L. "Report of the President for 1943", Maryland Historical Society, Baltimore, 1944.

8. Radcliffe, George L. Untitled Speech delivered, 1946.

9. Anderson, Patricia Dockman, ed., p. 474.

10. Anderson, Patricia Dockman, ed., p. 471.

11. "George L. Radcliffe (1877 – 1974). *News and Notes of the Maryland Historical Society.* (Baltimore, MD), Vol. 3, no. 2, Sept. 1974, p. 5.

12. Hopkins, Samuel. "Director Retires." *Maryland Historical Magazine* (Baltimore, MD), Vol. LXVII, 1972, page i.

13. Radcliffe, George L., Letter to Edwin H. Brown, Jr., 7 Sep 1934.

14. Foster, James W., Acting Secretary, "Report of Meeting of Committee on Maryland History in the Schools, at the Maryland Historical Society", 10 Jun 1944.

15. Anderson, Patricia Dockman, ed., pp. 475 – 77.

16. Anderson, Patricia Dockman, ed., pp. 478 – 480.

17. Numerous letters to county historical society officers over the years; Hopkins, Samuel. "George L. Radcliffe, 1877 – 1974." *Maryland Historical Magazine* 69 (1974), p. viii.

18. Maryland Historical Society. "Annual Report for the Year 1943." (Baltimore, MD), 1944, p. 2.

19. Maryland Historical Society, "Centennial Meeting Invitation and Programme." 21 Feb 1944.

20. Truman, Harry S. "Maryland and Tolerance." *Maryland Historical Magazine* (Baltimore, MD), Vol. XL, no. 2, June 1945, pp. 85 – 89.

21. Marshall, Gen. George C. "Some Lessons of History." *Maryland Historical Magazine* (Baltimore, MD), Vol. XL, no. 3, September 1945, pp. 175 – 84.

22. Maryland Historical Society. "Chesapeake Museum to be Opened at Maryland Historical Society", Press Release, Baltimore, MD, 18 Sep 1950.

23. "Historical Unit Obtains Key Original." *The Baltimore Sun* (Baltimore, MD), 28 Jun 1953, p. 28.

24. Dennis, Samuel K. "A Brief Summary of the Maryland Historical Society's Hundred Years." Maryland Historical Magazine (Baltimore, MD), Vol. XXXIX, no. 1, March 1944, p. 5.

- Source for the image of students entering the building: Maryland Center for History and Culture.

THE 200-POOUND BIRTHDAY CAKE

1. "Crippled Children Devour Roosevelt Birthday Cake." *The Evening Sun* (Baltimore, MD), 1 Feb 1934, P. 11.

2. Some recent research has suggested that his illness could have been Guillain-Barre Syndrome (GBS) due to his age and analysis of his symptoms. Whether it was Poliomyelitis or GBS is somewhat irrelevant as Roosevelt's disease initiated considerable fundraising and research. Goldman, Armond S. et al. "What was the cause of Franklin Delano Roosevelt's paralytic illness?" *Journal of Medical Biography*, 2003; 11: 232-240.

3. Radcliffe, George L. Letter to Mr. Basil O'Connor, President, The National Foundation, 10 Sep 1964.

4. "City Birthday Balls Heading for Record." *The Evening Sun* (Baltimore, MD), 29 Jan 1936, p. 32.

5. Radcliffe, George L. Letter to Dr. Howard Howe, Johns Hopkins Medical School, 7 August 1957. [Howe was one of the major researchers at Hopkins that did the research which laid the groundwork for Salk's vaccine.]

6. CDC. "What is Polio?" Centers for Disease Control and Prevention, https://www.cdc.gov/polio/what-is-polio/index.htm.

7. Smithsonian National Museum of American History. "The Iron Lung and Other Equipment", https://amhistory.si.edu/polio/howpolio/ironlung.htm.

8. Beaubien, Jason. "Wiping Out Polio: How the U.S. Snuffed Out a Killer." National Public Radio, 15 Oct 2012, https://www.npr.org/sections/health-shots/2012/10/16/162670836/wiping-out-polio-how-the-u-s-snuffed-out-a-killer.

9. Radcliffe, George L. Letter to Dr. Alan M. Chesney (Dean, Johns Hopkins Medical School), 22 Oct 1952.

10. "Decorators Take Over at Scene of Ball." *The Evening Sun* (Baltimore, MD), 29 Jan 1937, p. 44.

11. Birthday ball brochures for 1938 – 1939.

12. Powell, Eleanor. Letter to George L. Radcliffe, 15 Mar 1939.

13. Wrigley, Tom, Publicity Director. "Radcliffe, George L., Press Release." 8 Jan 1939.

14. Birthday ball brochures for 1940 – 1943.

15. "President's Birthday Ball Program, Here, To Be Varied." *The Baltimore Sun* (Baltimore, MD), 29 Jan 1943, p. 5.

16. Frost, Ernest M., National Director, March of Dimes. Letter to George L. Radcliffe, 9 July 1965.

THE PROMISE

1. Radcliffe, George L. Speech before the Maryland Historical Society, Baltimore, MD, 23 March 1935.

2. Grace Foundation of Taylor's Island, Inc. "About Historic Taylor's Island." http://www.gracefound.net/about-taylors-island.html. Accessed 3 Mar 2020.

3. Many accounts of this legend exist with slight variations in all. The basic core facts are the same, and this version is based on the written account of her grandson, Levi Dove Travers.

4. Spencer, Richard Henry, ed. "Thomas Broome Travers." *Genealogical and Memorial Encyclopedia of the State of Maryland*, The American Historical Society, Inc. (New York), 1919, pp. 262 – 265.

5. Radcliffe, George L. Letter to Guy Steele, 17 July 1950.

6. Ibid.

7. "Anniversary Services Grace Church, Taylor's Is.", Unknown Newspaper clipping. The event was on 31 May 1936.

8. Radcliffe, George L. Letter to Marguerite Ewell, 29 June 1950.

9. Radcliffe, George M. "Memories of the Formation of Grace Foundation of Taylor's Island, Inc. After 50 Years." 2001.

10. Radcliffe, George L. "Grace Foundation of Taylor's Island, First Annual Report." 20 Feb 1952.

11. Radcliffe, George L. "Grace Foundation of Taylor's Island, Sixth Annual Report." 15 May 1957.

THE DREAMS OF A TEN-YEAR-OLD CHILD

1. Hammond, Trevor. "The Great Blizzard of 1888 Hits the Northeast: March 11 – 14, 1888." Fishwrap (Blog of Newspapers.com), 1 Mar 2018. https://blog.newspapers.com/the-great-blizzard-of-1888-hits-the-northeast-march-11-14-1888/?xid=1564&utm_source=headline&utm_medium=email&utm_campaign=headline-march-18.

2. "The Blizzard and Its Effects." *The Baltimore Sun* (Baltimore, MD), 13 Mar 1988, p. 2.

3. Preston, Dickson. "Senator Radcliffe's Windmill." *The Sun Magazine* (Baltimore, MD), 20 May 1973, pp. 18 – 21.

4. Chaplain, Gordon W. "Windmill Birthday Gift Becomes Family Tribute." *The Sun* (Baltimore, MD), 23 Aug 1972, pp. C6, C24.

General Sources:

- Letters of George L. Radcliffe.

- Conversations with Thomas Howell.

- Megargee, Frank. "Senator's Dream Coming True." *The Sun* (Baltimore, MD), 27 Sep 1971, p. D1.

APPENDIX I:

- Maryland Historical Society, "The George L. Radcliffe Papers", MS 2280, http://www.mdhs.org/findingaid/george-l-radcliffe-papers-ca1895-1972-ms-2280.

- Andrews, Matthew Page. "George L. Radcliffe." *Tercentenary History of Maryland, Vol. III.* The S.J. Clarke Publishing Company (Chicago-Baltimore), 1925, pp. 750 – 752.

- Notes of George M. Radcliffe
- Letters of George L. Radcliffe
- Diaries of George L. Radcliffe

APPENDIX 3:

- Miles, Clarence W., Political Agent. The Man for U.S. Senator: George L. Radcliffe. 1934.

APPENDIX 9:

- Hopkins, Samuel. "George L. Radcliffe, 1877 – 1974." Maryland Historical Magazine 69 (1974), pp. v – ix.

www.ingramcontent.com/pod-product-compliance
Lightning Source LLC
Chambersburg PA
CBHW070945150426
42812CB00067B/3322/J